The Best of
COOKING
PLEASURES

A Recipe Treasury

Cooking Club of America

Minnetonka, Minnesota

The Best of Cooking Pleasures
A Recipe Treasury

Printed in 2006.

Tom Carpenter
Director of Book Development

Heather Koshiol
Managing Editor

Jen Weaverling
Book Development Coordinator

Teresa Marrone
Book Design

Contributing Writers
Bruce Aidells, Melanie Barnard, Penelope Casas, Jill Van Cleave, Jesse Cool, Stephen Durfee, Mary Evans, Elinor Klivans, Diane Kochilas, Nancy Maurer, G. Franco Romagnoli, Lisa Saltzman, Sharon Sanders, Mark Scarbrough, Jerry Tranufeld, Carolyn Weil, Bruce Weinstein and Eberhard Werthman.

Special thanks to:
Terry Casey, Janice Cauley, Lori Grosklags and Stafford Photography.

On the cover: Neapolitan Seafood Soup, page 41.
On page 1: Maple-Brined Rack of Pork, page 59.

1 2 3 4 5 6 7 8 9 10/ 10 09 08 07 06
©2006 Cooking Club of America
ISBN 1-58159-270-1

Cooking Club of America
12301 Whitewater Drive
Minnetonka, MN 55343
www.cookingclub.com

Table
of
Contents

Molasses-Mustard Barbecued Chicken, page 11.

Neapolitan Seafood Soup, page 41.

Beef and Mushroom Loaf, page 67.

Asparagus, Arugula and Radish Salad, page 77.

Cinnamon and Coffee Cake, page 101.

Lemon-Raspberry Cheesecake, page 130.

The Best of Cooking Pleasures
A Recipe Treasury

**Cooking ideas you will treasure <u>plus</u> lots of them adds up to
A Recipe Treasury that will guide you on exciting new culinary adventures!**

Pure and simple, good cooking revolves around good recipes.

Sure, we all like to "wing it" on occasion and create something of our own based on a recipe we saw once, or maybe even an old favorite we know inside and out. So every home chef can appreciate the effort and ingenuity it takes to develop and then perfect an all-new recipe from scratch ... a recipe that will turn out perfectly for you.

That's precisely why you're going to love *The Best of Cooking Pleasures — A Recipe Treasury*. Here is a sizable collection of the greatest recipes ever to appear in the pages of *Cooking Pleasures* magazine, all brought to you in one classy, hard-bound, four-color format.

To start, explore critical cooking techniques with recipes for grilling, slow-cooking and smoking. Then take a culinary tour of Greece, Hong Kong, Italy and Spain. Explore a variety of main dishes from pasta and roasts to meat loaf and special supper sandwiches. Work with savory feature ingredients such as asparagus, mushrooms, pork chops and sirloin steak. Have fun with sweet feature ingredients like cinnamon, pumpkin, rhubarb, white chocolate and butterscotch. Finally, revel in wonderful desserts from cheesecakes to restaurant classics, fruit creations, cool delights and autumn tummy-warmers.

You'll treasure the recipes in this book because they are so good, and you'll treasure how many of them there are to choose from. That's why it's *A Recipe Treasury* for the ages ... and for your own cookbook collection!

Grilled Herbed Trout, page 17.

Curry Meat Loaf with Potato Crust, page 65.

Turkey Sandwiches with Gorgonzola, Strawberries and
Chive Mayonnaise, page 71.

Peanut Brittle-Hot Fudge Sundae Squares, page 145.

TECHNIQUES

Chicken Piri Piri

Grilling Chicken to Perfection

Get out your grill to enliven an American favorite.

Text and Recipes by Melanie Barnard

Whenever cooks fire up their grills, there's a good chance they'll put boneless, skinless chicken breasts over the coals. Americans love poultry, particularly this cut. It's easy to see why: You can add flavor simply with a marinade or stuffing, and the chicken cooks to moist, tender perfection in no time. To showcase the meat's versatility, these recipes take their cues from global cuisines, from a Portuguese hot sauce to Indian spices. And for perfect chicken each time you grill, be sure to check out our grilling tips.

Chicken Piri Piri

Piri piri (pepper pepper) is a vinegar-based hot sauce from Portugal made with malaguetta peppers. Look for it in Portuguese, Hispanic or African markets. You can substitute other hot sauces, but if the sauce you use is not vinegar-based, add a teaspoon of vinegar to this recipe.

- ¼ cup orange juice
- 2 tablespoons olive oil
- 1 tablespoon red wine vinegar
- 1 tablespoon finely chopped fresh ginger
- 2 to 3 teaspoons piri piri or other hot pepper sauce
- 2 teaspoons paprika
- 1 teaspoon ground cumin
- 1 teaspoon grated orange peel
- ½ teaspoon ground coriander
- ½ teaspoon salt
- 2 tablespoons finely chopped onion
- 2 tablespoons chopped fresh parsley
- 4 boneless skinless chicken breast halves

1 In shallow glass or ceramic baking dish or in resealable plastic bag, stir together orange juice, oil, vinegar, ginger, piri piri, paprika, cumin, orange peel, coriander and salt. Stir in onion and parsley. Place chicken breasts between 2 sheets of plastic wrap; with flat side of meat mallet, pound to flatten chicken to ½ inch. Place chicken in marinade, turning to coat both sides. Refrigerate 2 to 4 hours.

2 Heat grill. Remove chicken from marinade; reserve marinade. Oil grill grates. Place chicken on gas grill over medium-high heat or on charcoal grill 4 to 6 inches from medium-high coals; cover grill. Grill 8 to 10 minutes or until no longer pink in center, turning once and brushing with marinade halfway through. Discard remaining marinade.

WINE Choose a white wine to temper the heat of this dish and complement the spices. Try Viña Carmen Sauvignon Blanc from Chile or the Raymond Estates Sauvignon Blanc from Napa Valley.

4 servings

PER SERVING: 190 calories, 7.5 g total fat (1.5 g saturated fat), 27 g protein, 2 g carbohydrate, 75 mg cholesterol, 225 mg sodium, .5 g fiber

Mushroom-Gorgonzola-Stuffed Chicken Breasts

Sautéed mushrooms, especially a combination of wild and domestic, along with heady Gorgonzola, make a particularly tasty stuffing for chicken. Or try mozzarella and sun-dried tomatoes, provolone and olive tapenade, or Boursin and prosciutto.

- 2 tablespoons olive oil, divided
- 2 cups chopped shiitake, button and/or crimini mushrooms (about 8 oz.)
- ¼ cup chopped shallots
- 2 tablespoons chopped fresh tarragon
- 1 tablespoon dry vermouth, Madeira or brandy, if desired
- ½ teaspoon salt, divided
- ¼ teaspoon freshly ground pepper, divided
- ¼ cup (1 oz.) crumbled Gorgonzola or other blue cheese
- 4 boneless skinless chicken breast halves
- Tarragon sprigs for garnish

1 Heat 1 tablespoon of the oil in large skillet over medium heat until hot. Add mushrooms and shallots; cook over medium heat 6 to 8 minutes, stirring frequently, or until mushrooms are tender and most of the liquid has evaporated. Stir in chopped tarragon, vermouth, ¼ teaspoon of the salt and ⅛ teaspoon of the pepper; cook and stir 1 minute. Remove from heat; cool to room temperature. Stir in cheese. (Filling can be made up to 8 hours ahead. Cover and refrigerate. Bring to room temperature before using.)

2 Heat grill. Place chicken breasts between 2 sheets of plastic wrap; with flat side of meat mallet, pound to flatten chicken to ½ inch. With small sharp knife, cut pocket in each chicken breast, cutting almost to other side but not all the way through. Fill each breast evenly with mushroom mixture; secure openings with toothpicks or small metal skewers. Brush chicken with remaining 1 tablespoon oil; sprinkle with remaining ¼ teaspoon salt and remaining ⅛ teaspoon pepper.

3 Place chicken on gas grill over medium-high heat or on charcoal grill 4 to 6 inches from medium-high coals; cover grill. Grill 10 minutes or until no longer pink in center, turning once. Remove toothpicks; garnish with tarragon sprigs.

WINE Try a Chardonnay such as Wyndham Estate Bin 222 from Australia or Concannon Selected Vineyard bottling from California, which has rich oak and fruit flavors.

4 servings

PER SERVING: 255 calories, 13 g total fat (3.5 g saturated fat), 30 g protein, 4 g carbohydrate, 80 mg cholesterol, 465 mg sodium, 1 g fiber

Hibachi Chicken with Wasabi Cream

Brining the chicken in soy sauce, sherry and other flavorful ingredients lends an Asian note and keeps the meat moist. The wasabi cream is the perfect finish. While wasabi has a horseradish-like taste and kick, it's tamed here with the addition of crème fraîche.

WASABI CREAM
  ½ cup crème fraîche or sour cream*
  1 tablespoon soy sauce
  2 teaspoons wasabi powder**
  3 tablespoons finely chopped green onions
CHICKEN
  ¼ cup dry sherry or orange juice
  ¼ cup soy sauce
  1 tablespoon minced fresh ginger
  1 tablespoon dark sesame oil
  1 teaspoon hot chili paste
  4 boneless skinless chicken breast halves
  1 tablespoon sesame seeds
  1 tablespoon finely chopped green onion

1 In small bowl, stir together crème fraîche, 1 tablespoon soy sauce and wasabi powder. Refrigerate at least 1 hour or up to 6 hours to blend flavors.
2 In shallow glass or ceramic baking dish or resealable plastic bag, stir together sherry, ¼ cup soy sauce, ginger, sesame oil and chili paste. Place chicken breasts between 2 sheets of plastic wrap; with flat side of meat mallet, pound to flatten chicken to ½ inch. Place chicken in marinade, turning to coat both sides. Refrigerate 2 to 4 hours.
3 Heat grill. Remove chicken from

Grilling Guide for Chicken

Uniform Pieces If the chicken breasts are equal in size, they'll cook evenly and in a short period of time, making it less likely the grill's high heat will dry them out. Choose breasts of equal size, usually 5 to 6 ounces each. Then flatten each piece with a meat mallet to about ½-inch thickness.

Flavoring Tips for Marinades and Stuffings

- Allow at least 1 hour marinating time but no longer than 4 hours, particularly if the marinade contains acid-based ingredients, such as citrus juice, wine or vinegar. The acid starts to break down the texture of the meat if it's marinated too long.

- Using small amounts of highly flavored ingredients for stuffings punches up the taste while making it easier to fill the pocket of the breast and seal it with toothpicks. Also, using less stuffing means it's less likely to drip out during cooking.

- Oil stuffed chicken to prevent it from sticking to the grill grate, to keep it from drying out and to give it an appealing golden exterior.

Cooking Tips for Chicken

- If the recipe doesn't call for coating the meat with oil, use tongs and a paper towel to oil the grate.

- Place the breasts 4 to 6 inches above the coals on a heated grate. The hot grate helps prevent sticking, plus it adds appealing grill marks to the meat.

- Don't overcrowd the grate. Leave a few inches between breasts to allow ample room for the heat to circulate.

- Cover the grill to maintain its temperature, ensuring fast, even cooking.

- Turn the chicken just once, halfway through grilling. If the chicken sticks to the grate when you try to turn it, let it cook a little longer until it releases without resistance.

- Don't pat or press the chicken with a spatula during cooking; you might release valuable juices.

- Brush with marinade just before turning. For food safety, don't brush on marinade within 5 minutes of the end of the cooking time. Discard any remaining marinade.

Doneness Test Because the chicken cooks so quickly, even an extra minute can result in overdone meat. It's best to use a watch to monitor grilling time. Grill temperatures vary, so test for doneness at the minimum recommended time. Chicken should be cooked just until it is white throughout. To check doneness, make a small slit in the center with a sharp knife at about the time you think it should be done. Remember that the meat continues to cook a bit after it's removed from the grill.

Molasses-Mustard
Barbecued Chicken

marinade; reserve marinade. Pat sesame seeds onto both sides of chicken. Oil grill grates. Place chicken on gas grill over medium-high heat or on charcoal grill 4 to 6 inches from medium-high coals; cover grill. Grill 8 to 10 minutes or until no longer pink in center, turning once and brushing with marinade halfway through. Discard remaining marinade.

4 Remove wasabi cream from refrigerator 20 minutes before serving. Just before serving, stir in 3 tablespoons green onions. Serve chicken topped with wasabi cream; sprinkle with 1 tablespoon green onions.

TIPS *Crème fraîche is a slightly tangy, thickened cream. It can be found in the dairy section of gourmet supermarkets.

**Wasabi is the root of an Asian plant and is very pungent in flavor, similar to the taste of horseradish. It is sold as a paste in tubes or in a powdered form. Powdered wasabi can be mixed with water to form a paste. It can be found in the Asian section of the supermarket or where sushi is sold.

WINE Pinot Grigio/Pinot Gris, which is dry, matches the flavors in this entree. Choose a California Pinot Grigio or a rich and flavorful Pinot Gris from Oregon.

4 servings

PER SERVING: 255 calories, 12.5 g total fat (5 g saturated fat), 29 g protein, 5 g carbohydrate, 90 mg cholesterol, 765 mg sodium, .5 g fiber

Molasses-Mustard Barbecued Chicken

American barbecued chicken is usually slathered with a tomato-based sauce. This variation skips the tomatoes but keeps the sweet and spicy kick. Molasses gives it a coffee-toffee flavor and that familiar sticky quality that's so appealing. Serve the chicken with creamy potato salad and corn on the cob.

    4   boneless skinless chicken
        breast halves
  1/3   cup molasses
    3   tablespoons whole-grain Dijon
        mustard
    2   tablespoons honey
    2   tablespoons chopped fresh
        thyme
 1 1/2 tablespoons cider vinegar
 1 1/2 tablespoons vegetable oil
  1/2   teaspoon salt
  1/4   to 1/2 teaspoon crushed red
        pepper

1 Place chicken breasts between 2 sheets of plastic wrap; with flat side of meat mallet, pound to flatten chicken to 1/2 inch. In shallow glass or ceramic baking dish or resealable plastic bag, stir together molasses, mustard, honey, thyme, vinegar, oil, salt and crushed red pepper. Add chicken, turning to coat both sides. Refrigerate 2 to 4 hours.

2 Heat grill. Remove chicken from barbecue sauce; reserve sauce. Oil grill grates. Place chicken on gas grill over medium-high heat or on charcoal grill 4 to 6 inches from medium-high coals; cover grill. Grill 8 to 10 minutes or until no longer pink in center, turning once and brushing with sauce halfway through. Discard remaining sauce.

BEER/WINE This dish pairs well with a spicy beer, such as Sierra Nevada Pale Ale from California, or a lightly spicy red wine, such as the Zinfandel from Pedroncelli in Sonoma.

4 servings

PER SERVING: 230 calories, 7 g total fat (1.5 g saturated fat), 27 g protein, 14.5 g carbohydrate, 75 mg cholesterol, 360 mg sodium, 0 g fiber

Melanie Barnard is the author of several cookbooks, including *A Flash in the Pan* (Chronicle), with Brooke Dojny.

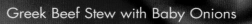
Greek Beef Stew with Baby Onions

Go with the Slow

No time to cook? No problem. Let a slow cooker do it for you.

Text and Recipes by Nancy Maurer

There is a natural comfort to slow-cooked food. But often we have to skip it because there just isn't time to monitor a pot of soup on the stove or a roast in the oven. If you crave the taste of long-simmered meals, pull out the slow cooker. Do a little preparation work the night before, fill the pot with the necessary ingredients in the morning, turn it on and return home later to the enticing aromas that signal dinner is just minutes away. You might not be able to devote more time to cooking, but you can eat as though you spent the day in the kitchen.

Greek Beef Stew with Baby Onions

Boneless beef chuck roast is gently stewed all day until it's fork-tender. The flavor is pumped up with plenty of fresh ingredients, including lemon peel and oregano, which are added at the end of the cooking time. Serve the stew over mashed potatoes or rice, or with a loaf of rustic bread for sopping up the sauce.

- 2 cups baby carrots, halved lengthwise if large
- 1 lb. pearl onions or small white boiling onions, peeled*
- 1 cinnamon stick
- 2 tablespoons olive oil
- 2 lb. boneless beef chuck roast, cut into 2- to 2½-inch pieces
- 4 medium garlic cloves, minced
- ½ teaspoon salt
- ½ teaspoon freshly ground pepper
- 2 (14½-oz.) cans diced plum tomatoes
- ⅓ cup tomato paste
- 1 tablespoon grated lemon peel
- 2 teaspoons chopped fresh oregano
- ¾ cup crumbled feta cheese

1 Place carrots, onions and cinnamon stick in 5- to 6-quart slow cooker. Heat oil in large skillet over medium-high heat until hot. Add beef, in batches if necessary; cook 5 to 7 minutes or until browned on all sides.

2 Place beef on top of vegetables in slow cooker. Sprinkle with garlic, salt and pepper; top with tomatoes. Cover and cook on low 8 to 10 hours or until beef and vegetables are tender.

3 Gently remove beef and vegetables with slotted spoon; place on plate. Discard cinnamon stick. Add tomato paste, lemon peel and oregano to slow cooker; stir to combine. Gently stir in beef and vegetables. Cover and cook on low 15 to 20 minutes or until thickened and heated through. Sprinkle each serving with cheese.

TIP *To easily peel onions, place in boiling water; boil 3 minutes. Drain; rinse with cold water to cool. Cut off root end and squeeze opposite end (onion should pop right out of its skin).

WINE Try a spicy, hearty red, such as Paul Jaboulet Aîné Côtes du Rhône Parallèle 45 or Yalumba "Y" Shiraz, which is flavorful without being too heavy.

4 servings

PER SERVING: 695 calories, 39.5 g total fat (15 g saturated fat), 55.5 g protein, 31 g carbohydrate, 165 mg cholesterol, 1215 mg sodium, 7 g fiber

Tuscan-Style Pork and Beans

Pork shoulder is slathered with a thick layer of herbs and seasonings and then left to cook for several hours, creating a melt-in-your-mouth meal. The beans are parboiled first to ensure they'll cook evenly. Slices of red onion and shreds of basil liven up each serving.

- 6 cups water
- 2 cups dried navy beans, rinsed
- 3 cups reduced-sodium chicken broth
- ¼ cup olive oil
- 6 large garlic cloves, finely chopped
- ¾ cup chopped fresh Italian parsley
- ¼ cup fennel seeds
- 1½ teaspoons kosher (coarse) salt
- 1 teaspoon freshly ground pepper
- 2½ lb. boneless pork shoulder roast (also known as Boston butt roast)
- ⅓ cup thinly sliced red onion
- ¼ cup shredded fresh basil

1 Bring water to a boil in large saucepan over high heat. Add beans. Reduce heat to medium-low; simmer, uncovered, 10 minutes. Remove from heat; drain and rinse with cold water. Place in 5- to 6-quart slow cooker; add broth.

2 Meanwhile, in medium bowl, stir together oil, garlic, parsley, fennel seeds, salt and pepper. Press mixture firmly onto pork.

3 Place pork on top of beans and broth in slow cooker. Cover and cook on low 7 to 9 hours or until beans are tender and pork pulls apart easily with fork. Serve pork and beans with broth; top with red onion and basil.

WINE Try Piccini Chianti, a lighter red made primarily from Sangiovese, or

Ruffino Fonte al Sole, a Sangiovese that has more depth of flavor and works beautifully with pork.

6 servings

PER SERVING: 600 calories, 26 g total fat (7 g saturated fat), 44.5 g protein, 46.5 g carbohydrate, 85 mg cholesterol, 730 mg sodium, 12.5 g fiber

Southwest Pulled Pork

This slightly spicy, Southwest-inspired dish is the perfect reason to pull out your slow cooker. The saucy pork can be wrapped in flour tortillas or spooned into crunchy taco shells. All it needs is a simple garnish of shredded lettuce and cheddar cheese. For the best consistency, purchase a mole that is very thick and paste-like.

- 2 tablespoons vegetable oil
- 2½ lb. boneless pork shoulder roast (also known as Boston butt roast)
- ½ teaspoon salt
- 1 medium onion, chopped
- 1 large green bell pepper, chopped
- ¾ cup chili sauce
- ½ cup purchased mole sauce*
- 1 teaspoon ground cumin
- 1 teaspoon chili powder

1 Heat oil in large skillet over medium-high heat until hot. Add pork; sprinkle with salt. Cook 4 to 6 minutes or until browned on all sides. Place pork, onion and bell pepper in 4- to 5-quart slow cooker.

2 Cover and cook on low 7 to 9 hours or until pork is tender. Remove pork and vegetables with slotted spoon; place on plate. Reserve ¾ cup of the liquid; discard remaining liquid. Return liquid to slow cooker; stir in chili sauce, mole sauce, cumin and chili powder. Shred pork; stir into sauce in slow cooker, along with vegetables. Cover and cook on low 15 to 20 minutes or until heated through.

TIP *Mole (pronounced MOH-lay) is an intricate, rich Mexican sauce with many versions. It usually contains chiles, ground nuts or seeds, spices and sometimes chocolate. Look for it in the Hispanic section of the grocery store or specialty markets. If you can't find mole sauce, substitute taco sauce. Because the consistency of taco sauce is much thinner than mole sauce, you may need to reduce the amount of reserved liquid to ⅓ to ½ cup.

BEER/WINE Negra Modelo, a dark, spicy Mexican beer, goes perfectly with the pork, as does Trapiche Malbec from Argentina, a spicy, hearty red wine.

6 servings

PER SERVING: 375 calories, 22 g total fat (6.5 g saturated fat), 30 g protein, 12.5 g carbohydrate, 85 mg cholesterol, 770 mg sodium, 3.5 g fiber

Asian Barbecued Short Ribs

In this Asian-flavored twist on traditional barbecued fare, ribs are cooked in a rich ginger-garlic broth studded with onions. This keeps the ribs moist and prevents them from

sticking to the bottom of the slow cooker. Ask your butcher to cut the ribs into pieces that are at least 1½ inches thick; they'll stand up better to the long cooking time.

1 tablespoon vegetable oil
3½ lb. beef short ribs (1½ to 2 inches thick)
¼ teaspoon salt
1 large onion, halved, sliced
4 large garlic cloves, minced
3 teaspoons grated fresh ginger, divided
1 (12-oz.) bottle chili sauce*
1 (7.25-oz.) jar hoisin sauce
3 tablespoons dark sesame oil
1 tablespoon red wine vinegar
¼ cup chopped fresh cilantro

1 Heat vegetable oil in large skillet over medium-high heat until hot. Sprinkle ribs with salt; add to skillet, in batches if necessary. Cook 6 to 8 minutes or until browned on all sides.
2 Place ribs, onion, garlic and 1½ teaspoons of the ginger in 5- to 6-quart slow cooker. Cover and cook on low 8 to 10 hours or until ribs are tender.
3 Meanwhile, in medium bowl, stir together remaining 1½ teaspoons ginger, chili sauce, hoisin sauce, sesame oil and vinegar; refrigerate until ribs are cooked.
4 Remove and discard excess liquid from ribs and onions. Pour reserved sauce over ribs in slow cooker. Cover and cook on low 15 to 20 minutes or until heated through. Sprinkle with cilantro before serving.
TIP *Use a standard chili sauce such as Heinz.
WINE Opt for a spicy red with these ribs. Two good choices are Jacob's Creek Shiraz from Australia or Pedroncelli Zinfandel California, which is quite elegant.
4 servings

PER SERVING: 645 calories, 36.5 g total fat (11 g saturated fat), 35.5 g protein, 42.5 g carbohydrate, 90 mg cholesterol, 2080 mg sodium, 8 g fiber

Nancy Maurer is a Cooking Pleasures kitchen tester and Minneapolis-based recipe developer.

Slow Cooker Basics

Slow cookers aren't complicated appliances, but following a few cooking tips will help you make the best use of them.

- Slow cookers work best when they're from one-half to three-fourths full. If the appliance is not full enough, it will cook the food too quickly; if it has too much food, it won't cook the food to a safe temperature quickly enough. In addition, some slow cookers cook hotter than others. Once you become familiar with yours, you may need to adjust cooking times slightly.

- Ingredients such as baby carrots, potatoes and root vegetables take a long time to cook, so they should be placed on the bottom of the pot, where there's more heat. To help them cook, cut up larger pieces.

- Less expensive cuts of meat work best. Beef short ribs, beef chuck roast, pork butt and pork shoulder roast benefit from the slow cooker's moist heat and low temperature. Trim away as much excess fat as possible to cut down on calories.

- Some ingredients, such as fresh herbs, citrus peel and vinegar, lose their potency when cooked all day in a slow cooker. For optimum flavor, add them during the last hour of cooking.

- For many recipes, ingredients can be prepared the night before and stored in the refrigerator. However, for food safety reasons, keep the ingredients in separate containers. In the morning, place the ingredients in the slow cooker in the order indicated in the recipe before turning on the appliance.

- If possible, turn meat such as beef short ribs halfway through the cooking process for even cooking. The portion of the meat that's submerged in liquid cooks faster.

- Resist the urge to peek at the food while it cooks. Lifting the lid can slow down the cooking time.

Grilled Herbed Trout

Fearless Grilling

A chef shares his secrets for cooking fish over fire.

Text by Jennifer Buege, Recipes by Eberhard Werthmann

Chef Eberhard Werthmann has been teaching people how to grill fish for more than eight years. For every class, he has one goal: to have his students leave saying, "I can do that!"

When people first walk into Eberhard's class, most are intimidated. Either they've tried grilling fish and have failed, or they're so uneasy, they don't know where to start. But cooking fish on the grill isn't difficult. In fact, it's an easy way to get dinner on the table quickly. And because fish and seafood make such a spectacular presentation, they're ideal for entertaining.

By the end of Eberhard's class, all nervousness disappears, and the students get to enjoy a variety of dishes that they helped grill. "Yum," says one as she bites into the seared tuna. "I can't wait to go home and make this." Mission accomplished.

Grilled Herbed Trout

Dried herbs can be substituted for the fresh ones in this dish. Use half the amount of herbs called for in the recipe. Sprinkle the dried herbs into the cavity of the trout, and refrigerate the fish for half an hour before grilling them. The moisture of the fish reconstitutes the herbs, making them more flavorful.

- 4 (8- to 10-oz.) whole boneless trout
- ½ teaspoon salt
- 1 teaspoon freshly ground pepper
- 4 teaspoons lemon juice
- 4 teaspoons soy sauce
- 1 tablespoon chopped fresh dill
- 1 tablespoon chopped fresh tarragon
- 1 tablespoon chopped fresh chives
- 1 teaspoon chopped fresh marjoram
- 1 teaspoon chopped fresh thyme
- 2 tablespoons olive oil

1 Place trout on rimmed baking sheet. Sprinkle cavities with salt and pepper; brush with lemon juice and soy sauce. Refrigerate 10 minutes.
2 Meanwhile, heat grill. In small bowl, stir together dill, tarragon, chives, marjoram and thyme.

Sprinkle inside of each trout with 1 tablespoon herb mixture. Brush outside of trout with olive oil.
3 Place trout on gas grill over medium heat or on charcoal grill 4 to 6 inches from medium coals. Grill 8 to 10 minutes or until fish just begin to flake, turning once.*
TIP *Placing trout in an adjustable grilling basket makes them easier to turn. You may need to increase cooking time 2 to 4 minutes.
WINE Serve Concha y Toro "Casillero del Diablo" Sauvignon Blanc from Chile or Silverado Napa Valley Chardonnay.

4 servings

PER SERVING: 300 calories, 17 g total fat (2.5 g saturated fat), 33 g protein, 1.5 g carbohydrate, 90 mg cholesterol, 715 mg sodium, .5 g fiber

Grilled Tuna with Porcini Mushrooms

Garnish this dish with chopped green onions or parsley. Use a lighter red wine, such as Beaujolais, in the sauce.

- 1 oz. dried porcini mushrooms
- 4 (6-oz.) tuna steaks (1 inch thick)
- ¾ teaspoon sea salt
- ½ cup red wine
- 3 tablespoons balsamic vinegar
- 1 tablespoon soy sauce
- 2 teaspoons minced garlic
- ½ teaspoon packed brown sugar
- 3 tablespoons olive oil, divided

1 Place mushrooms in medium bowl; cover with boiling water. Let stand 15 to 20 minutes or until softened. Drain; discard soaking liquid or save for another use. Slice mushrooms.
2 Place tuna in shallow baking dish; sprinkle both sides with salt. Refrigerate 10 minutes.
3 In small bowl, stir together mushrooms, wine, vinegar, soy sauce, garlic, brown sugar and 1½ tablespoons of the oil. Pour over tuna; refrigerate 15 minutes.
4 Heat grill. Remove tuna from marinade, scraping off mushrooms. Reserve mushrooms and marinade. Gently blot tuna with paper towel; brush lightly with remaining 1½ tablespoons oil.
5 Place tuna on gas grill over medium heat or on charcoal grill 4 to 6 inches from medium coals. Grill 6 to 8 minutes for medium-rare or until of desired doneness, turning once.
6 Meanwhile, place marinade and mushrooms in small saucepan. Bring to a boil over medium-high heat. Cook 1 to 2 minutes or until slightly thickened. Serve over tuna.
WINE Select a spicy, earthy red, such as Rancho Zabaco "Dancing Bull" Zinfandel from California or

Lemon-Spiced Salmon Steaks

Pedroncelli "Mother Clone" Zinfandel from Dry Creek Valley.

4 servings

PER SERVING: 325 calories, 19 g total fat (4 g saturated fat), 33.5 g protein, 3.5 g carbohydrate, 100 mg cholesterol, 645 mg sodium, .5 g fiber

Lemon-Spiced Salmon Steaks

The lemony marinade provides a nice foil for the richness of the salmon. After removing the skin from the steak, scrape off the grayish-brown fat between the skin and the fish; it sometimes has a fishy taste. Serve the salmon with a horseradish mayonnaise.

⅓ cup white wine
4 tablespoons vegetable oil, divided
2 tablespoons orange juice
1 tablespoon lemon juice
1 green onion, chopped
2 tablespoons grated lemon peel
1 teaspoon ground allspice
½ teaspoon salt
½ teaspoon freshly ground pepper
4 (8-oz.) salmon steaks (1 inch thick)

1 In small bowl, stir together wine, 2 tablespoons of the oil, orange juice, lemon juice, green onion, lemon peel, allspice, salt and pepper.
2 Place salmon in glass baking dish. Pour marinade over salmon; refrigerate 20 minutes, turning once.
3 Heat grill. Remove salmon from marinade; reserve marinade. Gently blot salmon with paper towel; brush with remaining 2 tablespoons oil.
4 Place salmon on gas grill over medium heat or on charcoal grill 4 to 6 inches from medium coals. Grill 7 to 10 minutes or until salmon just begins to flake, turning once and basting occasionally with reserved marinade during first 7 minutes of grilling.
WINE Serve Chardonnay with this dish: Casa Lapostolle from Chile or the earthy Edna Valley Vineyard "Paragon" from California.

4 servings

PER SERVING: 370 calories, 21 g total fat (4.5 g saturated fat), 41 g protein, 1.5 g carbohydrate, 125 mg cholesterol, 260 mg sodium, 0 g fiber

Seafood Kebabs with Saffron-Honey Glaze

A saffron glaze provides subtle flavor to the pineapple and seafood. Use long kitchen tongs to turn the skewers.

KEBABS
8 oz. swordfish, cut into 8 pieces
8 medium sea scallops (about 8 oz.)
8 shelled, deveined uncooked medium-large shrimp (16 to 20 count)
12 (1-inch) pieces fresh pineapple
2 tablespoons olive oil
1 tablespoon lemon juice
1 tablespoon Worcestershire sauce
1 teaspoon salt
½ teaspoon white pepper
GLAZE
½ cup white wine
Pinch saffron threads
3 tablespoons honey
¾ teaspoon ground cumin
GARNISH
Red Onion Salsa (pg. 19)

1 Place swordfish, scallops, shrimp and pineapple in large bowl. Add oil, lemon juice, Worcestershire sauce, salt and pepper; stir gently to combine. Refrigerate 15 minutes.

2 Meanwhile, combine wine and saffron in small saucepan. Bring to a boil over medium-high heat. Reduce heat to medium-low. Stir in honey and cumin; simmer 2 minutes.

3 Heat grill. Thread seafood and pineapple onto 4 (12- to 15-inch) skewers.

4 Place skewers on gas grill over medium heat or on charcoal grill 4 to 6 inches from medium coals. Grill 6 minutes or until scallops give slightly when pressed, swordfish flakes easily with fork and shrimp turn pink, turning skewers occasionally to grill all sides and brushing lightly with glaze. Serve with Red Onion Salsa.

WINE Chardonnay is the perfect choice. Try Jacob's Creek from Australia or Sterling Vineyards North Coast bottling.

4 servings

PER SERVING: 265 calories, 10.5 g total fat (2 g saturated fat), 20.5 g protein, 22 g carbohydrate, 60 mg cholesterol, 835 mg sodium, 1.5 g fiber

Red Onion Salsa
This salsa is best made a day ahead.

- ¾ cup finely diced red onion
- 2 tablespoons red wine
- 1 tablespoon balsamic vinegar
- 1 tablespoon chopped fresh cilantro
- ½ tablespoon honey
- ⅛ teaspoon salt
- ⅛ teaspoon freshly ground pepper

In small bowl, stir together all ingredients. Refrigerate at least 1 hour or up to 24 hours.

Jennifer Buege is senior editor of *Cooking Pleasures*. Eberhard Werthmann has been teaching cooking classes in Minneapolis and St. Paul, Minnesota, for more than 28 years.

Seafood Kebabs with Saffron-Honey Glaze

Preparing the grill Whether you use a gas or charcoal grill, make sure the grill is hot enough before adding the fish or seafood; the fish should sizzle a little when it's set on the grates. Don't use nonstick cooking spray to oil the grill because it can cause flare-ups. Rather, pour some oil onto a crumpled piece of paper towel, and, holding it with tongs, use it to oil the grates. Then lightly brush the fish or seafood with oil before putting it on the grill.

Washing fish There's no need to wash fish before grilling it. Instead, lightly scrape the surface of the fish with a knife. And don't worry—the fish will be cooked to a high enough temperature to kill any bacteria that may linger on the surface.

Basting Because fish loses a lot of moisture as it cooks, baste it as you go along. Basting prevents the outside of the fish from drying out and keeps the surface moist. Make sure to cook the fish 1 to 2 additional minutes after the last baste to avoid any problems with cross-contamination. Discard the baste.

Grease the grates with an oiled paper towel.

Cook fish until it just begins to flake.

Determining doneness Because fish cooks very quickly, it's easy to overcook it. A general guideline is to cook fish 10 minutes for each inch of thickness (measure fish at the thickest part). This is just an estimate, however. The best way to determine doneness is by the feel of the fish. Also, much like with meat, fish lets you know when it's ready to be flipped when it releases easily from the grate.

Whole fish, fillets and steaks For fillets and steaks, the most common way to determine whether fish has finished cooking is to press gently on the thickest part of the fish with a fork and see if it has started flaking. These recipes direct you to cook it until it just begins to flake; if it flakes easily, it's overdone. For whole fish, gently press down on the skin with your thumb or finger. You should feel the flesh start to separate slightly beneath the skin. This indicates that the fish is done cooking.

Scallops Because they're small and delicate, scallops are especially vulnerable to overcooking. Cook them until they just turn opaque in the centers. When pressed with a thumb or finger, they should give slightly.

Shrimp Cook shrimp until they turn pink.

Cleaning the grill The best way to clean the grill is to let it clean itself. Turn it to high heat, and close the cover for several minutes. Then turn off the grill. Once it has cooled down, scrape the grates with crumpled newspaper, aluminum foil or a grill brush. Don't scrub the grates in the sink. With use, they become seasoned, like a cast-iron pan; washing destroys some of the seasoning.

Tips for Success

Each of the recipes in this article features a different type of fish or seafood. Although the method for grilling each type is the same, there are fish-specific tips and tricks that will help you produce irresistible results.

Grilled Herbed Trout

- When choosing a whole fish, look for one with a fresh smell; it shouldn't have a strong fishy odor. If the gills are still attached, check to make sure they're bright red or pink and in good condition. (The gills are the best part of the fish to check because they're the first part to spoil.) Then look at the eyes; they should be bright and clear, not bulging, cloudy or indented. Finally, the scales should be firmly attached and shiny. Scales that come off easily are a sign that the fish isn't as fresh as it should be.

- Many people like to use a fish grilling basket. If you use a basket, make sure the fish fit in it snugly. You don't want them to move around when flipped.

- If you're grilling the fish directly on the grate, place the tail over the part of the grill with the least amount of heat, or wrap it in aluminum foil. Because it's so thin, the tail area quickly overcooks over high heat.

- To turn the fish, use a long, flexible spatula, such as an icing spatula.

Grilled Tuna with Porcini Mushrooms

- Before grilling tuna, lightly sprinkle both sides with salt. This helps firm up the fish by drawing out moisture.

- If grilling tuna to medium-rare, keep a close eye on the grill. Tuna can become overcooked quickly; even just an extra 30 to 60 seconds can cause it to be overdone.

Lemon-Spiced Salmon Steaks

- To check for freshness when purchasing, gently press down on the flesh of the steak; it should spring back. Avoid steaks that are brown or discolored around the edges.

- To test for doneness, insert a pointed object, such as the tip of a paring knife or metal skewer, into the backbone of the steak and jostle it slightly. When the backbone comes away from the meat, the fish is done.

- To remove the skin from cooked steaks, insert a fork tine at one edge of the steak between the skin and the fish, and roll it as you would spaghetti. Then scrape off the gray fat on the edge; it will taste fishy if left on.

Seafood Kebabs with Saffron-Honey Glaze

- Some people like to remove the shells from the tails of the shrimp before grilling them. We recommend keeping them on because they help prevent the tails from overcooking. Shrimp tails are thinner than other parts of the shrimp, which makes them cook faster.

- Use square metal skewers; the food is less likely to spin on the skewers, making them easier to turn than round ones. Also, metal conducts heat better than wood. If you use wooden skewers, make sure to soak them in water at least 30 minutes beforehand. And don't use skewers that are too long because they will take up too much room on the grill.

- Unless you like your fish well done, it should be threaded on the skewers so it touches the other ingredients. For well-done fish, leave a little space between each item on the skewer; this allows the fish to get completely cooked on all sides.

Stovetop-Smoked Salmon

Smoking on the Stove

It's easy to make moist, richly flavored smoked fish
with this low-tech indoor method.

Text and Recipes by Jerry Traunfeld

Salmon can be tasty prepared a number of ways, but when it's hot-smoked, it becomes truly luscious. Hot smoking imparts a rich, woodsy flavor and a moist, tender bite. Best of all, it's a top-of-the-range technique you can easily do at home, with little more than a cake pan, a cooling rack, wood chips and some foil. The foil serves as a tent, building up heat that roasts the salmon and confines the smoke. It's fast, it's easy and, once learned, there are plenty of other foods you can cook the same way, including fish, mussels, chicken breasts, duck breasts, even tomatoes.

Glistening salmon fillets, infused with the subtle aromatics of wood chips and cooked to perfection, all done indoors, without filling your kitchen with smoke—it's time to turn on the burners.

Stovetop-Smoked Salmon

Brining deepens the flavor and helps keep the salmon moist as it smokes. Be sure to tightly seal the foil around the rim of the pan to contain the heat and the smoke. Serve the salmon with just a squeeze of lemon or butter flavored with tarragon or dill.

- 1   cup water
- ¼   cup kosher (coarse) salt
- 2   tablespoons sugar
- 4   (3-inch) sprigs fresh thyme
- 2   bay leaves
- 1   cup ice cubes
- 1   (2-lb.) salmon fillet, skin removed, salmon cut into 6 pieces
- 1   cup dry hardwood chips or 1 cup dried herb stems, cut into 1-inch pieces

1 Place 1 cup water, salt, sugar, thyme sprigs and bay leaves in small saucepan; bring to a boil over high heat. Pour into 4-cup measuring cup. Add ice cubes; stir until melted. Add enough cold water to bring liquid to 4 cups.

2 Place salmon in large pan or resealable plastic bag; pour brine over salmon. Cover and refrigerate 2 hours.

3 Meanwhile, line bottom of lightweight to medium-weight 13x9-inch baking pan with foil. Brush wire rack (slightly larger than pan) with oil; place on baking sheet.

4 Remove salmon from brine; discard brine. Place salmon in large pan; cover with cold water. Gently stir water to release excess salt. Pour off and discard water. Pat salmon dry with paper towels. Place on oiled rack. Refrigerate, uncovered, at least 1 hour or up to 8 hours.

5 Spread dry wood chips or herb stems lengthwise down middle of pan; place rack with salmon on top of pan. Tent with heavy-duty foil, tucking foil tightly under rim of pan. (There should be at least 1 inch between salmon and foil.) Poke small slit in center of foil.

6 Position pan over 2 burners on stove. (Pile of chips should be over burners.) Place burners on high; if using electric stove, heat burners to high in advance. When smoke rises from slit (after about 2 minutes), begin timing salmon. Cook 5 minutes. Turn off heat; let stand 5 minutes. Remove foil. Fish should be golden colored and just beginning to flake. (If less done than preferred, replace foil; cook an additional 1 to 2 minutes.)

WINE Trapiche Chardonnay from Argentina is a great value, while the elegant and flavorful Oak Knoll Pinot Gris from Oregon is a fine match for salmon.

6 servings

PER SERVING: 215 calories, 8.5 g total fat (2.5 g saturated fat), 32 g protein, 0 g carbohydrate, 100 mg cholesterol, 315 mg sodium, 0 g fiber

Smoking Equipment and Method

The method used for stovetop smoking is called hot smoking. The salmon is placed close to the heat so that during the smoking process, the fish cooks completely. It's typically done outdoors with a smoker, but the method is easily adapted to the kitchen.

Simple Equipment To create the stovetop smoker, you need a 13x9-inch lightweight metal cake pan. It may warp over the high heat, so don't use an expensive one. You might find the perfect pan at a garage sale or thrift store for a few dollars. Old-fashioned graniteware pans (dark enamel speckled with white) also work well. You'll also need a rack that is slightly larger than the pan so that it sits on top of the pan without falling in. A rectangular cooling rack is perfect.

Brining The salmon is brined before smoking to add flavor and moisture. After it's brined, the fish is rinsed, patted dry and placed on the rack that will be used during smoking. Then the salmon and rack are placed, uncovered, in the refrigerator for up to 8 hours. This gives the fish time to form a skin, called a pellicle, which seals in the moisture and fat as the fish cooks and helps the fish pick up a smokier flavor.

Fuel Choices For the smoking fuel, use hardwood chips or dried herb stems. Wood chips give an assertive smoky flavor that varies with the type of wood. Woods that impart a milder flavor are best, such as apple, alder or maple; oak and hickory are too strong. You can purchase wood chips at grilling supply and cooking stores.

The smoke from herb stems is more aromatic than wood chips. Basil is best, but you also could use dried fennel, thyme, bay or lemon verbena stems. Stay away from rosemary and sage; they can be too resinous.

To prepare your own herb stems, pull up the plants in the fall and hang them upside down in a warm place to dry. Once dry, remove all leaves and snip the stems into pieces about 2 inches long.

Pan Setup For easy cleanup, line the smoking pan with foil. Spread a large handful of the chips or herb stems down the middle of the pan. Position the rack of fish on the pan, then tent the whole setup with a very large piece of heavy-duty foil so that there's at least 1 inch between the salmon and the foil. Tuck the

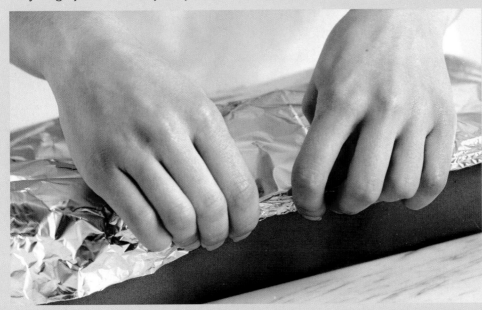

foil tightly under the rim of the pan. If your foil isn't wide enough to cover the pan, you can join two pieces together by making a seam. Poke a small slit in the top of the tent to monitor the smoke.

Cooking Method If you have gas burners, position the pan over two burners and turn them on to the high setting. If you have electric burners, heat them to high first, then place the pan on them. In about 2 minutes, you should see wisps of smoke coming through the slit. Leave the pan on high for an additional 5 minutes. Then turn off the heat (for an electric stove, transfer the pan to a cool burner), and let the fish stand and continue to smoke undisturbed for 5 minutes.

Lift the foil tent and inspect the fish. It should be golden-colored and just beginning to flake. If it is less done than you like, replace the foil, turn on the heat and cook an additional 1 to 2 minutes.

Jerry Traunfeld is a cooking instructor, cookbook author and the executive chef of The Herbfarm Restaurant near Seattle.

ETHNIC COOKING

Grilled Lamb Chops with Roasted Tomatoes
and Sheep's Milk Cheese

Celebrating Greece

Put the spotlight on the cuisine of this sunny country and the wonderful foods it produces.

Text and Recipes by Diane Kochilas

With its hospitable climate, Greece is home to a wealth of raw ingredients that have shaped the foods that appear on its tables. Each region has its specialties, but there are many foundation ingredients common to all Greek cooking. Olive oil runs like water throughout the country, serving as both a fat and flavoring agent. Garlic, lemons and pungent herbs season everything from bean dishes to lamb. Aromatic spices go into tomato-based stews and other sauces. Sweets are still based on the ancient duo of honey and nuts.

And Greek cuisine has a primal, no-nonsense element about it. Simple preparation makes it accessible to busy cooks. Plus, most ingredients, with the exception of a few regional cheeses, are easy to find in the United States.

Greek food is at once familiar and exotic, healthful and indulgent, easy and delicious. This menu demonstrates its appeal.

Grilled Lamb Chops with Roasted Tomatoes and Sheep's Milk Cheese

In Greece, the favorite way to season lamb is the simplest, with a little extra-virgin Greek olive oil, garlic and lemon juice. Topping these lamb chops with roasted tomatoes and sheep's milk cheese lends a slightly sweet and rich note to every tender bite.

LAMB

- ½ cup extra-virgin olive oil
- ½ cup fresh lemon juice
- 4 garlic cloves, minced
- 2 tablespoons dried marjoram or oregano
- 1 tablespoon dried rosemary
- 3 (1½-lb.) racks of lamb, cut into individual chops (about 24)
- ½ teaspoon kosher (coarse) salt
- ½ teaspoon freshly ground pepper

TOMATOES

- 6 large ripe but firm tomatoes, cut into 8 wedges
- ½ teaspoon kosher (coarse) salt
- ¼ teaspoon freshly ground pepper
- 2 tablespoons sugar
- 2 tablespoons extra-virgin olive oil
- 2 tablespoons balsamic vinegar

GARNISH

- 4 oz. firm aged sheep's milk cheese, such as Greek kefalograviera or kefalotyri, or Gruyère cheese, shaved*
- 4 cups fresh arugula leaves

1 In large bowl or resealable plastic bag, whisk together ½ cup oil, lemon juice, garlic, marjoram and rosemary. Add lamb chops; toss to coat. Cover and refrigerate at least 1 hour or up to 3 hours.

2 Meanwhile, heat oven to 400°F. Place tomatoes, skin side down, on lightly oiled rimmed baking sheet. Sprinkle with ½ teaspoon salt, ¼ teaspoon pepper and sugar; drizzle with 2 tablespoons oil and vinegar. Bake 30 to 35 minutes or until tomatoes are wrinkled and just beginning to char. Cool, saving accumulated juices.

3 Heat grill. Remove lamb from marinade; discard marinade. Sprinkle lamb with ½ teaspoon salt and ½ teaspoon pepper. Brush grill grate with oil. Place lamb on gas grill over medium heat or on charcoal grill 4 to 6 inches from medium coals; cover grill. Grill 6 minutes for medium-rare or until of desired doneness, turning once.

4 Place tomatoes in center of serving plates; arrange lamb over tomatoes. Top with cheese. Arrange arugula around lamb; drizzle with reserved tomato juices.

TIP *Shave cheese with vegetable peeler.

8 servings

PER SERVING: 330 calories, 21.5 g total fat (7 g saturated fat), 24 g protein, 10.5 g carbohydrate, 80 mg cholesterol, 315 mg sodium, 2 g fiber

Spicy Oven-Roasted Feta Cheese Squares

Spicy Oven-Roasted Feta Cheese Squares

Spiced-up feta is a favorite meze, or appetizer, in northern Greece. In this version, red pepper and cayenne provide some heat, which contrasts nicely with the creamy cheese and tangy lemon and herbs. The cheese softens during baking but stays firm enough to serve and eat easily. Accompany the dish with toasted pita wedges or bread.

1 (1-lb.) block Greek feta cheese
2 tablespoons extra-virgin olive oil
2 teaspoons crushed red pepper
¼ teaspoon cayenne pepper
1 tablespoon chopped fresh oregano
3 tablespoons chopped fresh Italian parsley
8 lemon wedges

1 Heat oven to 375°F. Lightly oil 8- or 9-inch shallow square baking dish. Cut feta into 8 equal slices; arrange slices in baking dish. Drizzle cheese with oil; sprinkle with crushed red pepper, cayenne pepper and oregano. Cover with foil.

2 Bake 15 to 20 minutes or until feta just begins to melt. Sprinkle with parsley; serve hot with lemon wedges.

8 servings

PER SERVING: 185 calories, 15.5 g total fat (9 g saturated fat), 8.5 g protein, 3.5 g carbohydrate, 50 mg cholesterol, 635 mg sodium, .5 g fiber

White Bean Salad

Bean salads in Greece almost always have pungent, raw onions added, usually the red variety. Lemon and parsley give this version a lively taste. And capers, also an island staple, add a pleasant saltiness. Be sure you don't overcook the beans; they should be slightly crunchy, not mushy.

- 1 cup dried navy or cannellini beans or 1 (15- or 19-oz.) can
- 1 bay leaf
- ½ cup chopped fresh Italian parsley
- ⅓ cup fresh lemon juice
- 3 tablespoons capers, rinsed, drained
- 1 medium red onion, finely chopped
- ½ teaspoon cayenne pepper
- ¼ teaspoon salt
- ½ cup extra-virgin olive oil

1 If using dried beans, place beans in large saucepan of cold water. Bring to a boil over medium-high heat; boil 3 minutes. Remove from heat; cover and let stand 1 hour. Drain; return beans to saucepan with enough cold water to cover. Bring to a boil. Add bay leaf. Reduce heat to low; simmer, uncovered, 1 hour or until beans are tender but not mushy. Drain; rinse under cold water. Remove bay leaf. (If using canned beans, drain and rinse with cold water.)

2 In large bowl, stir together beans, parsley, lemon juice, capers, onion, cayenne pepper and salt. Add oil; toss to coat. Let stand 1 hour. Drain slightly before serving. Serve cold or at room temperature. Store in refrigerator.

8 (½-cup) servings

PER SERVING: 215 calories, 14 g total fat (2 g saturated fat), 5.5 g protein, 18 g carbohydrate, 0 mg cholesterol, 165 mg sodium, 4.5 g fiber

Greek Summer Bread Salad

This colorful dish is a version of one of the best-known Greek dishes, the "village salad." The jalapeño and pepperoncini chiles give a pleasant amount of heat to the vegetables, while capers and feta contribute a salty flavor.

- ½ cup plus 2 tablespoons extra-virgin olive oil, divided
- 1 garlic clove, crushed
- 2 (6-inch) pita breads*
- ⅛ teaspoon salt
- 2 medium tomatoes, cut into ½-inch pieces
- 1 cup chopped red onion
- 1 large green bell pepper, diced
- 1 medium cucumber, peeled, cut into ½-inch pieces
- 1 jalapeño chile, veins and seeds removed, very finely chopped
- 3 pepperoncini, thinly sliced
- 2 tablespoons capers (preferably large), rinsed, drained
- ⅔ cup crumbled Greek feta cheese
- ½ cup Greek anthotyro cheese, fresh myzithra cheese or additional feta cheese**
- 1 teaspoon freshly ground pepper
- 1 teaspoon dried basil, divided
- 1 teaspoon dried oregano, divided
- ⅓ cup cracked green olives, pitted, halved***

1 Heat 2 tablespoons of the oil in large nonstick skillet over low heat until hot. Add garlic; cook 2 minutes or until it starts to brown. Remove garlic. Increase heat to medium-high. Cook pita breads, one at a time, in skillet 1 to 2 minutes or until golden brown, turning once. Remove from skillet; cool. Cut into bite-sized pieces; place in bottom of large serving bowl. Sprinkle with salt.

Ingredient Essentials

Greece's climate is ideal for producing a wide range of high-quality foods. It's worth seeking out these foundation ingredients to give this menu authentic Greek flavor.

Olive Oil Greece is the third largest producer of olive oil in the world, and more than 90 percent of Greek olive oil is extra virgin. Most olives are harvested by hand. The result is a high-quality product that the Greeks use with abandon, by itself and in cooking, from frying to desserts.

Olives Greece produces both table olives and oil olives. The main Greek table olives are the well-known Kalamatas, dark olives that range in color from deep brown to black and are distinguished by their almond shape and pointed tip. Another popular Greek olive is the Conservolia, a large, plump, oval variety that is the most versatile of all Greek olives. It can be processed both as a young green olive and as a mature dark one. In Greek shops, it's usually labeled not by the name of the actual variety but by the place from which it comes, such as Volos, Amphissa, Atalanti or Agrinio. Other favorite olives are the tangy, cracked green olive that is often found seasoned with garlic, herbs and lemon; and the wrinkled black olive from Thassos, which is deliciously thick-skinned and oily.

Nuts The best-known Greek dishes using nuts are the sweets, especially phyllo-based desserts, in which nuts are the filling. Baklava is the most recognized dish. Nuts also have a significant role in savory cuisine. Walnuts and almonds are the most popular, but chestnuts and pine nuts also are used.

Cheese One of the most surprising things about Greek cheeses is their sheer variety and regional diversity. There are at least 60 different types produced in the country. Although there are some cow's milk cheeses in Greece, most Greek cheese is made from sheep's milk or from a combination of sheep's and goat's milk. There are several categories:

- **Brine cheese** The best-known is feta, but there are other cheeses from different parts of the country that also are preserved in brine.

- **Semi-hard cheese** Many of these cheeses, such as kasseri, a mild sheep's milk cheese, and manouri, a delicious, creamy sheep's milk cheese that resembles pressed ricotta, are available in the United States.

- **Hard cheese** This is the broadest category of Greek cheese and can include graviera and kefalograviera, two nutty sheep's milk cheeses that can range in flavor from mild and sweet to sharp and peppery. There also are a whole range of regional cheeses that are aged or preserved in wine and olive oil.

- **Soft cheese** These cheeses are either naturally fermented and left to sour or aged long enough to acquire a fiery flavor and pungent scent. This category includes very mild curd cheeses as well as soft mold cheeses.

2 Layer tomatoes, onion, bell pepper, cucumber, jalapeño, pepperoncini and capers in bowl.

3 In small bowl, stir together feta cheese, anthotyro cheese, pepper, 1/2 teaspoon of the basil and 1/2 teaspoon of the oregano. Sprinkle over salad. Top with olives; drizzle with remaining 1/2 cup oil. Sprinkle with remaining 1/2 teaspoon basil and 1/2 teaspoon oregano; toss just before serving.

TIPS *Look for pita bread without pockets.

**Anthotyro and myzithra are fresh sheep's milk cheeses, similar to Italian ricotta cheese made with sheep's milk. The flavor is distinctive and nutty, and very different from the ricotta cheese widely available in supermarkets. These cheeses can be found in ethnic markets. If they are not available, substitute farmer's cheese or use additional feta cheese.

***Remove pits from olives by pressing olives with side of knife until olives split.

8 (1 1/4-cup) servings

PER SERVING: 70 calories, 5 g total fat (3 g saturated fat), 3.5 g protein, 3 g carbohydrate, 15 mg cholesterol, 405 mg sodium, .5 g fiber

Triple Nut-Poppy Seed Baklava

This baklava is based on a very old recipe from Crete. Almonds, pistachios and walnuts give it deep flavor; the honeyed syrup lends a touch of spice; and black pepper adds a hint of heat. For best results, thaw the phyllo overnight in the refrigerator.

SYRUP
- 1 1/2 cups honey (preferably Greek)
- 1/2 cup sugar
- 2 cups water
- 3 whole cloves
- 2 strips lemon peel
- 2 cracked black peppercorns
- 1 cinnamon stick

FILLING
- 2 egg whites
- 2 cups chopped walnuts
- 2 cups chopped raw pistachios
- 1 cup chopped slivered almonds
- 1 cup poppy seeds

- 1/2 cup sugar
- 1/2 teaspoon freshly ground pepper

PHYLLO
- 9 sheets frozen phyllo, thawed, room temperature
- 1/2 cup extra-virgin olive oil
- 1 tablespoon cold water

1 To make syrup, place honey, sugar and 2 cups water in medium saucepan; bring to a boil over medium-high heat. Reduce heat to low; add cloves, lemon peel, peppercorns and cinnamon. Simmer 12 to 15 minutes or until slightly reduced. Strain into medium bowl; cool completely. (For crisp baklava, make sure syrup is at cool room temperature before pouring over hot baklava.)

2 Heat oven to 400°F. Brush 13x9-inch baking pan with olive oil. In medium bowl, beat egg whites at medium-high speed until soft peaks form. In large bowl, stir walnuts, pistachios, almonds, poppy seeds, 1/2 cup sugar and pepper until blended. Stir in egg whites until nuts are moistened.

3 Cut phyllo sheets in half crosswise to form 18 sheets; cover with dry cloth. Layer 4 sheets in baking pan, brushing each lightly with olive oil. Sprinkle phyllo with 1 cup of the filling. Cover with 2 phyllo sheets, brushing each lightly with oil. Sprinkle with another cup of the filling. Continue until all the filling is used (you will have 6 layers of nuts). Top with 4 phyllo sheets, brushing each lightly with oil. Press down on baklava with palms of hands so baklava is compact. Cut diagonally into diamonds*; sprinkle with 1 tablespoon cold water.

4 Bake at 400°F. for 10 minutes. Reduce oven temperature to 325°F.; continue baking 1 hour 30 minutes to 1 hour 40 minutes or until golden brown and crisp.

5 Immediately pour cooled syrup over baklava, tilting pan so syrup evenly covers surface. Cool to room temperature, about 3 hours. Store in airtight container in cool dry place.

TIP *To cut baklava, make 3 lengthwise cuts to form 4 rows.

Diagonally cut each row into 8 pieces.

32 servings

PER SERVING: 260 calories, 16 g total fat (1.5 g saturated fat), 5 g protein, 28.5 g carbohydrate, 0 mg cholesterol, 25 mg sodium, 2.5 g fiber n

Cookbook author Diane Kochilas runs the Glorious Greek Kitchen Cooking School on the Greek island of Ikaria.

Stir-Fried Lobster with Spring Onions, Red Onions and Shallots

Savoring Hong Kong

These easy-to-make dishes capture the flavors of Hong Kong.

Text and Recipes by Janice Cole

My first glimpse of Hong Kong was through the window of a taxi coming from the airport. It was well after midnight, but the streets were crammed with neon-lit store-fronts showcasing shiny mahogany-skinned ducks, roast chickens and baskets of live crabs. Shoppers packed the sidewalks carrying bags; open restaurant doors gave glimpses of tempting roast pork and simmering soup. An exhilarating few days of nonstop food were in store for me.

I was in town to attend the Best of the Best Culinary Awards, an annual competition designed to recognize restaurants that serve the best Hong Kong dishes. The cuisine of this city is extraordinary and needs more than a few days to explore, but I did return to the United States with recipes that are easily prepared at home. They demonstrate the range of flavors and foods available, and offer a tiny glimpse into the exciting food scene of this Asian metropolis.

Stir-Fried Lobster with Spring Onions, Red Onions and Shallots

This deceptively simple dish, created by one of Hong Kong's premier restaurants, T'ang Court, was honored with the top award in Hong Kong's Best of the Best culinary awards. It highlights the essence of Cantonese cuisine. The ingredients blend to enhance, rather than overpower, the exquisite lobster taste.

LOBSTER
- 3 (6- to 8-oz.) lobster tails
- ½ small red onion, sliced lengthwise (¼ inch)
- 2 tablespoons Chinese rice wine, dry sherry or chicken broth
- 2 tablespoons soy sauce
- 6 green onions, cut into 2-inch pieces, cut lengthwise into thin strips

GARNISH
- 1½ tablespoons vegetable oil
- 2 medium shallots, thinly sliced

1 With large knife, Chinese cleaver or kitchen shears, cut lobster through shell in half lengthwise; cut crosswise into 1½-inch pieces, keeping shell on.
2 Heat wok over high heat until hot. Add oil and shallots; stir-fry 1 to 2 minutes or until golden brown. Remove wok from heat. Remove shallots using slotted spoon; place on paper towel-lined plate.

3 Return wok with oil to high heat; heat until oil is hot. Add lobster and red onion; stir-fry 4 to 6 minutes or until lobster is opaque but not firm. Add wine and soy sauce; stir until combined. Remove from heat; stir in green onions. Place on serving platter; top with shallots.

WINE Try a rich white, such as the Rosemount Diamond Chardonnay from Australia or the elegant Grove Mill Sauvignon Blanc from New Zealand.

4 servings

PER SERVING: 175 calories, 6 g total fat (1 g saturated fat), 24 g protein, 6.5 g carbohydrate, 80 mg cholesterol, 880 mg sodium, 1 g fiber

Chicken with Red Chile and Garlic

This recipe is based on a dish from the Hunan Garden restaurant in central Hong Kong. There, it arrives at the table with wok hay—the "breath of the wok"—still sizzling in the shallow cast-iron pot.

MARINADE
- 1 tablespoon soy sauce
- 1 tablespoon Chinese rice wine, dry sherry or chicken broth
- 1 lb. boneless skinless chicken breast halves, cut into 1½-inch pieces
- 2 teaspoons cornstarch

SAUCE
- ¼ cup reduced-sodium chicken broth
- 3 tablespoons soy sauce
- 3 tablespoons hoisin sauce
- 3 tablespoons red wine vinegar
- 1 teaspoon chili paste
- ½ teaspoon honey
- ¼ teaspoon dark sesame oil

SEASONINGS
- 1 tablespoon vegetable oil
- 4 large garlic cloves, sliced (⅛ inch)
- 1 tablespoon minced fresh ginger
- 10 whole dried red chiles
- 2 green onions, cut into 1½-inch pieces
- ½ teaspoon toasted ground Szechuan peppercorns or coarsely ground black pepper*

GARNISH
- 2 tablespoons coarsely chopped fresh cilantro
- 2 tablespoons peanuts

1 In medium bowl, stir together 1 tablespoon soy sauce and wine; stir in chicken to coat. Add cornstarch; stir until blended.
2 Meanwhile, in small bowl, stir

Chicken with
Red Chile and Garlic

together all sauce ingredients.

3 Heat wok or large skillet over high heat until hot. Add vegetable oil, garlic and ginger; stir-fry 30 seconds or until garlic and ginger turn golden brown, being careful not to let them burn. Add chicken, spreading in 1 layer, if possible. Stir-fry 3 to 5 minutes or until golden brown. Stir in chiles, green onions and ground peppercorns; stir-fry 1 to 2 minutes or until fragrant. Add sauce; stir to combine. Cook 1 minute or until sauce is hot and chicken is no longer pink.

4 Place on serving platter; garnish with cilantro and peanuts. Serve immediately.

TIP *Szechuan peppercorns are tiny

berries that add a unique pepper flavor with zing. This dish would typically use whole Szechuan peppercorns, but they currently can't be imported to the United States. If you can't find ground toasted Szechuan peppercorns, use freshly ground black pepper.

BEER/WINE To help rein in the heat of this chicken dish, try a refreshing pale ale, such as Coopers from Australia. For wine, select a Sauvignon Blanc from New Zealand, such as Villa Maria, which has a slight earthiness that works with the chile and garlic.

4 servings

PER SERVING: 285 calories, 11 g total fat (2 g saturated fat), 29.5 g protein, 17.5 g carbohydrate, 70 mg cholesterol, 1255 mg sodium, 2.5 g fiber

Chopstick Ribs in Dark Soy Sauce

The Chinese prepare pork in many ways, but braised ribs are one of their greatest achievements. The recipe for these spareribs is from Cecilia Au-Yang, owner of the Chopsticks Cooking Centre in Hong Kong. Blanching the pork first removes excess fat, which makes the sauce rich and glossy. Dark soy sauce, thicker and sweeter than regular soy sauce, adds deep flavor.

RIBS
- 1½ lb. pork spareribs, cut by butcher into 1½-inch lengths
- 4½ cups water
- 6 (¼-inch) slices fresh ginger, minced, divided
- 6 medium shallots, sliced (¼ inch), divided
- 3 teaspoons vegetable oil
- 3 tablespoons Chinese rice wine, dry sherry or chicken broth

SAUCE
- 3 tablespoons dark soy sauce*
- 3 tablespoons red wine vinegar
- 3 tablespoons sugar
- Scant ½ cup water

GARNISH
- 1½ teaspoons dark sesame oil
- 3 tablespoons sliced green onions

1 Cut spareribs between bones to form small bite-sized pieces. Bring 4½ cups water to a boil in large saucepan over high heat. Add pork, half of the ginger and half of the shallots; cook 1 minute or until pork turns gray. Drain. Rinse pork under running water; drain well.

2 In small bowl, stir together all sauce ingredients until blended.

3 Heat vegetable oil in large saucepan over high heat until hot. Add remaining ginger and shallots; cook 30 seconds or until fragrant, stirring constantly. Add pork; cook 2 to 3 minutes or until fragrant, stirring constantly. Add wine; bring to a boil. Stir in soy sauce mixture; bring to a boil. Reduce heat to low; cover and simmer 40 to 45 minutes or until pork is tender and easily pierced with chopstick or fork, turning pork halfway through cooking.

4 Remove pork from sauce; place in serving bowl. Skim any fat from surface of sauce. Bring to a boil over high heat; boil 2 to 3 minutes or until sauce is slightly thickened (bottom of saucepan will become visible while stirring). Pour sauce over pork. Drizzle with sesame oil; top with green onions.

TIP *Dark soy sauce is thicker and less salty than the soy sauce usually found in American supermarkets. Dark soy sauce is aged longer, and the color is very rich. Look for it in Asian markets, where it is also labeled "soy superior." Mushroom

Guide to Ingredients

All of the ingredients used in these recipes can be found in the Asian section of well-stocked grocery stores or in Asian markets. Visit www.cookingclub.com and go to Featured Links for online resources.

Chili Paste Red chiles are ground and combined with vinegar and spices to make chili paste.

Dark Sesame Oil Chinese sesame oil is made from toasted sesame seeds. Look for oil with dark color and rich fragrance.

Rice Wine Rice wine has a rich, nutty flavor and is used in Chinese dishes. You can substitute a good dry sherry, but avoid rice cooking wine; it has added salt.

Soy Sauce Soy sauce is an essential ingredient in Chinese cuisine, and it comes in both dark and light versions. Dark soy sauce is thicker and sweeter than regular soy sauce and also is less salty. It's used to add richness to hearty dishes. Light soy sauce refers to the color, not saltiness. It is actually saltier than dark soy but thinner and more delicate in flavor. If a recipe calls for soy sauce without indicating the type, use light soy sauce (but not reduced-sodium soy sauce). Hong Kong chefs make their own signature soy sauce blends by adding special seasonings and spices to purchased soy sauce, creating recipes they jealously guard.

soy is a flavored soy sauce that also can be used.

BEER/WINE A dark beer that isn't too heavy is fine here; we recommend the St. Pauli Girl Special Dark. For wine, look for a lighter Shiraz with good spice and not much tannin, such as Greg Norman Limestone Coast from Australia.

4 servings

PER SERVING: 370 calories, 25.5 g total fat (8 g saturated fat), 20.5 g protein, 14.5 g carbohydrate, 80 mg cholesterol, 465 mg sodium, .5 g fiber

The Hong Kong Food Scene

Dining out is serious business in Hong Kong, a city that has more than 9,000 restaurants, not counting the street vendors who sell everything from sweets to tonic soups. Much of the city's cuisine is typically Cantonese because most of the residents originally came from the Guangzhou area of China (formerly known as Canton). But it also is the meeting place for all of China, as well as other parts of Asia and the world. Today, every cuisine is represented. In fact, some say Hong Kong is the birthplace of fusion food.

Old and new The melding of past and present is evident everywhere. Modern skyscrapers built according to feng shui principles crowd the tiny island. The latest electronic gadgets are used in ancient food markets, which are, in turn, located next to high-tech businesses.

Freshness is key On this island of prosperity, each market displays the best of its goods: Young vegetables glisten in baskets, fresh seafood still wiggles on ice and chickens squawk in cages before they are selected by a buyer and prepared by the butcher. I was told, "You must be able to taste the freshness of the meat, not just an intricate sauce."

Balance is everything A delicate balance between textures and flavors is essential to every Hong Kong meal, but there also should be a balance in the properties of each food. According to the Chinese, each dish has innate characteristics that determine the combination of foods. A perfect example occurred one evening when I was presented with a Hong Kong seasonal delicacy, the hairy crab. This highly flavored freshwater crab lives in the depths of ponds, and its properties are considered cold (even though it was served warm). My host insisted I follow it with a ginger soup, whose properties are warm, to balance my digestion.

Tradition is honored Hong Kong cuisine is upscale, refined and innovative, but it rests on centuries of tradition. Dim sum chefs train for years to perfect the ornate delicate folds of their dumplings, for which Hong Kong is noted. Recipes are based on generations of use. While intricate dishes are enjoyed, the residents I talked to agree the most important dish in Hong Kong is simply soup. The rich, full-flavored broths I sipped convinced me of this wisdom. Interestingly, each tiny restaurant, some no bigger than the width of a table, had a bubbling soup pot displayed out front—apparently so customers can see exactly what the chef puts into the broth.

Warm Golden Custard Tarts

Warm Golden Custard Tarts

These jewel-like tarts are edible treasures in Hong Kong, whether ordered in a bustling dim sum restaurant or at the counter of a tiny bakery. The glistening bright-yellow custard looks like a quivering fresh egg, neatly enveloped in rich, flaky pastry. The Chinese call them egg custard tarts, and they are best served warm.

PASTRY
- ¾ cup all-purpose flour
- 1 tablespoon sugar
- ⅛ teaspoon salt
- 5 tablespoons unsalted butter, chilled, cut up
- 2 to 3 tablespoons ice water

GLAZE
- 1 egg, beaten

CUSTARD
- 2 egg yolks
- 3 tablespoons sugar
- ¾ teaspoon cornstarch
- ½ cup whipping cream
- 6 drops yellow food coloring, if desired*

1 In medium bowl, stir together flour, 1 tablespoon sugar and salt. With pastry blender or 2 knives, cut in butter until mixture resembles coarse crumbs with some pea-sized pieces. Add 2 tablespoons of the water; stir until dough starts to form, adding additional water, if necessary. Shape into thin flat round; cover. Refrigerate at least 30 minutes.

2 On lightly floured surface, roll dough to ⅛-inch thickness. Using 3-inch cutter, cut dough into 12 rounds, re-rolling dough scraps as necessary. Press dough into 12 (2¼-inch) tart pans, trimming pastry as necessary. Refrigerate 20 minutes or until firm.

3 Meanwhile, heat oven to 400°F. Place tart pans on baking sheet; line tart shells with foil and pie weights or dry beans. Bake 10 minutes; remove foil. Bake an additional 3 minutes or until pastry is lightly browned. Remove from oven; brush tarts lightly with glaze. Bake an additional 1 minute or until glaze is set. Remove from oven; reduce oven temperature to 325°F. Cool tart shells on wire rack 10 minutes or until room temperature.

4 Meanwhile, in medium bowl, whisk egg yolks, 3 tablespoons sugar and cornstarch until smooth. Whisk in cream and food coloring just until blended. Strain through fine strainer; let stand 15 minutes. Remove any excess bubbles and foam. Gently pour egg mixture into cooled tart shells. Bake 12 to 15 minutes or until custard is just set. Cool on wire rack 15 to 20 minutes; serve warm. (Tarts can be made up to 1 day ahead. Cover and refrigerate. To warm, heat tarts in 325°F. oven for 3 to 5 minutes or until warm.)

TIP *The custard tarts in Hong Kong are bright yellow in color. During the summer months, it's sometimes possible to get free-range, organic eggs with yolks that are often bright yellow-orange. Otherwise, food coloring helps create that color, but it's not necessary.

12 (2¼-inch) tarts

PER TART: 130 calories, 9 g total fat (5.5 g saturated fat), 2 g protein, 10.5 g carbohydrate, 75 mg cholesterol, 35 mg sodium, 0 g fiber

Janice Cole is food editor of Cooking Pleasures.

Neapolitan Seafood Soup

A Taste of Italy

Chase away chills with a warming bowl of zuppa.

Text and Recipes by Sharon Sanders

Italians have an antidote to sullen weather—a steaming bowl of soup, called zuppa. As my Italian friends would say, zuppa is more than soup. Zuppa is a meal, the creation of canny Italian home cooks who use bits of this and that to make it. These hearty soups may contain vegetables, legumes, mushrooms, broth or water, pasta or rice, grated cheese, and perhaps meat, fowl or seafood.

Even stale bread has a place in zuppa. Bread that's too hard to eat is placed at the bottom of the bowl. The soup is ladled over it. The bread thickens the soup and soaks up every last drop of savory juices. It becomes the prize when the soup is finished.

These versions of zuppa cook quickly. Accompany them with crusty bread and fresh fruit for dessert, for a perfect warming supper, the Italian way.

Neapolitan Seafood Soup

In Naples, tomato is the defining ingredient in soup broth. In keeping with the flexibility of Italian cooks, the clams, shrimp and scallops can be replaced with crab, mussels, lobster or baby squid.

- 3 large garlic cloves, divided
- 2 tablespoons extra-virgin olive oil
- 1 large onion, coarsely chopped (about 2 cups)
- 1 yellow or orange bell pepper, coarsely chopped
- 2 teaspoons dried oregano
- 1/4 teaspoon crushed red pepper
- 1 cup dry red wine
- 1 (28-oz.) can crushed plum tomatoes (not in puree)
- 3 cups water
- 2 (8-oz.) bottles clam juice
- 1/3 cup minced fresh Italian parsley
- 1/2 teaspoon salt
- 3/4 lb. shelled, deveined uncooked medium shrimp
- 3/4 lb. sea scallops
- 3/4 lb. chopped fresh clams
- 8 slices Italian bread (1 inch thick), toasted

1 Mince 2 of the garlic cloves. Heat oil in heavy large pot over medium heat until hot. Add onion, bell pepper, minced garlic, oregano and red pepper. Cover and cook 5 to 8 minutes or until soft, stirring occasionally. Add wine. Increase heat to medium-high; cook 5 minutes or until wine is reduced by half. Add tomatoes, water, clam juice, parsley and salt. Bring to a boil; reduce heat to low. Cover and cook 15 minutes, stirring occasionally.

2 Remove cover. Increase heat to medium-high; bring to a gentle boil. Add shrimp, scallops and clams. Cook 2 to 3 minutes or until shrimp turn pink and scallops and clams are opaque.

3 Meanwhile, rub toasted bread with remaining garlic clove. Place slice of bread in each soup bowl. Ladle soup over bread. Pass additional red pepper, if desired.

WINE The tomatoes and peppers in the soup necessitate a lighter red wine. Opt for either Terrale Primitivo from Puglia in southern Italy or Masi "La Vegrona" Bardolino.

8 (1 2/3-cup) servings

PER SERVING: 215 calories, 5.5 g total fat (1 g saturated fat), 21.5 g protein, 19.5 g carbohydrate, 85 mg cholesterol, 715 mg sodium, 2.5 g fiber

Cannellini Bean and Porcini Soup

Cannellini beans—white kidney beans—and wild porcini mushrooms are much beloved in Florentine kitchens. If you prefer, substitute great Northern or navy beans. Pass additional red pepper.

- 1 oz. dried porcini mushrooms
- 2 cups water
- 1/4 cup extra-virgin olive oil
- 1 1/2 tablespoons minced garlic
- 1 tablespoon minced fresh rosemary
- 10 oz. (5 cups) sliced cremini mushrooms
- 3 (14-oz.) cans reduced-sodium chicken broth
- 2 (15-oz.) cans cannellini beans, drained, rinsed
- 1 (14 1/2-oz.) can diced tomatoes, undrained
- 1/3 cup minced fresh Italian parsley
- 1/2 teaspoon salt
- 1/2 teaspoon crushed red pepper
- 6 slices Italian bread (1 inch), toasted
- 6 tablespoons (1 1/2 oz.) Parmesan cheese

Making Zuppa

Better ingredients, tastier soup.
Choose extra-virgin olive oil, Parmigiano-Reggiano cheese, pancetta, dense Italian bread, cannellini beans (white kidney beans) and dried porcini mushrooms. Use homemade broth or canned reduced-sodium broth.

Pancetta

A heavy pot for even cooking.
Use a heavy, 6-quart pot that's made of enameled cast iron, stainless steel over aluminum or anodized aluminum.

Sauté aromatic ingredients. Sautéing garlic, onion, peppers, herbs and other aromatics in olive oil or butter brings out the ingredients' natural flavors and sweetness. The Italians call this a soffrito (so-FREE-toh) and use it to flavor soups, sauces and other dishes.

Parmigiano-Reggiano

Add no starch before its time.
Pasta and other grains should never be mushy. Add the starch near the end of the cooking time. A zuppa may be made in advance, cooked up to the point of adding the pasta or grain, then cooled and refrigerated. Just before serving, return the zuppa to the pot and bring almost to a boil. Add the starch, and cook the zuppa until done.

1 Place porcini mushrooms and water in medium microwave-safe bowl. Cover with plastic wrap; make small cut in plastic wrap to vent. Microwave on high 2 to 3 minutes or until water is boiling. Let stand 10 minutes to soften.
2 Meanwhile, in heavy large pot, heat oil over medium heat until hot. Stir in garlic and rosemary until sizzling. Stir in cremini mushrooms. Cook 8 minutes or until mushrooms are browned, stirring occasionally. Add broth, beans, tomatoes with juice, parsley, salt and red pepper.
3 Drain porcini mushrooms into small bowl through fine sieve lined with paper coffee filter. Add porcini liquid to pot. Rinse porcini mushrooms; finely chop. Add to pot. Bring to a simmer over medium-high

heat. Reduce heat to medium-low. Partially cover and cook 30 minutes.
4 Place slice of toasted bread in each soup bowl. Ladle soup over bread; sprinkle with cheese.
WINE The ingredients in this dish call for an elegant Tuscan red. Barone Ricasoli "Formulae" is made entirely from the Sangiovese grape, while Brolio Chianti Classico is richer, yet still elegant enough for this soup.

6 (2-cup) servings

PER SERVING: 315 calories, 13.5 g total fat (3 g saturated fat), 16.5 g protein, 33.5 g carbohydrate, 5 mg cholesterol, 1280 mg sodium, 6.5 g fiber

Potato-Broccoli Soup with Prosciutto

The rich flavor of prosciutto is key to this robust dish, inspired by rustic winter soups from the Italian Alps. If making this soup ahead, wait to add the broccoli until just before serving.

- 3 tablespoons extra-virgin olive oil
- 4 oz. sliced prosciutto (1/8 inch thick), cut into 1/4-inch strips
- 1 1/2 tablespoons minced garlic
- 2 medium leeks, white and light green parts only, sliced (1/2 inch)
- 1 1/2 teaspoons dried sage
- 1 1/2 teaspoons dried thyme
- 2 bay leaves
- 1 1/2 lb. russet potatoes, peeled, cubed (1/2 inch)
- 3 (14-oz.) cans reduced-sodium chicken broth
- 3 cups water
- 1/2 teaspoon salt
- 1/2 teaspoon freshly ground pepper
- 4 cups broccoli florets, halved
- 6 tablespoons (1 1/2 oz.) grated Pecorino Romano cheese

1 Heat oil in heavy large pot over medium-low heat until hot. Add prosciutto and garlic; cook 5 minutes, stirring occasionally, or until any fat on prosciutto is melted. (If necessary, reduce heat so garlic doesn't brown.)
2 Add leeks, sage, thyme and bay leaves. Increase heat to medium-high. Cook and stir 5 minutes or until leeks soften. Add potatoes, broth, water, salt and pepper. Bring soup to a simmer; reduce heat to medium-low. Cover partially; simmer 20 minutes or until potatoes are tender. With back of large spoon, smash some potatoes against bottom and sides of pot to thicken broth.
3 Add broccoli. Cook, uncovered, 2 to 3 minutes or until broccoli is bright green. Remove and discard bay leaves. Ladle soup into bowls; sprinkle with cheese.
WINE Louis Latour Chardonnay from Ardeche in southern France is rich

Venetian Chicken-Rice Soup

enough for the prosciutto in this soup, while Pio Cesare Cortese di Gavi is a traditional northern Italian white that is ideal for bringing together this dish's flavors.

6 (1¾-cup) servings

PER SERVING: 265 calories, 12.5 g total fat (3 g saturated fat), 12.5 g protein, 27 g carbohydrate, 15 mg cholesterol, 835 mg sodium, 4 g fiber

Venetian Chicken-Rice Soup

Rice is an extremely popular grain in the Veneto region of Italy. If you're making this soup a day or two before serving, don't add the rice. At serving time, reheat the soup until almost boiling. Then add the rice and cook according to the recipe.

 2 tablespoons olive oil
 6 oz. pancetta, diced*
 1 large onion, chopped
 2 medium carrots, chopped
 2 ribs celery, chopped
 4 large garlic cloves, minced
 2 bay leaves
¼ teaspoon saffron threads, crushed

1½ lb. boneless skinless chicken thighs
 6 (14-oz.) cans reduced-sodium chicken broth
¾ cup medium- or long-grain rice
½ teaspoon freshly ground pepper
 3 tablespoons minced fresh Italian parsley
 1 tablespoon grated lemon peel

1 Heat oil in Dutch oven over medium heat until hot. Add pancetta; cook 5 minutes or until lightly browned. Add onion, carrots and celery; cook 8 minutes or until onion begins to brown. Add garlic, bay leaves and saffron; cook 30 seconds.
2 Add chicken and broth; increase heat to medium-high. Bring almost to a boil; reduce heat to medium-low. Partially cover and cook 12 to 15 minutes or until chicken is no longer pink in center and juices run clear. Remove chicken; cool slightly. Shred chicken meat.

3 Meanwhile, add rice and pepper to Dutch oven. Partially cover and cook

20 minutes or until rice is tender, stirring occasionally. Return chicken to pot; cook 5 minutes or until chicken is heated through. Remove and discard bay leaves.
4 In small bowl, stir together parsley and lemon peel. Ladle soup into bowls; sprinkle with parsley mixture.
TIP *Pancetta is an unsmoked, rolled Italian bacon that is cured with salt and spices. Prosciutto or ham can be substituted.
WINE Two Venetian whites are good selections for this soup. Canaletto Pinot Grigio marries well with the chicken and rice, as does Bolla Soave "Tufaie".

8 (1¾-cup) servings

PER SERVING: 450 calories, 28.5 g total fat (9.5 g saturated fat), 28 g protein, 18 g carbohydrate, 75 mg cholesterol, 795 mg sodium, 1 g fiber

Sharon Sanders, the author of *Cooking Up an Italian Life* (PergolaWest), heads a media lifestyle company devoted to Italian food and life.

Escarole, Tomato, Anchovy and Olive Salad with Xató Dressing
Sherry Roast Chicken with Black Currant Jam

A Toast to Spain

A hearty menu celebrates the tasty traditions of Spanish cuisine.

Text and Recipes by Penelope Casas

The foods and wines of Spain have long been a passion of mine. For years I have returned from that country with the foods I love best: splendid extra-virgin olive oils, the finest sherry vinegar, extraordinary cheeses, wonderful anchovies, unique piquillo peppers and plump Valencian rice.

What a pleasure now to finally find all these foods and so much more here in the United States with the click of a mouse, a quick phone call or a visit to a local gourmet shop. I often wonder why it took so long for Spain's cuisine to be embraced, although I know there were obstacles to overcome. Foremost among them was the notion that the cooking of Spain was one and the same as the cooking of Latin America. The word Spanish was loosely applied to dishes from any country where Spanish was spoken.

Today, Americans have begun to understand that the cooking of Spain is not hot and spicy, as some imagined it to be, but a health-giving Mediterranean diet based on olive oil, garlic, fish, grains and vegetables. *¡Que Aproveche!*, as they would say in Spain: Enjoy!

Escarole, Tomato, Anchovy and Olive Salad with Xató Dressing

Xató is a traditional sauce of garlic, nuts and dried red pepper from Catalonia. Although it is excellent with many dishes, including grilled fish and meats, it's a great dressing for a salad of escarole, tomatoes, anchovies and olives.

DRESSING
- 2 Spanish sweet dried red peppers (ñoras) or 1 mild dried red pepper (such as guajillo)*
- 10 blanched almonds
- 10 hazelnuts
- 1 small plum tomato, chopped
- 3 garlic cloves, minced
- ⅛ teaspoon kosher (coarse) or sea salt
- 6 tablespoons extra-virgin olive oil
- 2 tablespoons red wine vinegar

SALAD
- 6 cups torn escarole
- 24 grape or cherry tomatoes, halved if large
- 16 oil-cured ripe olives
- 8 anchovies
- 2 tablespoons minced fresh parsley

1 Heat oven to 450°F. Cut stems from dried peppers; shake out seeds. Place in small bowl of hot water; soak 20 minutes or until pliable.
2 Meanwhile, place almonds and hazelnuts on rimmed baking sheet. Bake 4 minutes or until almonds are light brown; cool. Place in food processor; process until finely ground. Scrape flesh from peppers; add to food processor with plum tomato, garlic and salt. Pulse until well combined. With motor running, slowly pour in oil and vinegar. Pour dressing through fine strainer into small bowl.
3 On individual salad plates, arrange escarole, cherry tomatoes, olives and anchovies. Drizzle with dressing; sprinkle with parsley.

TIP *Noras, Spanish dried, sweet red peppers, are available online or by mail order from Tienda.com (888-472-1022 or www.tienda.com) or from The Spanish Table (505-986-0243 or www.spanishtable.com). If they are unavailable, substitute a combination of 2 finely chopped pimientos and 2 teaspoons paprika.

4 servings

PER SERVING: 295 calories, 27 g total fat (3.5 g saturated fat), 5.5 g protein, 11.5 g carbohydrate, 5 mg cholesterol, 500 mg sodium, 4 g fiber

Sherry Roast Chicken with Black Currant Jam

Variations of this recipe are found frequently in Andalusian cooking. Don't let the long list of ingredients deter you. The recipe is easy and goes together quickly. For a perfect accompaniment, serve white rice cooked with chicken broth and seasoned with thyme, parsley and a few strands of saffron.

- 1 (3½-lb.) cut-up chicken
- 3 tablespoons extra-virgin olive oil, divided
- 1 large garlic clove, mashed
- ¼ cup black currant jam
- 2 tablespoons julienned orange peel
- 1 large garlic clove, minced
- ½ teaspoon ground cumin
- 2 tablespoons minced fresh parsley
- 2 tablespoons dry white wine or orange juice
- 1 tablespoon chopped fresh thyme or ½ teaspoon dried
- 1 tablespoon chopped fresh rosemary or ½ teaspoon dried
- ½ teaspoon kosher (coarse) or sea salt
- ¼ teaspoon freshly ground pepper
- ½ cup Oloroso (medium-sweet) sherry or apple cider

Chorizo- and Pimiento-Filled Fried Phyllo

1 Heat oven to 400°F. Using kitchen shears, cut chicken wings in half, divide breast into 4 pieces and halve each thigh.

2 In small bowl, stir together 2 tablespoons of the olive oil and mashed garlic. In another small bowl, stir together jam, orange peel, minced garlic, cumin, parsley and wine.

3 Grease shallow roasting pan with remaining 1 tablespoon olive oil; arrange chicken in pan, skin side up. Brush chicken with olive oil-garlic mixture; sprinkle with thyme, rosemary, salt and pepper. Pour sherry into pan; bake 30 minutes, basting occasionally.

4 Brush chicken with black currant mixture; bake an additional 15 minutes or until chicken is no longer pink and juices run clear. Place

chicken on platter. Skim off any fat from pan juices. If no liquid remains, add ¼ cup water or chicken broth. Place roasting pan over high heat; bring to a boil, scraping up browned bits from bottom of pan. Spoon sauce over chicken.

4 servings

PER SERVING: 550 calories, 30.5 g total fat (7 g saturated fat), 47.5 g protein, 18 g carbohydrate, 145 mg cholesterol, 335 mg sodium, .5 g fiber

Chorizo- and Pimiento-Filled Fried Phyllo

Phyllo pastry is typically brushed with butter and baked, but in Spain, it is more likely to be prepared without butter and fried in olive oil. The filling of chorizo, Spain's traditional garlic and paprika-scented sausage, and pimientos makes this appetizer perfectly Spanish.

- 2 teaspoons olive oil plus extra for frying
- 2 tablespoons minced onion
- 1 garlic clove, minced
- 1 tablespoon minced fresh parsley
- ¼ lb. sweet or spicy chorizo, skinned, finely chopped*
- 1 tablespoon dry red wine

Chorizo This is Spain's well-known, dry-cured sausage that is seasoned with paprika and garlic. In Spain, it is sliced and eaten as a tapa, but it is also used to season dishes, such as bean or chickpea stews.

Olive Oils Spain produces olive oils of the highest quality, the result of the country's ideal growing conditions and remarkable selection of olive varieties. The oils range from subtle and mild to fruity and robust.

Piquillo Peppers These delicate, wood-roasted, slightly piquant peppers have gained an enthusiastic following among chefs and home cooks. They are marvelous on their own, in salads or lightly sautéed, and most elegant when stuffed with meat or fish.

Noras These dried, sweet red peppers are used extensively in Spanish cooking to lend a distinctive earthy flavor to salad dressings, vegetables and sauces for fish.

Anchovies Spain's anchovies are among the world's best. Look for those in jars, which tend to be better quality and allow you to see what you are buying. Anchovies should be firm but succulent and not overly salty.

¼ cup minced Spanish pimientos del piquillo or roasted red bell peppers**
8 (17x12-inch) sheets frozen phyllo dough, thawed

1 Heat 2 teaspoons oil in medium skillet over medium heat until hot. Reduce heat to medium-low. Add onion, garlic and parsley; cook 3 minutes or until onion is wilted. Increase heat to medium-high. Add chorizo; cook and stir 1 minute or until it begins to release its oil. Stir in wine; bring to a boil. Boil 1 minute or until wine has evaporated. Stir in pimientos. Remove filling with slotted spoon; cool on paper towel-lined plate.
2 Cut 1 sheet phyllo dough in half lengthwise. (Keep remaining sheets

Sherry: The Quintessential Wine of Spain

Sherry is among the world's oldest wines, savored and praised over the centuries for its exceptional quality and distinctive taste. It's a uniquely Spanish wine made in the southern region of Spain called Andalucia, around the city of Jerez de la Frontera (jerez is the Spanish word for sherry). It requires the microclimate and the chalky albariza soil typical to that part of Spain. The sun shines brilliantly most days of the year, creating perfect conditions for sherry, which, unlike table wines, must be exposed to light and air during the aging process to achieve its unique flavor. The wine is then blended with older sherries and fortified to reach 16 to 20 percent alcohol.

Sherry is surely the world's most versatile wine, ranging from bone dry to syrupy sweet (it's the sweet sherry that gave sherry its image as a drink sipped by old ladies in staid British parlors). Cream and Oloroso sherries generally complement desserts, while pale, dry Fino, Manzanilla (a kind of Fino made in the nearby town of Sanlúcar de Barrameda) and Amontillado (dry, golden-colored and nutty) are apéritifs.

In southern Spain, well-chilled Fino and Manzanilla are considered the aristocrats of sherries and have traditionally been the wines of choice with tapas. Over the centuries, the custom developed of serving dry sherry with complementary nibbles—ideally, olives, almonds and shrimp. Indeed, once you have experienced sherry in its native setting, it is difficult to imagine a drink more sublime. In sherry country, time seems to stand still, and one is taken back to a more gracious and relaxed era. The magnificent weather, the slow pace of life that centers around outdoor cafes, and the warmth and friendliness of the people of Andalucia all contribute to the endurance of sherry as a part of the very fiber of Andalusian life. In America, sherry has finally come into its own as a delightful before-dinner alternative to white wines and cocktails.

Wines with This Menu

A well-chilled Fino sherry served with the appetizers gets the meal off to an authentically Spanish start. With the salad and chicken courses, serve a red Rioja wine. For dessert, serve a medium-sweet Oloroso sherry; it's the perfect complement to the apple custard tart. End on a festive note with Spanish cava, Spain's exceptional sparkling wine made using the champagne method.

covered with plastic wrap or cloth.) Place about 2 teaspoons of the filling in middle of one end of the phyllo strip. Fold sides over filling; roll up. Brush end with water to seal. Place on paper towel-lined baking sheet. Repeat with remaining phyllo and filling. Cover with plastic wrap.

3 Pour at least ½ inch oil into large skillet (or use deep-fryer); heat oil to 385°F. (cube of bread dropped in oil will quickly brown). Fry rolls in batches 1 to 1½ minutes or until golden brown, turning once. Drain on paper towels. If desired, place in 200°F. oven for up to 30 minutes to keep warm. (Phyllo rolls can be made up to 3 hours ahead. Cover and refrigerate. Reheat at 350°F. for 10 minutes or until crispy and warm.)

TIPS *Chorizo is a spicy pork sausage used in Mexican and Spanish cooking. Spanish chorizo is dry-cured and comes in links. It can be found in the meat department of some grocery stores or Latin markets. If unavailable, substitute other highly seasoned sausage.

**Pimientos del piquillo are delicate wood-roasted red peppers sold in jars.

16 appetizers

PER APPETIZER: 80 calories, 5.5 g total fat (1.5 g saturated fat), 2.5 g protein, 5.5 g carbohydrate, 5 mg cholesterol, 115 mg sodium, 0 g fiber

Basque Apple Custard Tart

This wonderful tart is found in many versions in Spain's Basque country. The flaky crust is a bit tricky, but it's worth the effort. The sliced apples tenderize nicely in the syrup, allowing for a shorter baking time. The tart is best when eaten the same day.

APPLES
- 2 Golden Delicious apples, peeled, quartered, cut into very thin slices (scant ⅛ inch)
- 1½ cups apple juice
- 3 tablespoons sugar
- 2 whole cloves
- ¼ teaspoon ground nutmeg

CRUST
- 1 cup all-purpose flour
- 2 tablespoons sugar

- ½ teaspoon baking powder
- 6 tablespoons unsalted butter, chilled
- 1 egg yolk
- 2 to 3 tablespoons heavy whipping cream

CUSTARD
- 1 cup milk
- ½ cinnamon stick
  Peel of ½ medium lemon, cut into wide strips*
- 2 egg yolks
- ¼ cup sugar
- 2 tablespoons cornstarch
- 2 teaspoons unsalted butter

GLAZE
- 2 tablespoons apricot preserves

1 Place apples in large shallow bowl. In medium saucepan, stir together all remaining apple ingredients. Bring to a boil over high heat. Reduce heat to medium-high; simmer 8 minutes or until reduced by half. Pour syrup over apples; let stand at room temperature 2 to 3 hours to infuse apples with syrup.

2 Heat oven to 350°F. In another large bowl, stir together flour, 2 tablespoons sugar and baking powder. With pastry blender or 2 knives, cut in butter until mixture resembles coarse crumbs with some pea-sized pieces. With fork, stir in egg yolk and cream. Turn out onto lightly floured work surface; work lightly until dough forms. Sprinkle with flour. Roll into 11-inch round. Line bottom and sides of 9-inch tart pan with removable bottom with dough. Prick all over with fork. Bake 15 to 18 minutes or until light brown. Cool on wire rack. Increase oven temperature to 450°F.

3 Meanwhile, in medium saucepan, bring milk, cinnamon stick and lemon peel to a boil over medium heat. Reduce heat to low. Cover and simmer 20 minutes. Cool 10 minutes; remove and discard cinnamon stick and lemon peel.

4 In medium bowl, whisk together 2 egg yolks and ¼ cup sugar. Whisk in cornstarch; slowly stir in warm milk. Return to saucepan; cook over medium heat, stirring constantly, 1 to 2 minutes or until thickened and smooth. Remove from heat; add 2 teaspoons butter. Cool, stirring occasionally.

5 Pour custard into crust. Remove

apples from syrup; discard syrup or save for another use. Arrange apples over custard in tightly overlapping rows. Bake at 450°F. for 10 minutes or until filling is set. (Filling will jiggle slightly when moved, and knife inserted between sides and filling will come out clean.)

6 Finely chop any large pieces of apricot in preserves. In small saucepan, heat preserves over low heat to liquify; brush over tart. Let stand until cool. Serve at room temperature. Store in refrigerator.

TIP *Use a vegetable peeler to remove lemon peel; avoid getting any white pith from under skin.

8 servings

PER SERVING: 275 calories, 13.5 g total fat (7.5 g saturated fat), 4 g protein, 35.5 g carbohydrate, 110 mg cholesterol, 55 mg sodium, 1 g fiber

Penelope Casas is the author of several books on Spain, including *The Foods and Wines of Spain* (Knopf).

MAIN DISHES

Linguine in Saffron-Lemon Sauce,
Belgian Endive, Watercress and Ginger Salad

Quick Pastas

Let's eat! I'm starving.

Text and Recipes by G. Franco Romagnoli

In Italy, a hungry worker phones home at the end of the day: "I'm coming, *butta giù la pasta!*" The call signals the cook at home that it's time to throw the pasta into the boiling water. The worker arrives home and dinner is ready—pasta and sauce.

These recipes debunk the notion that it takes hours to prepare an Italian sauce. While the pasta cooks, the sauce is prepared. Add a salad, and a satisfying meal is truly just minutes away. .

Linguine in Saffron-Lemon Sauce

Saffron and prosciutto add complex flavor and dramatic color to this delicate, aromatic sauce. You can substitute strips of thinly sliced ham for the prosciutto. Serve this dish with Belgian Endive, Watercress and Ginger Salad.

- 1 lb. linguine
- 1/2 cup whipping cream
- 1/4 cup vodka or chicken broth
- 2 tablespoons unsalted butter, cut up
- 1 1/2 teaspoons grated lemon peel
- 1/4 teaspoon ground nutmeg
- 1/4 teaspoon saffron threads, crushed
- 1/4 teaspoon salt
- 3 oz. sliced prosciutto, cut into thin strips*
- 3 tablespoons fresh lemon juice

1 Cook linguine in large pot of boiling salted water 8 to 10 minutes or until al dente; drain.
2 Meanwhile, place cream, vodka, butter, lemon peel, nutmeg, saffron and salt in large skillet. Cook over low heat 5 to 8 minutes or until hot and flavors have blended.
3 As soon as linguine is drained, add to skillet with prosciutto; increase heat to medium-high. Bring to a boil, gently stirring to combine. Remove from heat. Add lemon juice; toss.
TIP *Proscuitto is an Italian-style, salt-cured, unsmoked ham.
WINE Casa Lapostolle Sauvignon Blanc from Chile picks up on all the flavors here, as does Jacob's Creek Chardonnay from Australia.

4 servings

PER SERVING: 635 calories, 19 g total fat (10.5 g saturated fat), 20 g protein, 92.5 g carbohydrate, 60 mg cholesterol, 885 mg sodium, 4.5 g fiber

Belgian Endive, Watercress and Ginger Salad

- 3 heads Belgian endive, halved crosswise, cut into thin wedges
- 3 cups coarsely chopped watercress
- 2 tablespoons extra-virgin olive oil
- 1 tablespoon red wine vinegar
- 1 teaspoon water
- 1 teaspoon grated fresh ginger
- 1 small garlic clove, minced
- 1/4 teaspoon freshly ground pepper
- 1/8 teaspoon salt

1 In large bowl, toss together endive and watercress.
2 In small bowl, whisk together oil, vinegar, 1 teaspoon water, ginger, garlic, pepper and salt. Drizzle over endive and watercress; toss gently.

4 servings

PER SERVING: 115 calories, 7.5 g total fat (1 g saturated fat), 4.5 g protein, 11 g carbohydrate, 0 mg cholesterol, 145 mg sodium, 9.5 g fiber

Vermicelli with Clam Sauce

Anchovies heighten the clams' taste in the sauce. Toasted bread crumbs give a little crunch and help bind the sauce.

Mushroom-Parmesan Salad is the perfect accompaniment.

- 1 lb. vermicelli (thin strands of spaghetti)
- 6 tablespoons plus 1 1/2 teaspoons olive oil, divided
- 4 garlic cloves
- 3 anchovies
- 2 dried red chiles, veins and seeds removed, or pinch cayenne pepper
- 1/2 cup dry white wine
- 1 (10-oz.) can baby clams, drained, 5 tablespoons juice reserved
- 6 tablespoons unseasoned fresh bread crumbs*
- 1 tablespoon minced fresh Italian parsley

1 Cook vermicelli in large pot of boiling salted water 6 minutes or until al dente; drain.
2 Meanwhile, heat 6 tablespoons of the oil in large skillet over medium heat until hot. Add garlic, anchovies and chiles.** Cook, stirring occasionally, 3 to 5 minutes or until garlic and chiles are golden brown, watching carefully so they don't burn. While cooking, mash anchovies with fork or wooden spoon until almost melted into oil. Remove and discard garlic and chiles. Add wine and reserved 5 tablespoons of the clam juice. Bring to a boil; boil 2 to 3 minutes or until slightly reduced. Stir in clams; remove from heat. (Clams will get tough if overcooked.)
3 Place bread crumbs and remaining 1 1/2 teaspoons oil in small saucepan;

stir to coat bread crumbs. Cook and stir over medium-high heat 2 minutes or until golden brown.

4 Add drained vermicelli to skillet. Toss briefly over medium-high heat. Place on serving platter; sprinkle with bread crumbs and parsley.

TIPS *Toasted bread crumbs are used a lot in Italy for topping pasta. If desired, brown large batch of bread crumbs and keep in a jar in the refrigerator for up to 1 month.

**If using cayenne pepper, add with wine in this step.

BEER/WINE With its clean, refreshing flavors, Samuel Adams Boston Lager is a fine beer choice. For wine, go with the crisp Mezzacorona Pinot Grigio from northern Italy.

4 servings

PER SERVING: 720 calories, 25 g total fat (3.5 g saturated fat), 25 g protein, 96 g carbohydrate, 25 mg cholesterol, 665 mg sodium, 4.5 g fiber

Mushroom-Parmesan Salad

This salad is a study in contrast. The bright-red radicchio shines against the pale green of iceberg lettuce, while the crunchy texture of both offsets the tender mushrooms. Use a pleasantly fruity olive oil to blend the sweetness of the balsamic vinegar with the bitterness of the radicchio.

    2 cups thinly sliced radicchio
    2 cups thinly sliced iceberg lettuce
    4 oz. mushrooms, thinly sliced
    3 oz. Parmigiano-Reggiano cheese, shaved*
    2 tablespoons extra-virgin olive oil
    1 tablespoon balsamic vinegar
    ¼ teaspoon salt
    ¼ teaspoon freshly ground pepper

1 In medium bowl, toss together radicchio and lettuce. Divide evenly among 4 salad plates. Top with mushrooms and cheese.

2 In small bowl, whisk together oil, vinegar, salt and pepper. Drizzle over salad.

TIP *Shave cheese using vegetable peeler.

4 servings

PER SERVING: 175 calories, 13.5 g total fat (5 g saturated fat),

---

10 g protein, 4 g carbohydrate, 16.5 mg cholesterol, 550 mg sodium, 1 g fiber

Spaghetti with Fresh Mushroom-Caper Sauce

Mushrooms and anchovies give this uncooked sauce an earthy nature. Mayonnaise and mustard bind the sauce and lend it a creamy texture. This dish goes well with Tuscan Bean and Onion Salad.

    1   lb. spaghetti
    12   oz. button mushrooms, very thinly sliced
    2   anchovies, minced, if desired
    3   tablespoons minced fresh Italian parsley
    2   tablespoons capers, rinsed, drained, minced
    1   large garlic clove, finely minced
    ½   cup extra-virgin olive oil
    ¼   cup lemon juice
    1   teaspoon salt
    ¼   teaspoon white pepper
    1½   tablespoons mayonnaise
    1   teaspoon Dijon mustard

1 Cook spaghetti in large pot of boiling salted water 10 to 12 minutes or until al dente; drain.

2 Meanwhile, in large bowl, combine all remaining ingredients except mayonnaise and mustard; toss well. Let stand while spaghetti cooks.

3 When spaghetti is done, stir mayonnaise and mustard into mushroom mixture. Add spaghetti; toss.

BEER/WINE Dos Equis Amber from Mexico is a flavorful dark beer that works here. If you prefer wine, try Ruffino "Fonte al Sole" Sangiovese from Tuscany.

5 servings

PER SERVING: 605 calories, 27 g total fat (3.5 g saturated fat), 14 g protein, 77.5 g carbohydrate, 5 mg cholesterol, 990 mg sodium, 4.5 g fiber

Tuscan Bean and Onion Salad

    1   cup thinly sliced red onion
    1   (15-oz.) can cannellini or borlotti beans, drained, rinsed
    2   tablespoons extra-virgin olive oil

---

    1   tablespoon white wine vinegar
    ¼   teaspoon salt
    ¼   teaspoon freshly ground pepper

1 Place onion in medium bowl; cover with ice water. Let stand 20 minutes.

2 Just before serving, place beans in large bowl. Drain onions; add to large bowl. In small bowl, whisk together oil, vinegar, salt and pepper. Add to large bowl; toss.

4 servings

PER SERVING: 135 calories, 7 g total fat (1 g saturated fat), 4.5 g protein, 14.5 g carbohydrate, 0 mg cholesterol, 395 mg sodium, 4 g fiber

Spicy Tomato Penne

This is an uplifting dish, excellent for an alfresco spring dinner. You can adjust the heat to your tastes by cutting back on the chiles or cayenne. Serve this dish with Sicilian-Style Orange Salad *(page 57).*

    1   lb. penne (tube-shaped pasta) or ziti
    ¼   cup olive oil
    5   medium garlic cloves
    4   dried red chiles or 1 teaspoon cayenne pepper
    3   slices thick-sliced bacon, cut into ½-inch strips
    1   (14.5-oz.) can diced tomatoes, undrained
    6   tablespoons (1½ oz.) shredded Pecorino Romano cheese
    2   tablespoons minced fresh Italian parsley

1 Cook penne in large pot of boiling salted water 9 to 11 minutes or until al dente; drain.

2 Meanwhile, heat oil in large skillet over medium heat until hot. Add garlic and chiles;* cook 2 to 4 minutes or until golden brown, watching carefully so they don't burn. Remove and discard garlic and chiles.

3 Add bacon to pan; cook 5 minutes or until cooked but not browned and crisp. Add tomatoes. Bring to a boil; boil 1 to 2 minutes or until hot, mashing tomatoes with potato masher until sauce is blended and almost smooth.

Spaghetti with Fresh Mushroom-Caper Sauce,
Tuscan Bean and Onion Salad

Spicy Tomato Penne,
Sicilian-Style Orange Salad

4 Add drained penne to pan. Increase heat to medium-high; stir until blended. Place in serving bowl; sprinkle with cheese and parsley.

TIP *If using cayenne pepper, add in step 3 with tomatoes.

BEER/WINE If you prefer beer, try the Bass Ale from England. For wine, Badia a Coltibuono "Cetamura" Chianti is a fine option.

4 servings

PER SERVING: 735 calories, 29.5 g total fat (8 g saturated fat), 21.5 g protein, 95 g carbohydrate, 25 mg cholesterol, 860 mg sodium, 5.5 g fiber

Sicilian-Style Orange Salad

18 Kalamata olives
1 1/2 tablespoons lemon juice
 2 seedless oranges, peeled, thinly sliced
 2 blood oranges or seedless oranges, peeled, thinly sliced
 1/4 cup extra-virgin olive oil
 1/4 teaspoon salt
 1/4 teaspoon freshly ground pepper

1 In small bowl, combine olives and lemon juice; let stand 15 minutes.

2 Arrange oranges on large platter or individual salad plates. Drizzle with olive oil; sprinkle with salt and pepper. Let stand 15 minutes.

3 Press gently on some of the orange slices to release juices. Tilt plate; spoon juices over oranges. Sprinkle with olives; drizzle with olive marinade.

4 servings

PER SERVING: 205 calories, 15.5 g total fat (2 g saturated fat), 1.5 g protein, 17 g carbohydrate, 0 mg cholesterol, 305 mg sodium, 4 g fiber

Spring Spaghettini with Tuna

The light, fresh flavors in this sauce rely on high-quality canned tomatoes and albacore tuna. Accompany the pasta with Radicchio, Arugula and Fennel Salad.

 1 lb. spaghettini (very thin spaghetti)
 1/4 cup olive oil
 1 large onion, halved lengthwise, thinly sliced
 1 (14.5-oz.) can whole plum tomatoes, undrained
 1/2 teaspoon salt
 1/2 teaspoon freshly ground pepper
 1 (9-oz.) pkg. frozen baby peas, thawed
 1 (6-oz.) can albacore tuna in water, drained
 4 drops hot pepper sauce
 4 tablespoons minced fresh Italian parsley, divided

1 Cook spaghettini in large pot of boiling salted water 6 to 10 minutes or until al dente; drain.

2 Meanwhile, heat oil in large skillet over medium heat until hot. Add onion; cook 3 to 5 minutes or until soft. Add tomatoes; mash with fork. Stir in salt and pepper. Bring to a boil. Stir in peas; boil 1 minute. Add tuna, stirring until hot and blended. Remove from heat. Stir in hot pepper sauce and 2 tablespoons of the parsley.

3 Add drained spaghettini to skillet; stir over medium-high heat until combined. Sprinkle with remaining parsley.

BEER/WINE Grolsch from Holland is a clean, flavorful beer that works well with this dish. A good choice for wine is Guenoc "California" Sauvignon Blanc, with its light herbal flavors.

5 servings

PER SERVING: 545 calories, 13 g total fat (2 g saturated fat), 23 g protein, 83.5 g carbohydrate, 10 mg cholesterol, 870 mg sodium, 6.5 g fiber

Radicchio, Arugula and Fennel Salad

The anise-like qualities of fennel and the slightly sharp natures of radicchio and arugula add great depth to this salad. Soaking the fennel in ice water makes it crisp.

 1 fennel bulb, fronds and stems removed and discarded, bulb halved, cut into thin strips
1 1/2 cups thinly sliced radicchio
 3/4 cup julienned arugula
 1 tablespoon extra-virgin olive oil
1 1/2 teaspoons balsamic vinegar
 1/2 teaspoon Dijon mustard
 1/4 teaspoon salt
 1/4 teaspoon freshly ground pepper

1 Place fennel in medium bowl; cover with ice water. Let stand 15 minutes.

2 Divide radicchio and arugula among 4 salad plates. Drain fennel; divide among plates. In small bowl, whisk together oil, vinegar, mustard, salt and pepper; drizzle over salad.

4 servings

PER SERVING: 55 calories, 3.5 g total fat (.5 g saturated fat), 1 g protein, 5.5 g carbohydrate, 0 mg cholesterol, 190 mg sodium, 2 g fiber

G. Franco Romagnoli, a native of Rome, is a Boston-based food writer. His most recent cookbook is Cucino di Magro, Cooking Lean the Traditional Italian Way *(Steerforth Press).*

Maple-Brined Rack of Pork

Holiday Roasts

Creative seasonings lend spice to classic cuts.

Text and Recipes by Bruce Aidells

Like many, my family gathers with friends for the holidays to take part in the traditional feasting. As the meat expert, I get the task each year of cooking the centerpiece of the meal, a roast. Last year it was rack of lamb smothered in fresh herbs, but often we've chosen prime rib of beef, New York strip roast, pork loin roast or leg of lamb.

I'll share a secret: My job is the easiest. My wife and our friends spend several hours preparing the rest of the meal. Making the roast entails seasoning it properly, roasting it to a nice brown color and removing it from the oven at the right time. Effort is minimal, stress, nil. And the payoff is a delicious roast.

You can have equally great success. Start with a good piece of meat and follow the tips here. You just may carve a new tradition.

Maple-Brined Rack of Pork

Brining—soaking meat in a salt solution—improves the flavor and juiciness of pork. This brine contains water, salt, maple syrup and other flavorings. Some of the water is absorbed by the meat while the salt improves the flavor.

```
6   cups water
1/4 cup packed light brown sugar
1/2 cup kosher (coarse) salt
1/2 cup plus 2 tablespoons
    maple syrup, divided
1/4 cup malt vinegar
2   teaspoons vanilla extract
3   cups ice cubes
1   (8-rib) pork loin roast
    (about 5 lb.)
1   tablespoon chopped fresh
    rosemary
1   tablespoon freshly ground
    pepper
```

1 In 2-gallon resealable plastic bag, combine water, brown sugar, salt, 1/2 cup of the maple syrup, vinegar and vanilla; stir until completely dissolved. Stir in ice cubes. (This quickly lowers temperature of brine.) Place pork in brine; seal bag. Place in large pan. Refrigerate 24 hours.

2 Remove pork from brine; discard brine. (Pork can be wrapped in plastic wrap and refrigerated up to 1 day.) Heat oven to 350°F. In small bowl, stir together rosemary and pepper; sprinkle over roast. Place roast, rib side down, in shallow roasting pan. Bake 1 hour to 1 hour 15 minutes or until internal temperature reaches 140°F.

3 Remove pork from oven. Increase temperature to 425°F. Brush pork with remaining 2 tablespoons maple syrup; bake an additional 5 minutes to glaze outside.

4 Remove pork from oven. Cover loosely with foil; let stand 15 to 20 minutes. Carve between each rib bone so each person receives thick chop.

WINE A spicy California or Italian red is a good choice for this entree. Try Bogle Petite Sirah from California, which has lots of character for the price. Or, for a truly great red, choose Fattoria di Felsina Chianti Classico "Berardenga".

8 servings

PER SERVING: 370 calories, 16 g total fat (5.5 g saturated fat), 45.5 g protein, 9 g carbohydrate, 130 mg cholesterol, 1240 mg sodium, .5 g fiber

Prime Rib with Fennel and Sage Crust

While a standing rib roast makes for a stunning presentation, it is a lot easier to carve a boneless rib-eye roast. You still get the same great taste of prime rib without the bother of removing the bones before carving it.

```
1   (5- to 6-lb.) boneless rib-eye
    roast (boneless prime rib)
1   tablespoon olive oil
2   tablespoons minced garlic
2   tablespoons chopped fresh sage
1   tablespoon fennel seeds,
    crushed*
1   tablespoon kosher (coarse) salt
2   teaspoons freshly ground
    pepper
```

1 Heat oven to 450°F. Cut 12 slits (1/2 inch deep and 2 inches long) in top side of roast. Brush top and sides of roast with oil. In small bowl, stir together all remaining ingredients. Press some of the spice mixture into each slit; spread remaining mixture over top and sides of roast. Tie in several places with kitchen twine to help roast maintain shape during baking.

2 Place roasting rack in roasting pan; place roast on rack. Bake 15 minutes.

Tying Meat

To give your roast a neat appearance, tie it the professional way. Take a long piece of kitchen twine and tie one end of it into a knot around the end of the roast. Wrap the twine nearest the knot around your hand and slip your fingers into the loop that forms. Stretch the loop around the meat and pull securely. Continue wrapping the twine around your hand and looping it around the meat until the roast is secure, typically four to six times. When the last loop is completed, take the remaining twine and run it underneath the roast and tie it to the other end.

Rolling Leg of Lamb

When a boneless leg of lamb is unrolled, it has a rather irregular shape. For a stuffed version, such as Porcini-Spinach-Stuffed Leg of Lamb, you'll want to make it as cylindrical in shape as possible when you roll it up. Begin by opening the meat flat on the work surface. Spread the stuffing evenly over it. Starting with the thickest edge, roll up the meat. Adjust the meat as you work, to keep the ends even. Secure the meat in four places with kitchen twine to prevent it from unrolling as it bakes.

3 Reduce temperature to 350°F. Bake an additional 1 hour 15 minutes to 1 hour 30 minutes or until internal temperature reaches 125°F. for medium-rare.

4 Remove from oven; cover loosely with foil. Let stand 20 to 30 minutes. Thinly slice.

TIP *Crush fennel seeds with mortar and pestle, spice grinder or flat side of meat mallet.

WINE Prime rib and Cabernet Sauvignon are a classic match. Trapiche from Argentina is a good value. Benziger from Sonoma is more expensive, but it has a light, minty character that complements the fennel flavors.

12 servings

PER SERVING: 310 calories, 14.5 g total fat (5.5 g saturated fat), 41 g protein, 1 g carbohydrate, 110 mg cholesterol, 485 mg sodium, 0 g fiber

Porcini-Spinach-Stuffed Leg of Lamb

Boneless leg of lamb is often sold wrapped in netting. Cut away the netting and discard it. When rolling up the boneless leg after spreading the stuffing on it, try to form it into a cylindrical shape.

STUFFING
- 1 oz. dried porcini mushrooms
- 1 (10-oz. pkg.) fresh spinach
- 1 tablespoon olive oil
- 3 tablespoons chopped shallots
- 1 tablespoon finely chopped garlic
- 1 cup fresh bread crumbs*
- ½ cup (2 oz.) freshly grated Parmesan cheese
- 1 tablespoon chopped fresh thyme
- 1 egg, beaten

LAMB
- 1 (5- to 6-lb.) boneless leg of lamb
- 2 tablespoons grated lemon peel
- 2 tablespoons finely chopped Kalamata olives
- 1 tablespoon chopped fresh oregano
- 2 teaspoons salt

2 teaspoons freshly ground
    pepper
¼ cup olive oil

1 Heat oven to 350°F. Place mushrooms in medium bowl. Cover with boiling water; let stand 30 minutes or until soft. Drain; finely chop.

2 Cook spinach in large pot of boiling salted water 1 minute. Drain; rinse under cool running water. Squeeze out as much moisture as possible; coarsely chop.

3 Heat oil in small skillet over medium heat until hot. Add shallots and garlic; cook 5 minutes or until soft.

4 In medium bowl, combine mushrooms, spinach, shallots, garlic, bread crumbs, cheese, thyme and egg; mix until well combined.

5 Place lamb, fat side down, on work surface; spread stuffing evenly over lamb. Roll up lamb; tie in 4 places with kitchen string.

6 In small bowl, stir together all remaining lamb ingredients. Brush mixture over lamb; place in shallow roasting pan. Bake 2 hours to 2 hours 20 minutes or until internal temperature of thickest part of lamb reaches 145°F. for medium-rare. Loosely cover with foil; let stand 20 to 30 minutes. Carefully remove string; slice into ½-inch pieces.

TIP *To make fresh bread crumbs, tear whole-grain or white bread into pieces; place in food processor. Process 30 to 60 seconds or until coarse crumbs form. One bread slice yields about ¾ cup crumbs.

WINE The stuffing for the lamb pairs well with a robustly flavored red, such as the 1998 Bodega Norton Malbec from Argentina ($9) or the 1998 Peter Lehmann Shiraz from Australia ($20).

12 servings

PER SERVING: 385 calories, 20.5 g total fat (6.5 g saturated fat), 43.5 g protein, 4 g carbohydrate, 150 mg cholesterol, 620 mg sodium, 1 g fiber

Selecting the Best Roast

Because roasting is a dry-heat method of cooking, these recipes call for roasts that are inherently tender (tough cuts need moist heat to turn them into tender meat). Meat for roasting needs to be large enough so that it doesn't overcook while the exterior browns; roasts should be at least 2 to 3 inches thick. Make certain the meat is fresh; there should be no off odors, no yellow or brown discoloration on the fat, and no sticky feeling to the surface. And the meat should be bright in color, not dull with dark spots. Depending on the type of meat, there are factors in addition to freshness that affect the quality and taste of your roast.

Beef The grading of beef is based on the age of the animal, its physique and, most importantly, the amount of intramuscular fat, called marbling. Marbling improves juiciness and tenderness, and gives the meat superior flavor. The meat with the highest degree of marbling is labeled Prime; it's also the most expensive grade. However, only 2 percent of all beef is graded Prime, and much of that goes to restaurants. But if you can find Prime and can afford it, by all means purchase it. Otherwise, look for Choice or Select. The marbling in Choice varies considerably, but it has more than Select. Many supermarkets offer only Select beef. It produces an adequate roast if it's not cooked beyond medium-rare, but its lack of marbling means it will dry out when cooked much beyond that. And it's less juicy and tender than Choice meat. You also can look for certified beef, such as Certified Angus Beef. This kind of meat has adequate marbling and is worth paying a little more for. Whichever roast you choose, make sure that it has about a ¼-inch layer of external fat.

Pork This meat tends to be very lean with little marbling. It can vary, however, depending on the supplier, so ask a butcher to assist you in finding a roast that has the most marbling. The meat should be slightly moist, firm and pale reddish pink in color, with a fine grain. The fat should be creamy white and trimmed to ¼ inch thick. Because pork is so lean, watch it carefully when you cook it to make sure it's not overdone. It should be taken out of the oven when the meat reaches 140°F. to 145°F. As it rests, it will continue to cook a little more. It's fine if the meat is slightly pink. For pork loin that will be brined, do not purchase pork that has been pumped with salt, water or a phosphate solution. Check the label for these additives. Often such pork is labeled Tender and Juicy, or Flavor Enhanced.

Lamb Once associated with spring, because that's when it was available, lamb can be purchased year-round today. Look for meat that is light red and finely textured. The bones should be reddish and moist, and the fat smooth and white, never coarse and yellowish. Avoid strong-smelling meat. Ideally, purchase a bone-in leg and have a butcher bone it out for you. This gives you a larger roast than one sold boned, rolled and netted. But if that is all that is available, it works fine.

New York Strip Roast with
Bourbon Cream Sauce

New York Strip Roast with Bourbon Cream Sauce

The slightly sweet, smoky flavors of the bourbon complement and enhance the flavor of the beef. For a more intense contribution from the garlic-rosemary paste, spread it on the meat the night before, cover the meat with plastic wrap and refrigerate it until you are ready to cook the roast.

PASTE
- 2 tablespoons olive oil
- 2 tablespoons chopped fresh rosemary
- 2 tablespoons minced garlic
- 1 tablespoon salt
- 1 tablespoon freshly ground pepper

ROAST
- 1 (4- to 5-lb.) boneless New York strip roast, fat trimmed to 1/4-inch thickness

SAUCE
- 2 teaspoons cornstarch
- 2 tablespoons water
- 1/2 cup bourbon whiskey
- 2 tablespoons chopped shallots
- 1 cup reduced-sodium beef or chicken broth
- 1 tablespoon maple syrup
- 1 teaspoon Worcestershire sauce
- 1 tablespoon Dijon mustard
- 1/2 cup heavy whipping cream
- 1/4 teaspoon salt
- 1/8 teaspoon freshly ground pepper

Time and Temperature

The success of roasting depends on the internal temperature of the cooked meat and the temperature of the oven in which it is roasted. If you roast at a temperature that is too low, the meat will not brown. Roast at too high a temperature, and the outside of the meat may burn before the interior is cooked. The roasting temperatures for these recipes give the best caramelized exterior without compromising juiciness and tenderness.

Oven Temperature These recipes use one of two methods for roasting.

- **Two temperatures** This method works well for the *Prime Rib with Fennel and Sage Crust*, and *New York Strip Roast with Bourbon Cream Sauce*. First, the meat is roasted for a short time in a hot oven (450°F.) to aid in browning. Then the oven is turned to a moderate tempeature (350°F.) to complete the roasting. This method combines the advantage of high heat for flavor and moderate heat for tenderness and juiciness.

- **Moderate heat throughout** *Porcini-Spinach-Stuffed Leg of Lamb* and *Maple-Brined Rack of Pork* are best roasted in a moderate-temperature oven. The two-temperature method is not suitable for the lamb because the olive coating would burn. With the pork, a moderate temperature ensures juiciness because pork is prone to drying out.

Internal Temperature Only one factor determines doneness: the internal temperature of the roast. While roasting time affects doneness, using time alone to determine doneness is highly inaccurate due to variances among ovens. The best way to measure internal temperature is with an accurate thermometer that's placed in the center of the meat, away from the bone. The best type is called a remote thermometer. (One manufacturer is Polder.) It has a probe that is connected by a cable to a large digital readout. The probe stays in the roast the entire cooking time. The readout sits outside the oven. This thermometer allows you to set an alarm that will go off when the roast reaches the desired degree of doneness. Even though they cost $30 or more, they're worth it when you factor in the peace of mind you have knowing that the roast will be cooked just to your liking. One supplier of these thermometers is Sur La Table (800-243-0852 or www.surlatable.com).

If you don't use this type of thermometer, use an instant-read thermometer, and check the roast periodically.

Resting The roast should rest at least 15 minutes after it's removed from the oven; during that time, the residual heat completes the cooking, and juices are redistributed from the edges of the roast back into the center. This resting step results in juicy meat but not a lot of juices on the platter.

1 Heat oven to 450°F. In small bowl, combine all paste ingredients; spread over roast. Place on rack in shallow roasting pan.

2 Bake 15 minutes. Reduce oven temperature to 350°F.; bake an additional 45 to 55 minutes or until internal temperature reaches 125°F. for medium-rare or until of desired doneness. Place roast on platter; cover loosely with foil. Let stand 15 to 25 minutes.

3 Meanwhile, whisk together cornstarch and water until cornstarch is dissolved. Pour off any fat from pan juices. Add bourbon to roasting pan. Place pan over medium heat. Scrape any browned bits from bottom of pan, cooking until all browned bits are removed. (Be careful not to burn yourself because bourbon may flame during this process.)

4 Strain sauce into small saucepan; add shallots. Cook over medium-high heat 8 minutes or until sauce is reduced to 2 tablespoons. Add broth, syrup and Worcestershire sauce; bring to a boil. Whisk in mustard until smooth. Stir in dissolved cornstarch, cream, salt, pepper and any accumulated juices from roast. Bring to a boil; cook 1 to 2 minutes or until thickened.

5 Slice roast into 1/4- to 1/2-inch slices; serve with sauce.

WINE Any type of big red, from Merlot to Cabernet Sauvignon to Zinfandel, works here. Andretti "California" Merlot offers a lot of flavor for the price, while Rancho Zabaco Zinfandel from Dry Creek Valley is a spicier match.

12 servings

PER SERVING: 300 calories, 16 g total fat (6.5 g saturated fat), 33 g protein, 3 g carbohydrate, 95 mg cholesterol, 745 mg sodium, .5 g fiber

Bruce Aidells is the coauthor, with Denis Kelly, of *The Complete Meat Cookbook* (Houghton Mifflin).

Curry Meat Loaf with Potato Crust

Meat Loaf Multiplied

It's a perfect fit for today's busy cooks—versatile, satisfying and easy to make.

Text and Recipes by Jill Van Cleave

If you're a trendwatcher, you might have noticed a new item on restaurant menus: meat loaf. That humble standard, once popular but now nearly forgotten, has been revived. Restaurants know meat loaf has comfort appeal, but there are plenty of other reasons for the home cook to embrace this simple dish: It's quick to assemble, easy on the budget and extraordinarily versatile, readily adapting to a wide range of seasonings and treatments. And there's an added bonus: It yields leftovers (if you're lucky) that some people covet more than the hot loaf, fresh from the oven.

Consider the range of possibilities. Cajun flavors jazz up one meat loaf. Another version is infused with curry and topped with creamy mashed potatoes. A third is reminiscent of a rich stroganoff. By varying spices, meats and even shape, this homey standard moves full speed into the 21st century and onto the dinner table.

Curry Meat Loaf with Potato Crust

A mixture of beef and veal takes an exotic turn with curry powder and allspice. The loaf is partially baked, then crowned with a layer of mashed potatoes and returned to the oven. The potatoes provide a creamy contrast to the rich meat and help the meat loaf stay moist.

MEAT LOAF
- 2 teaspoons olive oil
- 1 onion, finely chopped
- 1 jalapeño chile, veins and seeds removed, finely chopped
- 1 large garlic clove, minced
- 1 1/2 tablespoons curry powder
- 1/2 teaspoon ground allspice
- 3/4 teaspoon salt
- 1/2 teaspoon freshly ground pepper
- 3/4 cup reduced-sodium vegetable broth
- 2 green onions, finely chopped
- 1 1/2 teaspoons finely chopped fresh thyme
- 2 eggs
- 3/4 cup unseasoned dry bread crumbs
- 1 1/2 lb. ground beef chuck
- 1/2 lb. ground veal

MASHED POTATOES
- 1 1/2 lb. red potatoes, peeled, cut into 1 1/2-inch pieces
- 1 teaspoon salt
- 1/4 cup reduced-sodium vegetable broth
- 2 tablespoons olive oil
- 1/4 teaspoon freshly ground pepper

1 Heat oven to 350°F. Heat 2 teaspoons oil in medium skillet over medium heat until hot. Add onion and chile; cook 5 minutes or until softened, stirring occasionally. Add garlic; cook 30 seconds or until fragrant. Stir in curry powder, allspice, 3/4 teaspoon salt and 1/2 teaspoon pepper; cook 1 minute. Add 3/4 cup broth; bring to a simmer. Reduce heat to low; cook 5 minutes. Remove from heat; stir in green onions and thyme. Place in large bowl; cool to room temperature.

2 Whisk eggs into vegetable mixture. Stir in bread crumbs. Add ground beef and ground veal; mix together by hand or with large fork until evenly blended. Press mixture into 2-quart casserole, smoothing top. Bake 30 minutes.

3 Meanwhile, place potatoes in large saucepan; fill with enough water to come 1 inch above potatoes. Add 1 teaspoon salt. Bring to a boil over high heat; reduce heat to medium to medium-low. Simmer 20 to 25 minutes or until tender. Drain, reserving 1/4 cup of the cooking water; place potatoes in bowl. Add reserved cooking water, 1/4 cup broth, 2 tablespoons oil and 1/4 teaspoon pepper; mash potatoes.

4 Remove meat loaf from oven; spread mashed potatoes over meat. Return to oven; bake an additional 30 minutes or until meat loaf is firm and juices run clear. Remove excess drippings with baster. Loosely cover with foil; let stand 15 minutes before slicing.

WINE Select a spicy red to pick up on the curry in this meat loaf. Lurton Syrah "Les Bateaux" from France's Pays d'Oc region is a good choice, as is Rosemount Estate Shiraz/Cabernet blend from Australia.

8 servings

PER SERVING: 385 calories, 20 g total fat (6.5 g saturated fat), 25 g protein, 26 g carbohydrate, 120 mg cholesterol, 595 mg sodium, 2.5 g fiber

Beef and Mushroom Loaf

Beef and Mushroom Loaf

Here's an all-beef meat loaf made with juicy sautéed mushrooms and a little sour cream, a winning combination of classic stroganoff-style flavors. It's very moist, so slice it thickly. Serve the leftovers on rye bread for sandwiches.

- 2 tablespoons butter
- 8 oz. thinly sliced button mushrooms
- ½ cup finely chopped onion
- 1 large garlic clove, minced
- 1 egg
- ⅓ cup reduced-fat sour cream
- 1 tablespoon Dijon mustard
- ½ cup unseasoned dry bread crumbs
- 1 teaspoon finely chopped fresh thyme
- ½ teaspoon salt
- ½ teaspoon freshly ground pepper
- 1½ lb. ground beef chuck
- 1 strip bacon

1 Heat oven to 350°F. Melt butter in large skillet over medium-high heat. Add mushrooms and onion; cook and stir 4 to 6 minutes or until mushrooms and onion are softened and liquid has evaporated. Stir in garlic; cook 30 seconds or until fragrant. Place in large bowl; cool to room temperature.

2 Stir egg, sour cream, mustard, bread crumbs, thyme, salt and pepper into mushroom mixture. Add ground beef; mix together by hand or with large fork until ingredients are evenly blended. Press into 8½x4-inch loaf pan or place freeform loaf in shallow baking pan; place bacon strip over top.

3 Bake 50 to 60 minutes or until meat loaf is firm and juices run clear. Remove from oven. Loosely cover with foil; let stand 15 minutes before slicing.

BEER/WINE Guinness Stout from Ireland is a rich beer that's perfect for this dish. For wine, Woodbridge Zinfandel from California is a fine value.

6 servings

PER SERVING: 355 calories, 23.5 g total fat (10.5 g saturated fat), 25 g protein, 10.5 g carbohydrate, 115 mg cholesterol, 415 mg sodium, 1 g fiber

Mixture Basics

In its simplest form, meat loaf is made with seasoned ground beef, chopped onion, egg and bread crumbs. But using a mixture of meats, spices and other additions gives the loaf more dimension in taste and texture.

Most grocery stores sell meat loaf mixes, which often contain equal parts ground beef, pork and veal. These are fine, but a mix made to your own proportions can be more interesting.

Increasing the proportion of beef to 50 percent when combined with two other meats gives a rich, beefy taste and firm meaty texture. The type of beef you choose makes a difference. Ground chuck, with a slightly higher fat content, is the preferred cut of beef for the best-tasting mix. Ground round is 85 percent lean or more, but that's too lean to retain moisture inside the baked loaf. The result is a loss of flavor and a drier texture. Using ground pork and ground veal in smaller and equal proportions (25 percent) will contribute milder flavor and a more tender texture.

Baked, Not Steamed

Ground meats need fat to produce a moist and flavorful loaf. But when you bake a meat loaf in a standard loaf pan, the juices and melted fat accumulate around the meat. As a result, the meat essentially steams

as it bakes, and it can become soggy as it cools in the pan. You can use a baster to remove excess drippings, or try these other methods.

Two-part loaf pan You can buy pans specifically designed for meat loaf. Typically nonstick, the pans consist of an outer pan that looks like a standard loaf pan and a perforated, removable insert that sits about 1 inch off the bottom of the pan. The meat is baked in the inner pan, where the holes funnel the juices away from the loaf. Look for this style of pan at cooking supply stores.

Freeform loaves Baking meat loaf in a freeform shape in a shallow-sided baking pan allows juices to drain away from the meat, toward the outer edges of the pan. Shape the meat loaf mixture by hand into a compact oval, similar to a football; place it in the pan and bake. Even as the meat cools in the pan, it is not sitting in its own juices. Because much of the meat's surface is exposed to air, this method produces a crusty exterior.

Classic Meat Loaf

This is the meat loaf to make when you long for a nostalgic taste of the foods of your childhood. It's moist, and the combination of beef, veal and pork gives it a rich, meaty flavor. It's equally good served warm from the oven or cold in sandwiches the next day.

MEAT LOAF
- 2 teaspoons olive oil
- 1 medium onion, chopped
- 2 garlic cloves, minced
- 2 eggs
- 2/3 cup unseasoned dry bread crumbs
- 1/4 cup finely chopped fresh parsley
- 1/2 cup whole milk
- 2 tablespoons Dijon mustard
- 1 tablespoon Worcestershire sauce
- 1/2 teaspoon hot pepper sauce
- 1 teaspoon finely chopped fresh thyme
- 3/4 teaspoon salt
- 1/2 teaspoon freshly ground pepper
- 1 1/2 lb. ground beef chuck
- 1/4 lb. ground veal
- 1/4 lb. ground pork

GLAZE
- 1/3 cup ketchup
- 2 tablespoons packed light brown sugar
- 1 tablespoon cider vinegar
- 1 tablespoon Dijon mustard

1 Heat oven to 350°F. Heat oil in medium skillet over medium heat until hot. Add onion; cook 5 minutes or until softened, stirring occasionally. Add garlic; cook 30 seconds or until fragrant. Place in large bowl; cool to room temperature.

2 Whisk eggs into onion mixture.

Stir in bread crumbs, parsley, milk, 2 tablespoons mustard, Worcestershire sauce, hot pepper sauce, thyme, salt and pepper. Add ground beef, ground veal and ground pork; mix together by hand or with large fork until evenly blended. Press into 9x5-inch loaf pan or place freeform loaf in shallow baking pan. To prevent glaze from dripping off pan during baking, mound meat in center with sloping sides.

3 In small bowl, stir together all glaze ingredients. Brush 1/4 cup of the glaze over top of loaf. Bake 45 minutes; remove pan from oven. Brush top of loaf with remaining 1/4 cup glaze. Bake an additional 15 to 20 minutes or until meat loaf is firm and juices run clear. Loosely cover with foil; let stand 15 minutes before slicing.

WINE Viña Santa Rita Merlot "120" from Chile is a nice choice to pair with this meat loaf, as is Torres Sangre de Toro from Spain, a slightly heartier red.

8 servings

PER SERVING: 330 calories, 18.5 g total fat (6.5 g saturated fat), 24.5 g protein, 16 g carbohydrate, 125 mg cholesterol, 585 mg sodium, 1 g fiber

Cajun Meat Loaf

Baking this meat loaf in a freeform shape gives it a delectable crust. Andouille sausage and Cajun seasoning infuse the meat loaf with smoky, spicy flavors.

- 2 teaspoons olive oil
- 1 cup finely chopped onion
- 1/2 cup finely chopped green bell pepper
- 1/4 cup finely chopped celery
- 2 garlic cloves, minced
- 2 eggs
- 1/2 cup unseasoned dry bread crumbs
- 1/4 cup finely chopped fresh parsley
- 1/2 cup spicy barbecue sauce, divided
- 1 tablespoon Worcestershire sauce
- 1 teaspoon Cajun seasoning
- 3/4 teaspoon salt
- 1 1/2 lb. ground beef chuck
- 1 lb. ground pork
- 4 oz. andouille or smoked sausage, diced (1/4 inch)

1 Heat oven to 350°F. Heat oil in large skillet over medium heat until hot. Add onion, bell pepper, celery and garlic; cook 5 minutes or until softened. Place in large bowl; cool to room temperature.

2 Whisk eggs into onion mixture. Stir in bread crumbs, parsley, 1/4 cup of the barbecue sauce, Worcestershire sauce, Cajun seasoning and salt. Add ground beef and ground pork; mix together by hand or with large fork until just blended. Add sausage; mix until thoroughly incorporated. Shape into compact oval loaf (approximately 10x5 1/2 inches); place in shallow baking pan.

3 Bake 30 minutes. Brush with 2 tablespoons of the barbecue sauce; bake 15 minutes. Brush with remaining 2 tablespoons barbecue sauce; bake 15 to 20 minutes or until meat loaf is firm and juices run clear. Loosely cover with foil; let stand 15 minutes before slicing.

BEER/WINE Try a spicy beer, such as Bass Ale from England, or a spicy red wine, such as Les Jamelles Syrah from Pays d'Oc in southern France.

8 servings

PER SERVING: 415 calories, 27 g total fat (10 g saturated fat), 30.5 g protein, 10.5 g carbohydrate, 145 mg cholesterol, 730 mg sodium, 1 g fiber

Italian Meat Loaf

Sausage, Parmesan cheese, ricotta cheese, tomatoes and oregano give this meat loaf a distinctly Italian accent. It's topped with a sauce that adds moisture and flavor during baking. Serve the meat loaf with a Caesar salad and a loaf of Italian bread.

SAUCE

- 1 cup canned crushed tomatoes in tomato puree
- 1/4 cup finely chopped sun-dried tomatoes in oil, drained

MEAT LOAF

- 2 teaspoons olive oil
- 1 medium onion, finely chopped
- 2 garlic cloves, finely chopped
- 2 eggs
- 1/3 cup whole milk ricotta cheese
- 3/4 cup unseasoned dry bread crumbs
- 1/3 cup plus 1/4 cup freshly grated Parmesan cheese, divided
- 2 teaspoons finely chopped fresh oregano
- 1/2 teaspoon salt
- 1/2 teaspoon freshly ground black pepper
- 1/4 teaspoon crushed red pepper
- 1 lb. ground beef chuck
- 1/2 lb. ground veal
- 1/2 lb. bulk mild Italian sausage

1 In medium bowl, stir together crushed tomatoes and sun-dried tomatoes.

2 Heat oven to 350°F. Heat oil in medium skillet over medium heat until hot. Add onion; cook 5 minutes or until softened, stirring occasionally. Add garlic; cook 30 seconds or until fragrant. Place in large bowl; cool to room temperature.

3 Whisk eggs into onion mixture. Stir in ricotta cheese until blended. Stir in 1/2 cup of the tomato sauce, bread crumbs, 1/3 cup of the Parmesan cheese, oregano, salt, black pepper and red pepper. Add ground beef, ground veal and sausage; mix together by hand or with large fork until evenly blended. Press into 9x5-inch loaf pan or place freeform loaf in shallow baking pan.

4 Stir remaining 1/4 cup Parmesan cheese into remaining tomato sauce. Spread sauce over top of meat loaf. Bake 1 hour or until meat loaf is firm and juices run clear. Loosely cover with foil; let stand 15 minutes before slicing.

WINE Try Piccini Chianti from Tuscany, a light red with a hint of spice. Santa Sofia Valpolicella from Italy's Veneto region is another value wine that's a perfect match with the meat loaf.

8 servings

PER SERVING: 335 calories, 20 g total fat (8 g saturated fat), 26 g protein, 12 g carbohydrate, 130 mg cholesterol, 635 mg sodium, 1 g fiber

Jill Van Cleave is a Chicago-based food writer and cookbook author.

Turkey Sandwiches with Gorgonzola,
Strawberries and Chive Mayonnaise

Sandwiches for Supper

The parameters of a sandwich are simple—bread and filling—but oh, the possibilities!

Recipes by Jesse Cool

When you start with interesting breads and add intriguing ingredients, the old lunchtime standard transforms into evening fare. Fresh strawberries and pungent blue cheese add punch to mild-mannered turkey. A spicy cherry topping gives a gentle kick to ham and Brie cheese. These aren't sandwiches you squeeze into a plastic bag and drop into a brown paper sack. They're groomed for dinner, pretty to look at … and delicious to eat!

Turkey Sandwiches with Gorgonzola, Strawberries and Chive Mayonnaise

This light, refreshing sandwich can be served as a main course or cut into smaller servings for an appetizer. If you have a little extra time, roast turkey thighs and use the meat in place of the turkey breast. The richer flavor of the dark meat is delicious with the pungent blue cheese and sweet strawberries.

- 1/4 cup mayonnaise
- 1 tablespoon finely minced chives
- 1/2 teaspoon sugar
- 1/4 teaspoon freshly ground pepper
- 8 slices sourdough bread
- 4 oz. Gorgonzola or other blue cheese, crumbled
- 4 to 6 large strawberries, thinly sliced
- 12 oz. sliced cooked turkey

1 In small bowl, stir together mayonnaise, chives, sugar and pepper.
2 Evenly sprinkle 4 slices of bread with Gorgonzola cheese; arrange strawberries over cheese. Top each sandwich with one-fourth of the turkey.
3 Spread each of the 4 remaining bread slices with one-fourth of the chive mayonnaise; place over turkey. Cut sandwiches in half.

4 sandwiches

PER SANDWICH: 700 calories, 27.5 g total fat (9 g saturated fat), 44 g protein, 65 g carbohydrate, 100 mg cholesterol, 1285 mg sodium, 4 g fiber

Cherry Tomato-Avocado Sandwiches on Olive Bread

- 1 cup chopped cherry tomatoes
- 2 tablespoons finely minced red onion
- 1 garlic clove, finely minced
- 1/2 cup chopped fresh basil
- 1 tablespoon capers
- 3 tablespoons extra-virgin olive oil
- 2 tablespoons red wine vinegar
- 1 large avocado, finely chopped
- 1/8 teaspoon salt
- 1/8 teaspoon freshly ground pepper
- 8 slices olive bread or 4 pita breads, split
- 4 butter lettuce leaves
- 3 tablespoons mayonnaise

1 In medium bowl, stir together tomatoes, onion, garlic, basil, capers, oil and vinegar. Let stand 15 minutes. Right before making sandwiches, gently stir avocado, salt and pepper into tomato mixture.
2 Mound tomato mixture with some of the juices on 4 bread slices; top with lettuce. Spread remaining bread with mayonnaise; place on top of lettuce. Press down lightly. Cut sandwiches in half.

4 sandwiches

PER SANDWICH: 380 calories, 26.5 g total fat (4 g saturated fat), 6 g protein, 32.5 g carbohydrate, 5 mg cholesterol, 435 mg sodium, 5 g fiber

Roast Beef and Rye Sandwiches with Horseradish Cream

The traditional roast beef on rye takes a spicy turn with fresh radishes and horseradish cream.

- 1/4 cup regular or low-fat sour cream
- 1 1/2 teaspoons prepared horseradish
- 1/2 teaspoon sugar
- 2 teaspoons chopped fresh chives
- 1 cup coarsely chopped watercress
- 1 tablespoon seasoned rice vinegar
- 1 tablespoon olive oil
- 12 thin slices rye bread (1/4 inch)
- 1/2 cup thinly sliced radishes
- 12 oz. thinly sliced roast beef

1 In small bowl, stir together sour cream, horseradish, sugar and chives. In another small bowl, toss watercress with vinegar and oil.
2 Spread horseradish sauce evenly on 4 slices of the bread. Arrange radishes over horseradish sauce; top with 4 slices bread. Evenly divide roast beef; place on top of bread. Arrange watercress mixture over beef; top with remaining 4 slices bread. Cut each sandwich in half.

4 sandwiches

PER SANDWICH: 430 calories, 21 g total fat (7.5 g saturated fat), 28.5 g protein, 30 g carbohydrate, 80 mg cholesterol, 470 mg sodium, 4 g fiber

Open-Faced Asparagus-Tuna Melts

Open-Faced Asparagus-Tuna Melts

If you have the time, use fresh tuna as called for in this sandwich. Otherwise, you can substitute drained water-packed canned tuna.

- 1 (8-oz.) fresh tuna steak
- 1/4 teaspoon plus 1/8 teaspoon salt, divided
- 1/8 teaspoon freshly ground pepper
- 1/2 cup finely chopped fennel bulb
- 2 green onions, finely sliced
- 1/2 cup mayonnaise
- 1 teaspoon Dijon mustard
- 1/8 teaspoon hot pepper sauce
- 4 slices rustic whole wheat bread
- 12 asparagus spears, cooked, chilled, halved crosswise

- 6 oz. sliced Emmentaler or Swiss cheese

1 Heat broiler. Spray shallow pan with nonstick cooking spray. Sprinkle tuna with 1/4 teaspoon of the salt and pepper. Broil 4 to 6 inches from heat 7 to 9 minutes or until fish just begins to flake, turning once. Cool.

2 Flake tuna; place in medium bowl. Stir in fennel, onions, mayonnaise, mustard, remaining 1/8 teaspoon salt and hot pepper sauce.

3 Place bread on small baking sheet; mound tuna salad on top of each piece of bread. Top with asparagus and cheese. Broil 1 to 2 minutes or until cheese is bubbly.

4 sandwiches

PER SANDWICH: 535 calories, 38 g total fat (12 g saturated fat), 30 g protein, 19.5 g carbohydrate, 75 mg cholesterol, 690 mg sodium, 3.5 g fiber

Ham and Brie Sandwiches with Spicy Cherry Compote

When buying sliced ham, look for a style that has been naturally smoked over wood.

COMPOTE
- 1 tablespoon olive oil
- 1/3 cup thinly sliced onion
- 1 cup dried cherries (about 4 oz.)
- 1/4 cup packed brown sugar
- 2 teaspoons grated orange peel
- 1/8 to 1/4 teaspoon crushed red pepper
- 1 cup reduced-sodium chicken broth or water

SANDWICHES
- 8 slices sourdough bread, toasted

8 oz. Brie cheese
12 oz. thinly sliced ham
2 tablespoons Dijon mustard

1 Heat oil in medium saucepan over medium heat until hot. Add onion; cook 5 minutes or until softened. Add cherries, brown sugar, orange peel, crushed red pepper and broth; bring to a boil. Reduce heat to low. Simmer, uncovered, 15 to 20 minutes or until cherries are soft and juices are reduced to a thick glaze, stirring occasionally. Cool to room temperature.

2 Spread 4 of the bread slices with generous amount of cherry mixture; top each with one-fourth of the cheese and ham. Spread remaining 4 bread slices with mustard; place over ham. Cut sandwiches in half.

4 sandwiches

Mayonnaise Multiplied

The difference between a good sandwich and a great one can be the subtle flavor of an interesting mayonnaise. Try these variations with your favorite sandwiches.

Chipotle Mayonnaise

Serve this spread with chicken, turkey, pork or egg salad sandwiches.

- ½ cup mayonnaise
- ½ teaspoon ground chipotle chile powder
- ½ teaspoon ground cumin
- 1 tablespoon minced red onion
- Dash salt
- Dash freshly ground pepper

In small bowl, stir together all ingredients. Store in refrigerator.

Honey-Mustard Mayonnaise

Use this mayonnaise with smoky meats, such as ham, bacon, smoked chicken or smoked turkey. It also goes well with salty, aged cheese.

- 1 tablespoon honey
- ½ cup mayonnaise
- 2 tablespoons Dijon mustard
- 2 teaspoons chopped fresh thyme
- 1 teaspoon rice wine vinegar
- Dash salt

Place honey in small bowl; gradually stir in mayonnaise. Stir in all remaining ingredients. Store in refrigerator.

Lemon-Garlic Mayonnaise with Parsley

This is a wonderful spread for fish, chicken and most vegetarian-based sandwiches. It also can be used as a sauce on grilled, flaky fish, such as halibut or cod.

- ½ cup mayonnaise
- 1 garlic clove, finely minced
- 1 tablespoon grated lemon peel
- 2 tablespoons chopped fresh Italian parsley
- ⅛ teaspoon paprika
- Dash salt
- Dash freshly ground pepper

In small bowl, stir together all ingredients. Store in refrigerator.

PER SANDWICH: 855 calories, 29 g total fat (13 g saturated fat), 42.5 g protein, 104.5 g carbohydrate, 100 mg cholesterol, 2440 mg sodium, 5 g fiber

Jesse Cool is a California restaurateur, food writer and cookbook author.

SAVORY INGREDIENTS

Asparagus, Arugula and Radish Salad

Here Come the Spears

Five delicious ways to enjoy this wonderful vegetable treat.

Text and Recipes by Mary Evans

For many cooks, spring means it's asparagus time. But with asparagus available much of the year now, it's no longer just a once-in-awhile purchase. Enjoy asparagus year round!.

A simple preparation of those tender green spears used to be enough: quick steaming, a little butter and a squeeze of lemon. After a time, however, unwilling to give up on this beloved vegetable, cooks search for alternative ways to prepare it. The appetizers, salads and main dishes here should please your palate and satisfy your cravings. And they'll keep the spotlight on this seasonal star a lot longer.

Asparagus, Arugula and Radish Salad

For a main dish variation, top this salad with one pound of cooked, shelled and deveined shrimp.

VINAIGRETTE
- 1 teaspoon grated orange peel
- 1 tablespoon orange juice
- 1 tablespoon lemon juice
- 1 teaspoon Dijon mustard
- 1/4 teaspoon salt
- 1/8 teaspoon freshly ground pepper
- 3 tablespoons canola oil

SALAD
- 1 lb. asparagus, peeled, halved diagonally
- 2 cups lightly packed arugula or mixed salad greens
- 2 cups torn leaf lettuce
- 8 radishes, thinly sliced

1 In small bowl, whisk together orange peel, orange juice, lemon juice, mustard, salt and pepper. Slowly whisk in oil.

2 In large skillet, bring 1 inch water to a simmer over medium heat. Add asparagus; cook 5 to 7 minutes or until asparagus is crisp-tender. Drain; place in shallow bowl. Cool; toss with 2 tablespoons of the vinaigrette.

3 In large bowl, toss arugula and leaf lettuce with remaining vinaigrette. Divide among 4 salad plates. Sprinkle with radishes. Arrange asparagus on top; serve immediately.

6 (about 1-cup) servings

PER SERVING: 80 calories, 7 g total fat (.5 g saturated fat), 1.5 g protein, 3 g carbohydrate, 0 mg cholesterol, 115 mg sodium, 1 g fiber

Asparagus and Oyster Mushroom Risotto

Arborio rice is the perfect foil for the woodsy flavor of spring asparagus and oyster mushrooms.

- 2 (14-oz.) cans reduced-sodium chicken broth
- 1 cup water
- 4 tablespoons butter, divided
- 2 (3.8-oz.) pkg. oyster mushrooms, sliced
- 1 lb. asparagus, tips removed and reserved, stalks peeled, cut into 1-inch pieces
- 1 small onion, chopped
- 1 1/2 cups Arborio rice
- 1/2 cup dry white wine
- 3/4 cup (3 oz.) freshly grated Parmesan cheese, divided
- 1/4 teaspoon salt
- 1/8 teaspoon freshly ground pepper

1 Place broth and water in medium saucepan; bring to a boil over medium-high heat. Reduce heat to medium or medium-low to keep at a simmer.

2 Meanwhile, melt 2 tablespoons of the butter in large skillet over medium heat. Add mushrooms; cook 3 to 5 minutes or until tender. Add asparagus

tips; cook 1 to 2 minutes or until just heated through and tips begin to turn bright green. Remove from heat.

3 Melt remaining 2 tablespoons butter in large heavy saucepan over medium heat. Add onion; cook 3 to 5 minutes or until softened. Stir in rice; cook 1 to 2 minutes or until rice is hot. Stir in wine and 1/2 cup of the hot broth; cook until liquid is absorbed, stirring constantly. Continue adding broth, 1 cup at a time, cooking and stirring until broth is absorbed before adding more; adjust heat if necessary to keep rice simmering gently. Cook until rice is creamy and tender with a slight bite.

4 Stir in 1/2 cup of the Parmesan, asparagus pieces, mushrooms, salt and pepper. Divide among 4 bowls. Sprinkle with remaining 1/4 cup Parmesan.

WINE The earthiness of the asparagus and mushrooms in this risotto matches well with a Sauvignon Blanc. Try Pedroncelli from Dry Creek Valley or Pascal Jolivet Sancerre from France.

4 (1 1/2-cup) servings

PER SERVING: 535 calories, 19.5 g total fat (11.5 g saturated fat), 20.5 g protein, 68.5 g carbohydrate, 45 mg cholesterol, 985 mg sodium, 3 g fiber

Asparagus and Goat Cheese Bruschetta

Bruschetta, or garlic-rubbed toast slices, form the base for many popular Italian appetizers that are then topped

Peeling Asparagus

When asparagus is added to a dish with other delicate ingredients, as in *Asparagus and Oyster Mushroom Risotto*, it's a good idea to peel off the tough outer skin of the stalk. Peeling helps asparagus cook faster and makes it more tender. To peel asparagus, trim the end. Then hold the spear with your fingers or place it on a counter. Use a vegetable peeler and start just below the tip.

with a tasty spread. Use thin asparagus spears in this recipe.

BRUSCHETTA
- 16 slices baguette (½ inch), or 8 slices Italian-style country loaf, halved
- 1 large garlic clove, crushed
- 4 teaspoons extra-virgin olive oil

TOPPING
- ¾ lb. asparagus, cut into 2-inch pieces
- 1 tablespoon extra-virgin olive oil
- 4 oz. soft goat cheese
- 1 teaspoon grated lemon peel

1 Heat broiler. Place baguette slices on rimmed baking sheet. Broil 4 to 6 inches from heat 2 to 3 minutes or until lightly browned, turning once. Cool. Rub one side of each slice with crushed garlic; brush with ¼ teaspoon olive oil.

2 Heat oven to 425°F. Place asparagus on same baking sheet; toss with 1 tablespoon olive oil. Bake 10 to 12 minutes or until tender. Cool.

3 In small bowl, stir together goat cheese and lemon peel. Spread over bread slices; top with asparagus.

16 appetizers

PER APPETIZER: 80 calories, 5 g total fat (2 g saturated fat), 3.5 g protein, 6 g carbohydrate, 10 mg cholesterol, 85 mg sodium, .5 g fiber

Roasted Asparagus with Warm Basil-Mint Vinaigrette

You can use either thick or thin spears in this simple but elegant side dish. If you use thick spears, peel them before roasting.

ASPARAGUS
- 1 lb. asparagus
- 1 tablespoon extra-virgin olive oil

VINAIGRETTE
- 1 tablespoon heavy whipping cream
- ½ teaspoon Dijon mustard
- ⅛ teaspoon salt
    Dash freshly ground pepper
- 2 tablespoons finely chopped fresh basil
- 1½ teaspoons finely chopped fresh mint
- 3 tablespoons extra-virgin olive oil
- 2 tablespoons minced shallots
- 1 tablespoon white wine vinegar

1 Heat oven to 425°F. Place asparagus in shallow baking pan; toss with 1 tablespoon olive oil. Bake 10 to 12 minutes or until tender.

2 Meanwhile, in small bowl, whisk together cream, mustard, salt and pepper; stir in basil and mint. Place 3 tablespoons olive oil and shallots in small skillet. Cook over low heat 4 to 5 minutes or until shallots are tender. Add vinegar; cook 30 seconds. Whisk hot oil mixture into cream mixture until smooth.

3 Place roasted asparagus on platter; drizzle with warm vinaigrette. Serve immediately.

4 servings

PER SERVING: 150 calories, 15 g total fat (2.5 g saturated fat), 2 g protein, 3.5 g carbohydrate, 5 mg cholesterol, 80 mg sodium, 1.5 g fiber

Asparagus Pesto Pasta with Pine Nuts

Using buttermilk instead of oil to bind the pesto makes this dish lighter. The creamy tang of the buttermilk complements the slightly nutty notes of the asparagus.

- 2 lb. asparagus
- ¼ cup chopped fresh chives
- ¼ cup chopped fresh parsley
- 1 tablespoon chopped fresh tarragon
- ½ cup (2 oz.) freshly grated Parmesan cheese
- ¾ cup pine nuts, divided
- ½ teaspoon salt
- ⅛ teaspoon freshly ground pepper
- ⅓ cup buttermilk
- 1 tablespoon lemon juice
- 12 oz. fettucine
- 1 cup julienned carrots (about 1½ inches long)

1 Remove tips and next 1½ inches from asparagus; reserve. Place remaining asparagus in steamer basket. Set basket in large pot over boiling water; cover and steam 6 to 8 minutes or until tender.

2 Place steamed asparagus, chives, parsley and tarragon in food

Asparagus Pesto Pasta with Pine Nuts

processor. Pulse until chopped. Add Parmesan, ¹/₂ cup of the pine nuts, salt and pepper; pulse until finely chopped. Add buttermilk and lemon juice; process until smooth but some texture remains. Place in large bowl.

3 Meanwhile, cook fettuccine in large pot of boiling salted water according to package directions or until al dente. During last 4 to 5 minutes of cooking time, steam reserved asparagus and carrots in covered steamer basket over boiling water until crisp-tender.

4 Drain pasta, reserving ¹/₄ cup pasta cooking water. Stir water into pesto. Add pasta; toss. Top with asparagus

and carrots; sprinkle with remaining ¹/₄ cup pine nuts.

WINE This dish calls for a dry Italian white with some earthiness. You'll be fine with either Argiolas Vermentino from Sardinia or the Leonildo Pieropan Soave Classico.

4 (2¹/₄-cup) servings

PER SERVING: 540 calories, 22 g total fat (5.5 g saturated fat), 23 g protein, 70 g carbohydrate, 85 mg cholesterol, 940 mg sodium, 8.5 g fiber

Mary Evans is a food writer and cookbook author based in Minneapolis.

Rosemary Pan-Grilled Pork Chops

Chop, Chop!

Timing is everything when it comes to juicy, moist pork chops.

Recipes by Bruce Aidells

There are some foods that live or die by the clock. An extra minute in the oven can be disastrous for cookies. A few too many seconds on the stove can burn caramel. Many meats tend to be more forgiving, but some cuts have to be watched carefully. That's especially true of pork chops. Because they're lean and cook quickly, a minute or so longer on the heat can turn them dry and tough. Luckily, you can become adept at knowing when chops are done. It just takes a little practice. Once you learn that lesson, you can concentrate on the many different ways to prepare this versatile meat. Then *moist, tender* and *flavorful* will be the delicious rule with pork chops, not the exception.

Rosemary Pan-Grilled Pork Chops

These big, juicy chops are coated with a zesty rosemary-black pepper rub. Fresh sage, thyme, savory or marjoram also would pair well with the pork. The key is to marinate the chops long enough so that the herbs sufficiently flavor the meat.

RUB
- 2 tablespoons extra-virgin olive oil
- 1 tablespoon chopped fresh rosemary
- 2 teaspoons kosher (coarse) salt
- 2 teaspoons freshly ground pepper

PORK
- 4 boneless center-cut loin pork chops (1 to 1¼ inch thick)

1 In small bowl, stir together all rub ingredients. Press onto all sides of chops. Place chops in large resealable plastic bag; seal bag. Refrigerate at least 8 hours or up to 24 hours.
2 Remove chops from bag, leaving most of the rub on chops. Lightly spray ridged grill pan or heavy skillet with nonstick cooking spray; heat over high heat until hot. Add chops; cook 2 to 4 minutes or until chops are browned, turning once.
3 Reduce heat to medium; cook an additional 2 to 4 minutes or until chops are pale pink in center, turning once. Place chops on platter; cover loosely with foil. Let stand 5 to 7 minutes before serving.

WINE A medium-bodied, lightly spicy red is a nice choice with the pork. Select Blackstone Zinfandel from California or opt for Chateau Souverain Zinfandel from Dry Creek Valley in Sonoma.

4 servings

PER SERVING: 235 calories, 15 g total fat (4 g saturated fat), 23.5 g protein, 1 g carbohydrate, 70 mg cholesterol, 810 mg sodium, .5 g fiber

Sautéed Boneless Pork Chops with Apple Pan Sauce

This recipe uses rib pork chops, which have a bit more fat and, therefore, a deeper taste. It's quick to prepare and relies on ingredients from the pantry, making it perfect for a weeknight meal. Butter whisked into the apple cider reduction gives the sauce a smooth, subtle richness.

PORK
- 1 teaspoon kosher (coarse) salt
- 1 teaspoon freshly ground pepper
- 1 teaspoon chopped fresh sage
- ⅛ teaspoon ground nutmeg
- 4 boneless rib pork chops (1 to 1¼ inches thick)
- 1 tablespoon olive oil

SAUCE
- ½ cup finely chopped onions
- 1 Granny Smith or Pippin apple, peeled, thinly sliced
- ½ cup apple cider or apple juice
- ½ cup reduced-sodium chicken broth
  Dash ground cinnamon
  Dash ground ginger
- 2 tablespoons butter
- ⅛ teaspoon kosher (coarse) salt
- ⅛ teaspoon freshly ground pepper

1 In small bowl, stir together 1 teaspoon salt, 1 teaspoon pepper, sage and nutmeg. Sprinkle over both sides of chops.
2 Heat oil in large skillet over medium-high heat until hot. Add chops; cook 2 to 4 minutes or until browned, turning once. Reduce heat to medium; cover and cook an additional 2 to 3 minutes or until chops are pale pink in center. Place chops on platter; cover loosely with foil.
3 Add onions to same skillet; cover and cook over medium heat 2 minutes or until soft, stirring occasionally. Add apple; cook 2 to 3 minutes or until tender. Add apple cider, broth, cinnamon and ginger. Increase heat to high; bring to a boil, scraping up any browned bits from bottom of skillet. Boil 3 to 5 minutes or until slightly thickened and syrupy. Whisk in butter, ⅛ teaspoon salt and ⅛ teaspoon pepper. To serve, spoon sauce over chops.

WINE This dish pairs best with a lighter red. Meridian Pinot Noir from Santa Barbara is a choice match and a good value, while Georges Duboeuf Morgon, a Beaujolais, plays well with

Parmesan-Crusted Pork Chops

the apple and pork flavors.

4 servings

PER SERVING: 285 calories, 17 g total fat (6 g saturated fat), 22 g protein, 10.5 g carbohydrate, 75 mg cholesterol, 655 mg sodium, 1.5 g fiber

Parmesan-Crusted Pork Chops

Using thin pork chops ensures the meat will just finish cooking when the Parmesan crust turns golden brown. Squeezing lemon wedges over the chops cuts some of the richness from the crust. For a quick-to-fix accompaniment, serve a salad of baby greens or arugula lightly dressed with extra-virgin olive oil and lemon juice.

    2   cups fresh bread crumbs*
    ½   cup (2 oz.) freshly grated
        Parmesan cheese
    1   teaspoon finely chopped fresh
        oregano

    1   teaspoon kosher (coarse) salt
    ½   teaspoon freshly ground pepper
    ¼   cup all-purpose flour
    2   eggs, beaten
    8   boneless thin-cut pork loin
        chops (¼ inch thick)
    4   tablespoons olive oil, divided
        Lemon wedges

1 In small shallow bowl, stir together bread crumbs, cheese, oregano, salt and pepper. Place flour in another shallow bowl; place beaten eggs in third shallow bowl. Place wire rack over baking sheet.

2 Dip each chop in flour, shaking off any excess. Dip in egg; dip in bread crumb mixture, patting both sides to make sure mixture adheres well. Place chops on rack over baking sheet. Refrigerate at least 30 minutes or up to 6 hours.

3 Heat 2 tablespoons of the oil in large skillet over medium-high heat

until hot. Add half of the chops; cook 2 to 3 minutes or until golden brown, turning once. Keep warm in 250°F. oven while cooking remaining chops. Repeat with remaining 2 tablespoons oil and chops. Serve with lemon wedges.

TIP *To make fresh bread crumbs, tear day-old whole-grain or white bread into pieces; place in food processor. Pulse 30 to 60 seconds or until coarse crumbs form. One bread slice yields about ¾ cup crumbs.

WINE A dry white hits all the right notes with this dish. Try Château Julien Barrel Fermented Chardonnay from California or Letrari Pinot Bianco from Trentino in northern Italy.

4 servings

PER SERVING: 470 calories, 29 g total fat (8 g saturated fat), 34.5 g protein, 17 g carbohydrate, 175 mg cholesterol, 795 mg sodium, 1 g fiber

Pork Chop Primer

It's easy to cook pork chops to juicy, tender and tasty perfection if you start out with a high-quality cut of meat and don't overcook it.

Freshness counts Good chops are moist but never sticky. They have no off colors, blemishes or brown spots, and they're distinguished by close-grained meat and creamy white fat. Chops may vary from pale grayish pink to light reddish-brown. Avoid dark reddish brown meat with a dry surface, an indication that the pork was improperly processed. And don't purchase chops that are extremely pale grayish pink, exceedingly soft to the touch and sitting in a pool of pink liquid. This pork is known as PSE (pale, soft, exudative); it comes from pigs improperly handled during processing. When it's cooked, it will continue to throw off excessive liquid, resulting in tough, tasteless and dry meat even when it isn't overcooked.

No enhancements Many stores are selling pork that has been injected with a solution of salt, sodium phosphate and water. This pork must be labeled as such, often noted as "flavor enhanced," "tender and juicy," "extra tender" or "guaranteed tender." Pork manufacturers inject salty water because it makes the meat more juicy, even if it's overcooked. As the buyer, you're paying for pork chops that are 10 percent or more salt water. While some cooks may perceive enhanced chops as tender and juicy, others find the meat soft, spongy and rubbery, with a slightly bitter and acrid taste.

Better cuts The best and most tender chops are cut from the loin, the muscle that runs across the back of the pig. Center-cut loin chops are cut from the center of the loin and include rib chops with a rib bone attached or loin chops, which have a characteristic T-shaped bone and include some of the tenderloin. Thick-cut chops (1 1/4- to 1 1/2-inch thick) cut from the rib area are best. These have a little more fat than the T-bone loin chops. Bone-in chops seem to have more flavor than boneless ones, but boneless chops are easier to cook evenly. Boneless chops can come from any area of the loin, but the best come from the rib area. It's difficult to tell where boneless chops are from once in their packaging, so ask your butcher for help.

Thick or thin? Pork chops should be at least 3/4-inch thick if cooked uncoated; otherwise, there's a risk they'll cook too quickly and become dry. Chops that are 1- to 1 1/4-inches thick are ideal for stovetop cooking or grilling; 1 1/4- to 1 1/2-inch-thick cuts are good for baking. If you do wish to cook thin pork chops (less than 1/2-inch thick), coat them first. This technique protects the chops and gives the meat a crispy, brown crust (see Parmesan-Crusted Pork Chops).

Don't overcook Because pork is much leaner today than in the past, it's very easy to overcook it. To ensure the meat doesn't become dry and chewy, watch cooking times and remove it from the heat when the meat is pale pink in color.

Baked Pork Chops Stuffed with Apricots and Leeks

Baked Pork Chops Stuffed with Apricots and Leeks

These thick pork chops are bursting with stuffing. The mixture of sweet, salty, smoky and savory sensations pumps up the flavor and keeps the chops moist as they bake. When choosing pork chops to stuff, look for ones that are about 1½ inches thick.

STUFFING
½ cup chopped dried apricots
2 slices thick-cut bacon, chopped
½ cup finely chopped leeks
¼ cup finely chopped celery
1 cup cubed dried bread*
1 egg, beaten
½ teaspoon finely chopped fresh thyme
¼ teaspoon salt
¼ teaspoon freshly ground pepper
Dash ground cinnamon
PORK
4 bone-in center-cut rib pork chops (1½ inches thick)
1 teaspoon finely chopped fresh thyme
½ teaspoon salt
½ teaspoon freshly ground pepper
2 tablespoons olive oil

1 Place apricots in small bowl of hot water. Let stand 10 minutes; drain.
2 Cook bacon in medium skillet over medium heat until it just begins to brown. Add leeks and celery; cover and cook 5 minutes or until vegetables are soft, stirring occasionally. Place in large bowl; stir in all remaining stuffing ingredients. Refrigerate at least 30 minutes or until chilled.

sheet; bake 15 to 20 minutes or until stuffing is hot and chops are pale pink in center. Place chops on platter; cover loosely with foil. Let stand 7 to 10 minutes before serving.

TIP *Use dried bread from purchased stuffing mix or dry your own. Bake 2 bread slices on baking sheet at 350°F. for 7 to 10 minutes or until dry and crisp.

WINE For a lighter red that's very soft, select Louis Jadot Beaujolais-Villages. Or try La Crema Pinot Noir from the Sonoma Coast, a medium-bodied wine with fresh fruit flavors and a light spiciness.

4 servings

PER SERVING: 405 calories, 24 g total fat (7 g saturated fat), 30 g protein, 17 g carbohydrate, 135 mg cholesterol, 625 mg sodium, 2 g fiber

Brined Pork Chops with Aromatic Spice Rub

Coffee is the surprise ingredient in this brine. It provides a subtle bitterness that's almost undetectable, but it balances well with the sweetness of the brown sugar. It's important to use thick pork chops because they're better suited for this gentle cooking method.

BRINE
- 2 cups water
- 1 1/2 cups strong coffee, room temperature
- 6 tablespoons packed dark brown sugar
- 1/4 cup kosher (coarse) salt
- 1 tablespoon Worcestershire sauce
- 1 cup ice cubes

PORK
- 4 bone-in center-cut rib pork chops (1 1/4 to 1 1/2 inches thick)
- 2 tablespoons olive oil, divided

SPICE RUB
- 2 teaspoons minced garlic
- 1 teaspoon chopped fresh thyme
- 1 teaspoon paprika
- 1 teaspoon freshly ground pepper
- 1/2 teaspoon ground allspice
- 1/2 teaspoon ground cardamom
- 1/2 teaspoon ground ginger
- 1/4 teaspoon ground nutmeg

1 In large bowl, stir together water, coffee, brown sugar and salt until salt and brown sugar are dissolved. Stir in Worcestershire sauce. Stir in ice cubes until melted.

2 Place chops in large resealable plastic bag; pour in brine. Seal bag. Refrigerate at least 4 hours or up to 6 hours.

3 Meanwhile, in small bowl, stir together all spice rub ingredients.

4 Heat oven to 400°F. Remove chops from brine; pat dry. Discard brine. Brush chops with 1 tablespoon of the oil; press spice rub onto all sides of chops.

5 Heat 1/2 to 1 tablespoon of the remaining oil in large skillet over medium-high heat until hot. Add chops; cook 4 to 6 minutes or until browned on all sides. (If necessary, add chops in batches, cleaning skillet between batches.)

6 Place chops on rimmed baking sheet; bake 15 to 20 minutes or until chops are pale pink in center. Place chops on platter; cover loosely with foil. Let stand 7 to 10 minutes before serving.

WINE Try a spicy red with enough character to stand up to the spice rub, such as Alamos Malbec from Argentina or Marietta Zinfandel from Sonoma.

4 servings

PER SERVING: 280 calories, 16.5 g total fat (4.5 g saturated fat), 27.5 g protein, 4.5 g carbohydrate, 80 mg cholesterol, 645 mg sodium, .5 g fiber

Bruce Aidells is author of *Bruce Aidells's Complete Book of Pork* (HarperCollins), due out this fall.

3 Heat oven to 350°F. With small sharp knife, cut pocket in side of each chop, cutting to the bone. Stuff each chop with one-fourth of the stuffing. (Chops will be very full.)

4 In small bowl, stir together 1 teaspoon thyme, 1/2 teaspoon salt and 1/2 teaspoon pepper; press onto both sides of chops.

5 Heat oil in large skillet over medium-high heat until hot. Add chops, in batches if necessary; cook 6 to 8 minutes or until browned on all sides.

6 Place chops on rimmed baking

Morel Mushroom and Asparagus Pasta

The Mushroom Boom

These earthy treasures add a deep, rich taste to dishes.

Text and Recipes by Mary Evans

White button mushrooms have a lot of company these days in the produce department. Where they once were the only fresh choice, now you often find them sharing shelf space with many other varieties, such as oysters, shiitakes and portobellos. In specialty markets, lesser-known types, such as chanterelles, are becoming more common. And in the dried section, the choices seem almost limitless, with porcinis and morels now available year-round.

That's good news for cooks because mushrooms are a magical ingredient. Even when used in small amounts, they can transform a dish with their rich, earthy flavors and meaty textures. And because mushrooms are enormously versatile, you can vary their impact by choosing milder-tasting types, combining several kinds or substituting one for the other.

These recipes demonstrate mushrooms' flexibility, from a simple soup to a rich bread pudding. So start foraging. Mushrooms are waiting to be discovered.

Morel Mushroom and Asparagus Pasta

Because fresh morel mushrooms have such a short season in spring, using dried morels mixed with fresh button mushrooms is a more practical alternative.

- 1 (14-oz.) can reduced-sodium chicken broth
- ½ oz. dried morel mushrooms (½ cup)
- 1 lb. asparagus, peeled, cut into 2-inch lengths (3 cups)
- 2 tablespoons butter
- ½ cup diced shallots
- 8 oz. button mushrooms, sliced
- 12 oz. fettuccine
- ⅛ teaspoon freshly ground pepper
- 1 cup (4 oz.) freshly shredded Parmesan cheese

1 Place broth in small saucepan; bring to a boil over medium heat. Remove from heat; stir in morel mushrooms. Let stand 30 minutes.

2 Meanwhile, fill large skillet half full with water; bring to a simmer over medium heat. Add asparagus. Reduce heat to medium-low; simmer 8 to 10 minutes or until just tender. Drain; rinse under cold water to cool.

3 Remove morels with slotted spoon; halve or quarter, depending on size. Strain soaking liquid through coffee filter; reserve.

4 Melt butter in large skillet over medium-low heat. Add shallots; cook 4 to 5 minutes or until softened. Add button mushrooms. Increase heat to medium; cook 3 to 4 minutes or until mushrooms begin to soften, stirring frequently. Add morel mushrooms and all but ¾ cup of the mushroom soaking liquid. Cook 6 to 9 minutes or until all liquid is absorbed.

5 Cook fettuccine in large pot of boiling salted water according to package directions; drain. Place in large shallow bowl.

6 Meanwhile, add remaining ¾ cup mushroom liquid to skillet; stir in asparagus and pepper. Bring to a simmer. Pour over pasta in bowl; toss to coat. Sprinkle with cheese.

WINE Tiziano Chianti from Tuscany is a fine value, while Allegrini "La Grola" Veronese from the Veneto is a medium-bodied wine with noticeable spice and a slightly earthy finish.

4 servings

PER SERVING: 510 calories, 17.5 g total fat (9 g saturated fat), 26.5 g protein, 63.5 g carbohydrate, 110 mg cholesterol, 1070 mg sodium, 4.5 g fiber

Shiitake-Stuffed Chicken Breasts

Meaty, intensely flavored shiitake mushrooms marry particularly well with the tomato paste, ginger and garlic in this dish. Shiitake stems tend to be tough, so remove and reserve them for flavoring stocks. The chicken breasts can be assembled earlier in the day and refrigerated, covered, until you're ready to cook them.

- 2 (3.5-oz.) pkg. fresh shiitake mushrooms
- 1 teaspoon minced fresh ginger
- ½ teaspoon minced garlic
- 2 tablespoons canola oil, divided
- 2 tablespoons dry sherry, divided
- ½ teaspoon soy sauce
- 1 tablespoon tomato paste
- 4 boneless skinless chicken breast halves
- ¼ teaspoon salt
- ⅛ teaspoon freshly ground pepper
- ¼ cup water

1 Remove and discard stems from shiitake mushrooms. Reserve 8 of

Guide to Mushrooms

While different types of mushrooms can be used almost interchangeably, flavor and texture do vary.

Chanterelle These mushrooms look like small calla lilies. They range in color from yellow to golden-orange. Fresh ones may not always be available, but if you can find them, their chewy texture and mellow, nutty flavor make them a wonderful addition to any dish. Look for them dried as well.

Crimini and portobello Crimini, also called baby portobellos, are smaller versions of the mature portobello mushroom; they're sold fresh. Brown and firm, these readily available and reasonably priced mushrooms provide a meatier, more flavorful option than button mushrooms. They darken considerably when cooked.

Morel A sign of spring, morel mushrooms have wrinkled, conical domes; they're related to the truffle and are harvested mostly in the wild. Morels are pricey whether fresh or dried, but their distinctive, slightly smoky flavor means they can be used sparingly.

Oyster Shaped like a slightly curled fan with ruffled edges, oyster mushrooms are commonly available and can be used in almost any mushroom recipe. Their pleasant flavor is mild when cooked, and their unique shape and texture add interest to dishes using multiple mushroom varieties. They're available fresh and dried.

Portobello

Oyster

Dried porcini

Dried morel

Crimini

White button

Porcini Called cèpes in France, these mushrooms are easier to find dried than fresh. When reconstituted, porcinis provide a deep, succulent flavor, allowing them to be used in small quantities.

Shiitake These firm, meaty mushrooms have a distinctive taste that permeates a recipe, making them best used alone or paired with neutral-flavored mushrooms, such as button. They are readily available both fresh and dried. The stems are tough and should be removed before cooking.

White button Universally available, their neutral, earthy taste blends well with other mushrooms; use them to augment more expensive varieties. When sautéed and simmered with the soaking liquid from reconstituted dried mushrooms, button mushrooms take on the flavor of the dried variety. They're available fresh.

When purchasing mushrooms, look for firm, whole caps without darkened areas. Button mushrooms and crimini mushrooms should have closed caps; portobello mushrooms should show their gills but not look wilted or moist.

Chanterelle

Shiitake

Fresh mushrooms can be stored for several days in the refrigerator, loosely covered with a damp paper towel. To clean them, quickly rinse and dry. If necessary, brush them with a paper towel to remove residual grit, and trim any woody stems.

To use dried mushrooms, cover them with hot water and soak them for 20 to 30 minutes or until softened. Remove them with a slotted spoon, and then strain the soaking liquid through a coffee filter or paper towel to remove fine dirt particles. The liquid can be used in a recipe or added to soups or risotto for an extra hit of flavor. Trim any tough portions from the mushrooms before using them.

the smallest caps. Place remaining mushrooms in food processor with ginger and garlic; pulse until finely chopped or chop by hand.

2 Heat large skillet over medium-high heat until hot. Add 1 tablespoon of the oil; heat until hot. Add chopped mushrooms; cook 2 to 3 minutes or until softened, stirring frequently. Add 1 tablespoon of the sherry and 1/2 teaspoon soy sauce; cook 1 to 2 minutes or until liquid has evaporated and mushrooms form paste. Stir in tomato paste. Place in small bowl; cool.

3 Place chicken breasts on flat surface. Slice chicken almost in half horizontally, cutting to about 1/2 inch from edge. Open; press to flatten slightly. Spread one-fourth of the mushroom mixture over 1 side of chicken. Fold breasts in half over mushroom mixture; tuck in pointed end of breast. Seal with toothpicks; sprinkle with salt and pepper.

4 Heat same skillet over medium-high heat until hot. Add remaining 1 tablespoon oil; heat until hot. Add chicken; cook 3 to 4 minutes or until golden brown. Turn; add reserved mushroom caps, cap side down. Cook 3 to 4 minutes or until golden brown. Reduce heat to low; cover and cook 8 to 10 minutes or until chicken is no longer pink in center, turning mushrooms and chicken once. Place chicken on platter.

5 Add water and remaining 1 tablespoon sherry to skillet; increase heat to high. Bring to a boil, scraping up any browned bits from bottom of skillet. Boil 1 to 2 minutes or until slightly reduced. Serve chicken with mushroom caps and sauce.

WINE Try a medium- to full-bodied red that has spice but won't overpower the chicken, such as Barone Ricasoli Brolio Chianti Classico from Tuscany or Beaulieu Vineyard "Napa" Zinfandel.

4 servings

PER SERVING: 230 calories, 11 g total fat (1.5 g saturated fat), 28.5 g protein, 4 g carbohydrate, 75 mg cholesterol, 285 mg sodium, 1 g fiber

Three-Mushroom Soup

A mixture of three types of mushrooms gives this soup its rich depth of flavor. Crimini sometimes are labeled baby portobellos.

2 (14-oz.) cans reduced-sodium beef or vegetable broth, divided
1 oz. dried porcini mushrooms
3 tablespoons butter
2 cups chopped leeks, white and pale green parts (2 to 3 leeks)
12 oz. crimini mushrooms, coarsely chopped
2 (3.8-oz.) pkg. fresh oyster mushrooms, coarsely chopped
3/4 cup red wine
2 teaspoons finely chopped fresh rosemary or 3/4 teaspoon dried, crumbled
1/8 teaspoon freshly ground pepper
Dash ground cinnamon

1 Pour 1 can of the broth in small saucepan; bring to a boil over medium heat. Remove from heat; stir in porcini mushrooms. Let stand 30 minutes. Remove mushrooms with slotted spoon; coarsely chop. Strain soaking liquid through coffee filter; reserve.
2 Melt butter in Dutch oven or large pot over medium-low heat. Add leeks; cook 6 to 8 minutes or until soft and tender, stirring frequently. Add crimini mushrooms and oyster mushrooms; cook 5 to 8 minutes or until mushrooms begin to soften and release juices. Stir in remaining 1 can broth, porcini mushrooms, reserved soaking liquid, wine, rosemary, pepper and cinnamon until blended. Increase heat to medium; bring just to a boil. Reduce heat to low; simmer 30 minutes or until mushrooms are tender and broth has rich flavor.

4 (1 1/2-cup) servings

PER SERVING: 160 calories, 10 g total fat (5.5 g saturated fat), 8 g protein, 12 g carbohydrate, 25 mg cholesterol, 205 mg sodium, 3.5 g fiber

Wild Mushroom Salad with Sherry Vinaigrette

If you can't get fresh chanterelles, substitute another type of fresh mushroom or use more crimini or oyster mushrooms.

SALAD
2 tablespoons butter
2 tablespoons canola oil
1/4 cup minced shallots
1 (6-oz.) pkg. crimini mushrooms, sliced
2 (3.8-oz.) pkg. fresh oyster mushrooms, sliced
1 (3.5-oz.) pkg. fresh chanterelle mushrooms, sliced
12 cups torn mixed salad greens
VINAIGRETTE
2 tablespoons minced shallots
2 tablespoons sherry wine vinegar
1 teaspoon Dijon mustard
1/2 teaspoon salt
1/4 teaspoon freshly ground pepper
1/3 cup canola oil

1 Heat butter and 2 tablespoons oil in large skillet over medium heat until sizzling. Add 1/4 cup shallots; cook 1 minute. Add crimini, oyster and chanterelle mushrooms; cook 6 to 8 minutes or until mushrooms are tender and most of the liquid has evaporated.
2 In small bowl, whisk together 2 tablespoons shallots, vinegar, mustard, salt and pepper. Slowly whisk in 1/3 cup oil. Stir about 3 tablespoons of the vinaigrette into hot mushroom mixture. Toss greens with enough of the remaining vinaigrette to coat; divide among 6 salad plates. Top with mushroom mixture; serve with remaining vinaigrette.

6 servings

PER SERVING: 220 calories, 21 g total fat (3.5 g saturated fat), 4.5 g protein, 7.5 g carbohydrate, 10 mg cholesterol, 275 mg sodium, 3.5 g fiber

Mushroom Bread Pudding with Tarragon-Cream Sauce

Although this dish takes a little time to prepare, you'll be amply rewarded when you taste the results. The tarragon-cheese sauce adds an elegant touch, making the bread pudding perfect to serve for a fancy brunch.

BREAD PUDDING
1 oz. dried porcini mushrooms (1 cup)
1 cup boiling water
1 (1-lb.) loaf stale challah or brioche, cubed (1 1/2 inches)*
2 tablespoons balsamic vinegar
1 teaspoon salt, divided
1/4 teaspoon freshly ground black pepper, divided
2 tablespoons canola oil
12 oz. portobello mushrooms, chopped (3/4 inch)
1 red onion, chopped (1/2 inch)
8 eggs, lightly beaten
3 cups milk
8 oz. Gruyère or Emmantaler cheese, diced (generous 1/4 inch)
SAUCE
2 tablespoons butter
2 tablespoons all-purpose flour
2 cups milk
2 teaspoons Dijon mustard
1/4 teaspoon salt
1/8 teaspoon white pepper
1/2 cup (2 oz.) grated Gruyère or Emmantaler cheese
2 tablespoons chopped fresh tarragon

1 Place porcini mushrooms and boiling water in small bowl; let stand 30 minutes. Remove mushrooms with slotted spoon; chop into 1/2-inch pieces. Strain soaking liquid through coffee filter; reserve 1/4 cup. Discard remaining soaking liquid or reserve for another use.
2 Heat broiler. Butter bottom and sides of 13x9-inch (3-quart) glass baking dish. Place bread cubes in shallow 15x10-inch jelly-roll pan; broil 4 to 6 inches from heat 1 minute or until tops are toasted. Place in baking dish.

Mushroom Bread Pudding with Tarragon-Cream Sauce

3 In small bowl, whisk together reserved 1/4 cup mushroom soaking liquid, balsamic vinegar, 1/2 teaspoon of the salt and 1/8 teaspoon of the black pepper; whisk in oil. Place portobello mushrooms and onion in jelly-roll pan; drizzle with balsamic mixture. Stir to coat. Broil 4 to 6 inches from heat 8 to 10 minutes or until mushrooms are tender and most of the liquid has evaporated, stirring every 2 minutes. Stir in porcini mushrooms. Spoon mixture over bread.

4 Heat oven to 325°F. In medium bowl, whisk eggs, milk, and remaining 1/2 teaspoon salt and 1/8 teaspoon pepper until combined. (Bread pudding can be made to this point up to 1 day ahead. Cover liquid and mushroom mixture separately; refrigerate. When ready to bake, continue as directed. Baking time may need to be increased 5 to 10 minutes.) Pour over bread; stir gently to combine. Sprinkle with 8 oz. Gruyère; stir gently to combine. Cover with foil; bake 50 minutes. Remove foil; bake 20 to 25 minutes or until puffed, edges are bubbly and internal temperature reaches 170°F.

5 Meanwhile, melt butter in medium saucepan over medium heat; whisk in flour. Cook 2 minutes, stirring constantly. Remove from heat; slowly whisk in milk until smooth. Whisk in mustard, 1/4 teaspoon salt and white pepper. Return to medium heat; bring to a boil, whisking frequently. Boil 2 to 3 minutes or until thickened, whisking frequently. Remove from heat; stir in 1/2 cup Gruyère and tarragon until smooth. Serve with bread pudding.

TIP *Challah and brioche are rich yeast breads made with eggs. Look for them in your local bakery.

WINE This dish needs a lighter red with some earthiness to complement the mushrooms. Try Bolla Sangiovese from northern Italy or Masi Valpolicella, a lightly spicy red from the Veneto.

12 servings

PER SERVING: 365 calories, 19.5 g total fat (8.5 g saturated fat), 19.5 g protein, 28.5 g carbohydrate, 195 mg cholesterol, 520 mg sodium, 1.5 g fiber

Mary Evans is the author of *Bistro Chicken* (Broadway).

Ranch-Style Steak with Bourbon Sauce

To Sirloin with Love

Rich, satisfying and easy—with sirloin steaks, every bite is a delight.

Text and Recipes by Jill Van Cleave

For cooks who crave satisfying steaks, boneless beef sirloin is a natural choice. In addition to having great flavor, sirloin is attractively priced for the budget-minded, quick to cook for the time-pressed and wonderfully lean for the health- and value-conscious. It's not as tender as the more expensive cuts, but a little marinating and proper slicing take care of that.

How you cook sirloin is up to you. It can be perfectly prepared in various ways—under the broiler, on the grill or on the stovetop. When it's serving time, sirloin's texture and taste favor rich accompaniments that complement rather than smother its deep nuances. It comes down to this: When it's sirloin for dinner, let the star steal the show.

Ranch-Style Steak with Bourbon Sauce

Top sirloin steaks are praised for their natural tenderness but are even tastier when marinated before cooking. Here's a marinade made with a simple paste of garlic and black pepper. The accompanying bourbon-spiked sauce benefits when a homemade stock or quality beef broth is used. Pair this dish with fluffy, buttered baked potatoes.

STEAK
- 1½ lb. boneless top sirloin steak, 1 inch thick
- 4 teaspoons olive oil, divided
- 1 teaspoon coarsely ground black peppercorns
- 8 medium garlic cloves, minced

SAUCE
- 1 tablespoon butter
- 2 large shallots, minced
- ½ cup bourbon whiskey
- 1 tablespoon all-purpose flour
- 1 cup reduced-sodium beef broth
- 2 teaspoons Worcestershire sauce

1 Pat steak dry with paper towels. Brush steak with 2 teaspoons of the oil. In small bowl, stir together peppercorns and garlic; press evenly onto both sides of steak. Place in single layer in shallow dish. Cover and refrigerate at least 2 hours or up to 8 hours.

2 Melt butter in medium saucepan over low heat. Add shallots; cook 2 minutes or until softened. Add bourbon. Increase heat to medium; bring to a boil. Boil 2 to 3 minutes or until reduced to about ¼ cup. Stir in flour; cook 1 minute. Whisk in broth; bring to a boil. Add Worcestershire sauce; simmer 7 to 10 minutes or until thickened.

3 Heat large cast-iron or other heavy skillet over medium-high heat until hot. Add remaining 2 teaspoons oil; swirl pan to coat bottom. Add steak; cook 10 to 12 minutes for medium-rare or until of desired doneness, turning once. Place on cutting board; let stand 5 minutes. Cut across the grain into ¼-inch slices. Serve with sauce.
WINE A hearty red works well here. Try Torres "Sangre de Toro" Penedes from Spain or Dry Creek Cabernet Sauvignon from Sonoma County.
4 servings

PER SERVING: 295 calories, 13 g total fat (4.5 g saturated fat), 35.5 g protein, 5.5 g carbohydrate, 100 mg cholesterol, 155 mg sodium, .5 g fiber

Steak House Broil

Marinating steaks cut from the bottom sirloin section of beef with an acid-based mixture makes them tender and tasty. To complete a hearty steak-house presentation, pair the meat with sautéed mushrooms and potatoes.

- 1½ lb. boneless bottom sirloin steak (bottom butt, tri-tip or tip, or ball tip), ¾ to 1 inch thick
- 1 medium onion, coarsely chopped
- 6 medium garlic cloves, coarsely chopped
- 1 cup dry red wine
- ¼ cup olive oil
- 2 tablespoons soy sauce
- 2 tablespoons chopped fresh Italian parsley
- ½ teaspoon kosher (coarse) salt

1 Place steak in single layer in shallow dish. Sprinkle onion and garlic over meat.
2 In medium bowl, whisk together wine, oil, soy sauce and parsley; pour over steak, lifting meat to allow liquid to spread evenly underneath. Cover and refrigerate 4 hours, turning once.
3 Remove meat from marinade. Strain marinade, discarding onions and garlic; reserve marinade.
4 Heat broiler and broiler pan until hot. Sprinkle steak with salt. Place on hot broiler pan; broil 4 to 6 inches from heat 6 to 8 minutes for medium-rare or until of desired doneness, turning once. Place meat on cutting board; let stand 5 minutes. Cut across the grain into ¼-inch-thick slices.
5 Meanwhile, pour reserved marinade into small saucepan. Bring to a boil over medium heat; cook 5 to

Sirloin Cooking Tips

The best methods for cooking sirloin steaks are broiling, grilling, pan-broiling or pan-frying. Because sirloin is lean, it benefits from marinades and quick cooking over medium to high heat.

Seasoning and Tenderizing Marinades are primarily flavor enhancers that may be wet (liquids and oil) or dry (herbs and spices). If the marinade has an acidic ingredient, such as lemon, vinegar or wine, it also tenderizes the meat. Use a liquid marinade on sirloin steaks for at least 2 hours for flavor purposes and at least 4 hours to tenderize it. Do not marinate more than 24 hours because the cooked meat texture may become mushy. Use a dry marinade (also called a rub) for less time—no more than 1 hour for 1-inch-thick steaks.

Doneness Most sirloin steaks should be 3/4 to 1 inch thick. This allows them to cook quickly and evenly. All sirloin steaks, top or bottom cuts, should be cooked to medium-rare to medium doneness (145°F. to 160°F.), but not beyond. That's because sirloin is very lean muscle meat without the self-basting benefit of marbling. Prolonged cooking dries out the meat and makes it tough. As a rule, cook 1-inch-thick steaks 8 to 10 minutes, turning once. To tell if the meat is done, make a small slit near the center.

Slicing Once cooked, cut sirloin steaks across the grain into relatively thin slices, about 1/4 inch thick. The thin pieces of meat will seem more tender in the mouth. If you hold the knife at a 45-degree angle when carving the meat, you will cut the meat across the grain and obtain wider slices.

---

8 minutes or until slightly thickened. Stir in any accumulated carving juices. To serve, spoon sauce over steak.

WINE Try a young Cabernet Sauvignon-based wine here, such as Viña Santa Rita from Chile or Geyser Peak from Sonoma.

4 servings

PER SERVING: 330 calories, 19 g total fat (3.5 g saturated fat), 34.5 g protein, 1.5 g carbohydrate, 90 mg cholesterol, 775 mg sodium, 0 g fiber

Spiced Sirloin Skewers with Roasted Onion-Tomato Salsa

Dry marinades, also called rubs, are not intended to tenderize meat, but they do add considerable flavor. Because it is primarily the outside of the steak that benefits from a rub, the rub will be more effective if you slice the steak before cooking it and then apply the rub. Serve the skewered steak with the oven-roasted salsa and warm corn tortillas.

STEAK
- 2 tablespoons paprika*
- 1 tablespoon packed light brown sugar
- 1 1/2 teaspoons ground cumin
- 1 teaspoon ground allspice
- 1 teaspoon ground coriander
- 1/2 teaspoon kosher (coarse) salt
- 1/2 teaspoon freshly ground pepper
- 2 lb. boneless bottom sirloin roast (tri-tip or triangle roast, or ball tip roast)
- 2 tablespoons vegetable oil

SALSA
- 2 large onions, quartered, separated
- 2 large tomatoes
- 4 serrano chiles
- 4 large garlic cloves, unpeeled
- 2 tablespoons vegetable oil
- 2 tablespoons balsamic vinegar
- 2 teaspoons packed light brown sugar
- 1/2 teaspoon kosher (coarse) salt

1 In small shallow bowl, stir together paprika, 1 tablespoon brown sugar, cumin, allspice, coriander, 1/2 teaspoon salt and pepper.

2 Cut roast into 1/2-inch-thick slices. Cut each slice into 1 1/2-inch-wide strips.** Coat all sides of meat with spice rub. Place in shallow baking pan; cover. Refrigerate at least 30 minutes.

3 Meanwhile, heat oven to 450°F. Place onions, tomatoes, chiles, garlic and 2 tablespoons oil in large bowl; toss to coat vegetables with oil. Place in single layer on foil-lined rimmed baking sheet; do not clean bowl.

4 Bake vegetables 20 minutes or until chiles are blistered, garlic is soft and onions and tomatoes are browned and tender, stirring halfway through. Cool; scrape roasting juices into reserved large bowl.

5 When cool enough to handle, remove skin and seeds from chiles and tomatoes. Squeeze garlic pulp from cloves. Coarsely chop onions, chiles and garlic together; add to reserved large bowl. Chop tomatoes; add to bowl.

6 In small bowl, stir together vinegar and 2 teaspoons brown sugar until sugar dissolves. Add to vegetable mixture. Sprinkle with 1/2 teaspoon salt; stir to mix thoroughly.

7 Heat broiler. Thread steak onto 6 (8- to 10-inch) metal skewers; place on foil-lined baking sheet. Brush steak lightly with 2 tablespoons vegetable oil; broil 4 to 6 inches from heat 5 to 7 minutes for medium-rare or until of desired doneness, turning once. (Do not cook beyond medium or meat will dry out.) Serve with warm or room temperature salsa.

TIPS *If available, use Hungarian or Spanish paprika for this recipe. **For easier slicing, place meat in freezer about 30 minutes before slicing.

Roquefort Steak with Caramelized Onions and Radicchio

WINE The spices and chiles in this dish call for a spicy red, such as Zinfandel. Two great choices are Rancho Zabaco "Dancing Bull" or De Loach "Russian River" bottling, which is rich and loaded with flavor.

6 servings

PER SERVING: 325 calories, 14.5 g total fat (3 g saturated fat), 32.5 g protein, 16.5 g carbohydrate, 80 mg cholesterol, 325 mg sodium, 2.5 g fiber

Roquefort Steak with Caramelized Onions and Radicchio

Top sirloin and top butt steaks are the primary cuts used in French bistros for steak frites. Because they're thin, they cook fast and are less chewy than thick steaks. A rich Roquefort cheese butter tops the meat.

ROQUEFORT BUTTER

- 1 cup (4 oz.) crumbled Roquefort cheese
- 2 tablespoons unsalted butter, softened

- 1 garlic clove, chopped
- 1 teaspoon dry mustard
- 1/4 teaspoon Worcestershire sauce

RADICCHIO AND STEAK

- 3 tablespoons olive oil, divided
- 1/2 lb. sliced sweet onions (2 cups)
- 1/2 teaspoon sugar
- 1/2 lb. radicchio, coarsely chopped (6 cups)*
- 1/4 teaspoon freshly ground pepper, divided
  Dash salt
- 4 boneless top sirloin steaks (1 1/2 lb.), 1/2 inch thick

1 In small bowl, stir together all Roquefort butter ingredients until combined.

2 Heat large skillet over medium-high heat until hot. Add 2 tablespoons of the oil; heat until hot. Add onions and sugar; cook 5 to 7 minutes or until onions are light golden brown, stirring frequently. Add radicchio; cook 30 to 60 seconds or until lightly wilted but color remains. Sprinkle with 1/8 teaspoon of the

pepper and salt.

3 Heat large cast-iron or other heavy skillet over medium-high heat until hot. Add remaining 1 tablespoon oil; swirl pan to coat bottom. Add steaks; cook 5 minutes for medium-rare or until of desired doneness, turning once.

4 To serve, place each steak on bed of warm radicchio-onion mixture; sprinkle with remaining 1/8 teaspoon pepper. Top with Roquefort butter.

TIP *Radicchio is a red-leafed member of the chicory family. Its small, tight heads resemble miniature cabbages. The slightly bitter leaves are often used in mixed salad greens.

WINE Paul Jaboulet Aîné Côtes du Rhône "Parallel 45" is a fine partner for this bistro-style steak, as is St. Supéry Cabernet Sauvignon from Napa Valley.

4 servings

PER SERVING: 495 calories, 31 g total fat (13 g saturated fat), 43 g protein, 9 g carbohydrate, 130 mg cholesterol, 625 mg sodium, 2 g fiber

Teriyaki Steak with Soba Noodle Salad

Teriyaki Steak with Soba Noodle Salad

Besides adding great flavor, the teriyaki marinade acts as a glazing sauce for beef. When cooked in a grill pan, the meat chars slightly and produces an authentic outdoor grill taste. Soba noodles are tossed with an Asian-style dressing to complement the smoky flavor of the meat. Serve this dish at room temperature.

STEAK
1 1/2 lb. boneless bottom sirloin steak (tip or bottom butt), 3/4 to 1 inch thick

1/2 cup teriyaki sauce
4 teaspoons vegetable oil, divided
1/2 teaspoon Asian chile sauce*

SALAD
1 (8-oz.) pkg. soba noodles**
1 1/2 teaspoons vegetable oil
10 shiitake mushrooms, stems removed and discarded, caps sliced
1 bunch (10 oz.) fresh spinach
1/4 cup water
2 cups sliced bok choy
1/4 cup sliced green onions

VINAIGRETTE
3 tablespoons teriyaki sauce
2 tablespoons rice vinegar
1 tablespoon dark sesame oil

2 garlic cloves, minced
2 teaspoons hoisin sauce
1/4 teaspoon Asian chile sauce

1 Place steaks in single layer in shallow dish. In small bowl, whisk together 1/2 cup teriyaki sauce, 2 teaspoons of the vegetable oil and 1/2 teaspoon chile sauce; pour evenly over steaks. Cover and refrigerate at least 3 hours or up to 24 hours.
2 Cook noodles in large pot of boiling salted water 6 to 8 minutes or until just tender. (Be careful not to overcook.) Drain; rinse under cold running water to cool. Place in large bowl.

Guide to Sirloin

While boneless sirloin is very popular, there are so many names for various cuts of this steak that it can be confusing.

Sirloin comes from a cow's hip area, between the short loin and the rump. This area is divided into several sections. Boneless sirloin comes from the sections labeled top and bottom sirloin.

Confusion comes in several forms. First, the sirloin section can be butchered several different ways, so similar cuts of meat can have several names. Second, names vary regionally in the United States.

The top sirloin section produces the most tender boneless cuts. Called top sirloin steak, it comes from the top portion of the hip that butts up to the very tender short loin area, in the middle of the back. This is a steak with firm texture and outstanding flavor. While top sirloin steak is its official name, other names include top butt, sirloin butt, culotte or center-cut.

The bottom sirloin section is found at the bottom area of the full loin, which is located near the rump. Cuts from this section include the bottom sirloin butt, ball tip, tip, tri-tip (also called triangle, for the triangle shape of the muscle portion found in the lower end of the bottom sirloin) or steaks simply labeled sirloin. Ball tip is more commonly known in food service, but it is sold in certain retail markets.

---

3 Heat 1 1/2 teaspoons oil in large nonstick skillet over medium-high heat until hot. Add mushrooms; cook 5 minutes or until tender. Place in bowl with noodles. To same skillet, add spinach and water; cook 1 to 2 minutes or until just wilted, stirring constantly. Add spinach to bowl. In same skillet, cook bok choy, adding a little more water if necessary, 2 to 3 minutes or until barely tender. Add bok choy and green onions to noodles; toss to combine.

4 In medium bowl, whisk together all vinaigrette ingredients. Pour over salad; toss to combine.

5 Heat nonstick grill pan or large cast-iron skillet over medium heat until hot; brush with remaining 2 teaspoons oil. Remove steak from marinade; discard marinade. Place steak on grill pan; cook 8 to 10 minutes for medium-rare or until of desired doneness, turning once. Place steak on cutting board; let stand 5 minutes. Cut across the grain into 1/4-inch-thick slices. Arrange steak over salad; drizzle with any accumulated carving juices.

TIPS *There are many types of Asian-style chile sauces on the market. Look for them in the Asian section of the grocery store.

**Soba noodles are Japanese noodles made with buckwheat and wheat flour. They are gray-brown in color and have a nutty taste.

BEER/WINE If you prefer beer, try an amber ale, such as Anchor Liberty Ale, which isn't too sweet. For wine, try Guenoc Petite Sirah from Northern California; it's rich and slightly spicy but won't overpower this dish.

4 servings

PER SERVING: 510 calories, 14.5 g total fat (3 g saturated fat), 47.5 g protein, 51 g carbohydrate, 90 mg cholesterol, 1190 mg sodium, 10 g fiber

Jill Van Cleave is a Chicago-based food writer and cookbook author.

SWEET INGREDIENTS

Cinnamon and Coffee Cake

Cinnamon Secrets

Take a fresh look at a familiar friend.

Text and Recipes by Stephen Durfee

Often in the pursuit of new spices and seasonings to enliven our cooking, we find there's much to learn about some of our old favorites. Cinnamon is one spice ripe for rediscovery. The choices have expanded, and the once humble jar of ground cinnamon now shares shelf space with previously unavailable varieties—exotic cousins with distinct, developed flavors and rich culinary histories. Plus, applying some simple techniques, such as toasting and grinding, can add further nuance to this wonderful spice. Cinnamon is still the perfect choice for home-baked apple crisp, cinnamon rolls or coffee cake, but now you have more options.

Cinnamon and Coffee Cake

This cake has a wonderfully buttery flavor, with the perfect balance of cinnamon and espresso. Don't be surprised when it doesn't rise very high; it should only come halfway up the sides of the tube pan.

STREUSEL
- ¼ cup packed brown sugar
- ¼ cup sugar
- ¼ cup unsalted butter, softened
- ½ cup all-purpose flour
- 2 teaspoons freshly ground cinnamon*
- 1 teaspoon finely ground espresso coffee beans
- Dash salt

FILLING
- ¾ cup finely chopped pecans
- 1 tablespoon packed brown sugar
- 1 tablespoon sugar
- 1 teaspoon freshly ground cinnamon*
- 1 teaspoon finely ground espresso coffee beans
- ¼ teaspoon salt

CAKE
- ¾ cup unsalted butter, softened
- 1 cup sugar
- 1 egg
- 2 egg yolks
- 2 cups cake flour, sifted
- ½ teaspoon baking powder
- ½ teaspoon baking soda
- ½ teaspoon salt
- ¾ cup buttermilk
- 2 tablespoons canola oil
- Powdered sugar

1 Heat oven to 350°F. Butter and flour 10-inch plain tube pan with removable bottom. In medium bowl, beat ¼ cup brown sugar, ¼ cup sugar and ¼ cup butter at medium speed 1 to 2 minutes or until blended. Beat in all remaining streusel ingredients until combined.

2 In small bowl, stir together all filling ingredients. In large bowl, beat ¾ cup butter and 1 cup sugar at medium speed 2 to 3 minutes or until creamy. Beat in egg and egg yolks until combined.

3 In another large bowl, stir together cake flour, baking powder, baking soda and ½ teaspoon salt. At low speed, beat flour mixture into egg mixture until combined. Beat in buttermilk and oil 30 seconds or until smooth and well combined, occasionally scraping down sides of bowl.

4 Spoon half of the batter into pan; smooth with spoon. Sprinkle filling evenly over batter. Spoon remaining batter over filling. Sprinkle streusel topping evenly over batter. Bake 45 to 55 minutes or until light golden brown and toothpick inserted in center comes out clean.

5 Cool in pan on wire rack 15 minutes. Remove cake from pan by lifting center tube, leaving cake on base; cool completely. Invert onto plate; remove base. Place cake upright on serving plate. Sprinkle with powdered sugar.

TIP *To grind cinnamon, break sticks into smaller pieces. Grind in coffee grinder until finely ground; sift through fine strainer to remove any pieces. (You will need about 4 cinnamon sticks for this recipe.)

12 servings

PER SERVING: 425 calories, 24.5 g total fat (10.5 g saturated fat), 4.5 g protein, 49 g carbohydrate, 95 mg cholesterol, 265 mg sodium, 1.5 g fiber

Cinnamon-Caramel Swirl Ice Cream

With the rich, full flavor of toasted cinnamon and caramel and a smooth, creamy texture, this ice cream took first place with everyone who tasted it. If you'd like to experiment with a different type of cinnamon, try using freshly ground Ceylon cinnamon. It provides a pleasant citrus aroma that is nicely matched by a garnish of tangy orange slices.

CUSTARD
- 2 cups milk
- 2 cups whipping cream
- ⅔ cup sugar, divided
- 1 teaspoon ground toasted cinnamon*
- 9 egg yolks

CARAMEL CREAM
- ⅔ cup whipping cream
- 1 cinnamon stick
- ½ cup sugar
- 2 tablespoons water

Types of Cinnamon

Ceylon cinnamon

Cassia

There are two main types of cinnamon, Ceylon and cassia. They come from different tropical evergreen trees that are part of the laurel family. Cinnamon comes from the smooth, sweetly scented inner bark of these trees. The bark is harvested twice a year. The upper branches of the trees are cut off, and the inner bark is removed and dried in the sun. As the bark dries, it's formed into long sticks called quills, which are then cut into shorter cinnamon sticks. Large chunks of the lower bark and broken pieces are ground into powder or distilled for their essential oil; it's the oil that carries the spice's distinct flavor.

Ceylon cinnamon Although quite different, both Ceylon cinnamon and cassia are sold in the United States under the name "cinnamon," which can cause some confusion. Ceylon cinnamon, often called "true cinnamon," is native to Sri Lanka (formerly known as Ceylon). You can recognize these buff-colored, aromatic and mildly sweet cinnamon sticks by their papery quills, which are tightly rolled, one inside the other. Ceylon cinnamon is the preferred spice throughout Europe and Mexico, where it is known as "canela." It's part of the reason why desserts and pastries from these regions have such a unique flavor. The low volatile oil content of this cinnamon provides a subtle, complex flavor that marries especially well with other spices. Ceylon cinnamon, in stick or powder form, can be found in Mexican or Asian markets.

Cassia Many Americans find Ceylon cinnamon to be too timid in flavor for their palates. They're more familiar with the stronger flavor of cassia, which is what's usually found on store shelves labeled as "cinnamon." It's darker in color and deeper in flavor than Ceylon cinnamon, and its quills are slightly thicker, single-layered and spongy. Sticks cut from these quills are generally used in canning or as a stirring stick for hot drinks. Cassia is highly aromatic and warm, and is often described as bittersweet. Because it contains a greater percentage of essential oil than Ceylon cinnamon (up to 4 percent), its flavor is more assertive and pungent. Cassia grows throughout Asia, notably in China. When choosing cassia, look for sticks labeled "Batavia," an Indonesian variety that is considered the most fragrant.

Other varieties Other species—hundreds of them, in fact—do exist. Few make it to the United States. If they do, they're most likely mixed in with ground cassia and marketed as an anonymous cinnamon product, or used in the packaged food industry. One exception is a Vietnamese variety of cassia, usually called Saigon cinnamon; it can be found in certain Vietnamese groceries. If using this type of cinnamon in recipes, use only two-thirds the amount called for because it's very strong.

The varieties are interchangeable; use whichever one you prefer.

1 In medium saucepan, stir together milk, 2 cups cream, 1/3 cup of the sugar and ground cinnamon. Bring to a boil over medium-high heat; remove from heat. Let stand 30 minutes.
2 In medium bowl, whisk egg yolks and remaining 1/3 cup sugar until combined. Beat on medium speed about 5 minutes or until pale yellow.

3 Bring milk mixture to a simmer over medium heat; remove from heat. Slowly pour hot milk mixture into egg yolk mixture, whisking constantly. Return mixture to saucepan; cook over medium heat 3 to 4 minutes or until custard thickens and coats back of spoon (temperature should be 170°F.).
4 Immediately strain custard through fine sieve into large bowl; place in

bowl of ice water to chill, stirring occasionally.
5 Meanwhile, to make caramel cream, place 2/3 cup cream and cinnamon stick in small saucepan. Bring to a boil over medium-high heat. Remove from heat; let stand 30 minutes. Remove and discard cinnamon stick.
6 In heavy large saucepan, combine 1/2 cup sugar and water. Cook over

high heat, without stirring, until sugar turns deep golden brown. Watch carefully or mixture will burn; if necessary, remove saucepan from heat occasionally to stop cooking. Carefully add cream to caramel (if added too quickly, mixture could spatter and burn). Swirl mixture around saucepan to blend evenly. Remove from heat; refrigerate until completely cool.

7 Freeze in ice cream maker according to manufacturer's directions. Remove from container; gently stir caramel cream into ice cream (do not overstir or you will lose any swirl pattern). Place in airtight container; store in freezer.

TIP *To toast cinnamon sticks, place them on small baking sheet. Bake at 350°F. for 5 minutes or until you can smell toasted aroma of cinnamon. Do not overbake or sticks will burn and cinnamon will be bitter. Cool completely. Break sticks into smaller pieces; grind in coffee grinder until finely ground. Sift through fine strainer to remove any pieces. (You will need about 1 1/2 cinnamon sticks for this recipe.)

12 (1/2-cup) servings

PER SERVING: 295 calories, 21 g total fat (12 g saturated fat), 4.5 g protein, 23.5 g carbohydrate, 220 mg cholesterol, 45 mg sodium, 0 g fiber

Cinnamon Stars

The uniqueness of these traditional European holiday cookies is that they are baked with the frosting on. Using freshly ground Ceylon cinnamon accents the fruity quality of the almonds.

COOKIES
    2 cups slivered almonds
    3/4 cup sugar
    1 tablespoon freshly ground
        cinnamon*
        Dash salt
    1 tablespoon honey
    1 egg white

ICING
    1 cup powdered sugar
    1 egg white
        Edible glitter or sprinkles,
        if desired**

Cinnamon Stars

1 In food processor, combine almonds, sugar, cinnamon and salt; pulse 2 to 3 minutes or until very finely ground. Add honey; pulse to distribute. Add 1 egg white; pulse several seconds or until dough pulls together and forms ball. Pat out dough between 2 sheets of parchment or waxed paper to about 1/2-inch thickness. Roll dough to 1/4-inch thickness (about 12x10-inch rectangle). Be careful not to let paper bunch up and wrinkle underneath. Refrigerate 1 hour or until firm.

2 Meanwhile, in medium bowl, stir together all icing ingredients except edible glitter; beat at medium-high speed 5 to 7 minutes or until stiff but spreadable. Press plastic wrap

directly onto icing to prevent skin from forming.

3 With offset spatula, spread thin layer of icing onto chilled dough. Discard any remaining icing. Sprinkle with edible glitter or sprinkles, if desired. Refrigerate dough 10 minutes or until icing is set.

4 Heat oven to 400°F. Line 2 baking sheets with parchment paper. Cut out cookies using 2-inch star-shaped cutter. (Dip cutter into water before each use, shaking off excess.) If cookies are difficult to remove from cutter, tap edge of cutter against baking sheet until cookies release.

5 Place cookies on baking sheets. Bake one sheet at a time 5 to 6 minutes or until cookies have risen slightly (icing should remain white).

Cinnamon Lollipops

a boil over medium-high heat. Boil 12 to 18 minutes or until reduced to 1/4 cup. Remove and discard cinnamon sticks.

3 Stir in sugar. Bring to a boil, brushing sides of pan with pastry brush dipped in water to wash down any sugar crystals. Stir in corn syrup. Cook 7 to 10 minutes or until candy thermometer reaches 295°F.

4 Immediately remove from heat; pour syrup into glass measuring cup. Gently pour syrup into molds or over ends of lollipop sticks on parchment.

TIP *To toast cinnamon sticks, place on small baking sheet. Bake at 350°F. for 5 minutes or until you can smell toasted aroma of cinnamon. Do not overbake or cinnamon will burn and become bitter. Cool completely.

24 lollipops

PER LOLLIPOP: 60 calories, 0 g total fat (0 g saturated fat), 0 g protein, 15.5 g carbohydrate, 0 mg cholesterol, 10 mg sodium, 0 g fiber

Cinnamon Rum Soufflé

This recipe is an optimal choice for entertaining. Not only does a soufflé make an impressive presentation, but most of the work can be done in advance. For best results, use a clean bowl and whisk, and make sure your egg whites are at room temperature; they'll whip up the fullest.

CUSTARD
- 1/4 cup plus 1 tablespoon sugar, divided
- 1 tablespoon cornstarch
- 1 teaspoon freshly ground cinnamon*
- 1/2 cup milk
- 2 egg yolks
- 1 tablespoon dark rum
- 6 egg whites

WHIPPING CREAM
- 1 cup whipping cream
- 1 tablespoon sugar
- 2 teaspoons dark rum

1 In small heavy saucepan, stir together 1/4 cup of the sugar, cornstarch and cinnamon. In small bowl, whisk together milk and egg yolks; whisk into sugar mixture. Bring

Cut and bake remaining dough scraps, if desired. Cool cookies completely on wire rack. (Cookies can be made up to 1 week ahead. Store in airtight container.)

TIPS *To grind cinnamon, break sticks into smaller pieces. Grind in coffee grinder until finely ground; sift through fine strainer to remove any pieces. (You will need about 4 cinnamon sticks for this recipe.) **Edible glitter, an all-natural gum arabic, adds beautiful sparkle to cookies.

30 cookies

PER COOKIE: 85 calories, 4.5 g total fat (.5 g saturated fat), 2 g protein, 11.5 g carbohydrate, 0 mg cholesterol, 15 mg sodium, 1 g fiber

Cinnamon Lollipops

These delicately flavored cinnamon lollipops are as much fun to make as they are to eat. You can find inexpensive lollipop molds and sticks at kitchen supply or craft stores.

- 2 cups water
- 6 cinnamon sticks, toasted*
- 1 cup sugar
- 2/3 cup light corn syrup

1 Place lollipop sticks in plastic or metal lollipop molds, or arrange sticks 3 inches apart on greased parchment paper.

2 In medium saucepan, combine water and cinnamon sticks. Bring to

Cinnamon Techniques

When cooking with any spice, keep in mind that freshness is important. Ground spices of any type have a limited shelf life, generally one year from the date of opening. After that, the volatile oils will be subdued. Resist the temptation to buy a jumbo-sized package of spice unless you plan to use it up.

Toasting Both ground cinnamon and cinnamon sticks can benefit from some slight toasting before use, especially if they've been on your shelf for a while.

- Warm ground cinnamon in a small skillet over gentle heat, stirring with a wooden spoon, until its fragrance becomes noticeable.

- For recipes that ask for a cinnamon infusion, reassert the aromatic qualities of cinnamon sticks by toasting them in a 350°F. oven or on the stovetop for several minutes. Be careful not to let the sticks burn because they will take on a very bitter flavor.

Cassia sticks used in infusions often are reusable. Wash them under warm running water and let them dry out thoroughly at room temperature before repackaging them. Because of the many layers of Ceylon cinnamon sticks, they're harder to reuse. They need to be cleaned well, especially if they've been infused in cream, and thoroughly dried.

Grinding The best way to enjoy cinnamon's rich fragrance is to grind it yourself. Toast the sticks briefly, then grind them in an electric coffee mill dedicated to spice grinding, or with a mortar and pestle. Sift the ground spice before measuring it to ensure a fine, even grind. One 4-inch-long cinnamon stick yields about 1 teaspoon ground cinnamon. Because home-ground cinnamon is more pungent than packaged ground cinnamon, you may wind up using less of it than the recipe calls for.

Cinnamon sources

Penzeys Spices: www.penzeys.com, (800) 741-7787
The Spice Hunter: www.spicehunter.com, (800) 444-3061
The Spice House: www.thespicehouse.com, (414) 272-0977

---

to a boil over medium-high heat, stirring constantly. Reduce heat to medium; cook 30 seconds or until thickened. Remove from heat; stir in rum. Place mixture in large bowl; place plastic wrap directly on surface of custard. Let stand 2 hours or until cool. (Mixture can be made up to 1 day ahead. Cover and refrigerate.)

2 Heat oven to 400°F. Brush 6 (6-oz.) ramekins with softened butter; sprinkle generously with sugar. Shake ramekins to remove excess sugar; wipe rims clean. Place on baking sheet; refrigerate while preparing soufflés.

3 Whisk egg yolk mixture until well blended. In large bowl, beat egg whites at medium-high speed until soft peaks form. Add remaining 1 tablespoon sugar; beat until stiff, but not dry, peaks form. Stir one-fourth of the egg whites into egg yolk mixture. Fold in remaining egg whites.

4 Divide batter among ramekins; wipe off any mixture on edges of ramekins. (Soufflés can be made to this point up to 3 hours ahead. Refrigerate.) Place baking sheet with soufflés in oven. Bake 17 to 20 minutes or until tops of soufflés are puffed up and sides feel slightly firm. (Soufflés will not start to rise until after 10 to 12 minutes.)

5 Meanwhile, in small bowl, beat all whipping cream ingredients at medium-high speed until soft peaks form. Serve with soufflés.

TIP *To grind cinnamon, break sticks into smaller pieces. Grind in coffee grinder until finely ground; sift through fine strainer to remove any pieces. (You will need about 1¹/₂ cinnamon sticks for this recipe.)

6 servings

PER SERVING: 225 calories, 14.5 g total fat (8.5 g saturated fat), 6 g protein, 16.5 g carbohydrate, 115 mg cholesterol, 80 mg sodium, 0 g fiber

Stephen Durfee is the former pastry chef at The French Laundry in Yountville, California. He currently is a pastry instructor at the Culinary Institute of America's Greystone (Napa Valley) campus.

Pumpkin-Pecan Cake with Brown Sugar Frosting

Sweet on Pumpkin

Five scrumptious desserts feature this fall favorite.

Recipes by Carolyn Weil

Fall means that change is in the air. Light summer desserts get tucked away for the season. In their place—inhale deeply now—are richer offerings with mingling aromas of cinnamon, ginger and a favorite autumn ingredient, pumpkin. Its deep color and flavor along with its sweet nature make pumpkin an amiable ingredient in more desserts than you have time to make. But it's fun trying. Treat your family to a creamy pumpkin cheesecake. Take a spicy pumpkin cake to a potluck supper. Or serve a pumpkin chiffon pie to dinner guests. From lunchbox-casual to party-elegant, pumpkin's versatility makes it a baker's sweetheart.

Pumpkin-Pecan Cake with Brown Sugar Frosting

This deeply flavored pumpkin-and-spice cake is the perfect make-ahead dessert. Olive oil keeps it moist, and our testers found it tasted even better on the second day.

CAKE
- 2¾ cups all-purpose flour
- ½ cup finely chopped toasted pecans*
- 1 tablespoon ground cinnamon
- 2 teaspoons baking powder
- 2 teaspoons ground ginger
- ¾ teaspoon ground cloves
- ½ teaspoon finely ground pepper
- ½ teaspoon salt
- 2¼ cups packed brown sugar
- 1 cup light olive oil
- 4 eggs
- 1 (15-oz.) can pure pumpkin
- 2 teaspoons grated orange peel

FROSTING
- ¼ cup unsalted butter
- ½ cup packed brown sugar
- 3 tablespoons milk
- 1¼ to 1½ cups powdered sugar, sifted

1 Heat oven to 325°F. Grease 12-cup Bundt pan with shortening.
2 In medium bowl, whisk flour, pecans, cinnamon, baking powder, ginger, cloves, pepper and salt to distribute all ingredients evenly.
3 In large bowl, beat 2¼ cups brown sugar and oil at low speed until well mixed. Add eggs one at a time, beating well after each addition. Add pumpkin and orange peel; beat at low speed until blended. With mixer on low, slowly add flour mixture, beating just until incorporated. Spoon batter into Bundt pan.
4 Bake 60 to 65 minutes or until skewer inserted in center of cake comes out clean. Cool on wire rack 15 minutes; invert onto wire rack. Remove from pan; cool completely before placing on serving plate.
5 Meanwhile, melt butter in medium saucepan over medium heat. Stir in ½ cup brown sugar; bring to a full boil. Whisk in milk until smooth. Remove from heat; whisk in 1¼ cups of the powdered sugar until smooth and of glaze consistency. Add additional ¼ cup powdered sugar, if necessary. Place in container with pouring spout. Immediately pour over cooled cake. Frosting sets up almost immediately, so slowly pour frosting over cake in one motion.** For a smooth look, do not go back over frosting with spoon or spatula.
TIPS *To toast pecans, spread on baking sheet; bake at 350°F. for 7 to 10 minutes or until light golden brown. **If frosting begins to thicken too much while pouring, place container in bowl of hot water and stir until thinner.

12 servings

PER SERVING: 610 calories, 27.5 g total fat (6 g saturated fat), 6 g protein, 88.5 g carbohydrate, 80 mg cholesterol, 225 mg sodium, 2.5 g fiber

Pumpkin Brûlée

For a spectacular presentation, the pumpkin brûlée is spooned into miniature pumpkins and caramelized before serving. It also can be made more traditionally in individual ramekins.

- 2 cups heavy whipping cream
- 1 (2-inch) piece vanilla bean, split lengthwise
- 8 egg yolks
- ½ cup sugar
- ¼ teaspoon ground cinnamon
- ⅛ teaspoon salt
- ½ cup canned pure pumpkin
- 6 mini pumpkins*
- ¼ cup turbinado sugar**

1 Heat oven to 325°F. Place 11x8½-inch glass baking dish in shallow roasting pan. (If using ramekins instead of mini pumpkins, place 6 (½-cup) ramekins in roasting pan.) In medium saucepan, heat cream and vanilla bean over medium heat until tiny bubbles appear around edges.
2 In medium bowl, whisk egg yolks, ½ cup sugar, cinnamon and salt until pale. Whisk in pumpkin. Slowly whisk in hot cream mixture. Strain through fine sieve into baking dish or ramekins. Fill roasting pan with enough hot water to come ½ inch up sides of baking dish or ramekins.
3 Place roasting pan in oven. Bake 25 to 30 minutes or until custard is set but still quivery like gelatin. Remove from water bath; cool to

Pumpkin Cheesecake with Bourbon-Butter Sauce

room temperature. Refrigerate 3 hours or until chilled. (If using ramekins instead of pumpkins, skip to Step 5.)
4 Meanwhile, slice tops off pumpkins. Scrape seeds from insides to create bowl for crème brûlée; discard seeds. Rinse; dry well. Refrigerate until needed. Gently spoon chilled custard into pumpkins (do not stir custard), smoothing top of custard with back of spoon.
5 Place turbinado sugar in food processor; process until finely ground. Sprinkle 2 teaspoons turbinado sugar over custard in each pumpkin or ramekin. With kitchen torch, caramelize sugar until golden brown.*** Refrigerate brûlées briefly before serving, to set caramel. (Brûlées can be made up to 4 hours ahead.) Store in refrigerator.
TIPS *If mini pumpkins aren't available, custard can be made in 6 (¹/₂-cup) ramekins.
**Turbinado sugar is large, pale brown crystals of pure cane sugar. It has a mild brown sugar flavor. If you can't find turbinado sugar, substitute white granulated sugar.
***Kitchen torches are small, open-flame torches used to caramelize the sugar for crème brûlée. They can be found in kitchen supply stores. Any

blowtorch (designed for home repair) can be used, but use extra caution with the larger blowtorches.
6 servings

PER SERVING: 450 calories, 36.5 g total fat (20.5 g saturated fat), 5.5 g protein, 27 g carbohydrate, 390 mg cholesterol, 90 mg sodium, .5 g fiber

Pumpkin Cheesecake with Bourbon-Butter Sauce

Cheesecake meets pumpkin pie in this rich, creamy, wonderful dessert. A perfect blend of spices enlivens the cheesecake, and a buttery caramel sauce tops it. Make sure to tightly wrap the foil around the springform pan so that water doesn't seep in while the cheesecake bakes.

CRUST
  1¹/₂ cups graham cracker crumbs
  ¹/₄ cup sugar
  1 tablespoon grated orange peel
  1 teaspoon ground nutmeg
  ¹/₃ cup unsalted butter, melted
FILLING
  3 (8-oz.) pkg. cream cheese, softened
  1 cup sugar
  3 eggs

  ¹/₂ cup sour cream
  1¹/₂ cups canned pure pumpkin
  ¹/₂ teaspoon ground cinnamon
  ¹/₂ teaspoon ground ginger
  ¹/₂ teaspoon salt
  ¹/₄ teaspoon ground nutmeg
SAUCE
  ¹/₂ cup unsalted butter
  1 cup packed dark brown sugar
  ¹/₂ cup whipping cream
  2 tablespoons bourbon whiskey or 1 tablespoon vanilla extract

1 Heat oven to 350°F. Spray bottom of 9-inch springform pan with nonstick cooking spray (do not spray sides). Wrap outside of pan with heavy-duty aluminum foil. In medium bowl, stir together graham cracker crumbs, ¹/₄ cup sugar, orange peel and 1 teaspoon nutmeg. Add ¹/₃ cup melted butter; stir until crumbs are well-moistened. Press mixture evenly over bottom and ¹/₂ inch up sides of springform pan. Bake 10 minutes or until golden brown.
2 In large bowl, beat cream cheese at medium-low speed until smooth. Beat in 1 cup sugar until smooth. Add eggs one at a time, beating just until combined. Beat in sour cream, pumpkin, cinnamon, ginger, salt and

¼ teaspoon nutmeg. (Do not overbeat.) Pour into springform pan.

3 Place springform pan in large shallow roasting pan or broiler pan. Fill roasting pan with enough hot water to come ½ inch up sides of springform pan.

4 Bake 65 minutes or until edges are puffed and top looks dull and is dry to the touch. Center should be less set than edges and will move when pan is tapped. It should not ripple as if liquid.

5 Remove from oven; remove from water bath. Cool completely on wire rack. Refrigerate at least 4 hours or overnight.

6 To make sauce, melt ½ cup butter in medium saucepan over medium heat. Whisk in brown sugar until mixture is smooth. Whisk in cream and bourbon; bring to a boil. Pour into medium bowl; cool completely. Serve with cheesecake. Refrigerate leftovers.

WINE Try a sweet Marsala, a fortified dessert wine from southern Italy, such as the nonvintage Pellegrino.

12 servings

PER SERVING: 585 calories, 40 g total fat (24 g saturated fat), 7 g protein, 52 g carbohydrate, 165 mg cholesterol, 355 mg sodium, 1 g fiber

Pumpkin Chiffon Pie with Ginger Crust

Pumpkin Chiffon Pie with Ginger Crust

The crust in this pie offers a double hit of ginger's bold character with gingersnaps and crystallized ginger. The lightly spiced, fluffy filling provides a gentle contrast.

CRUST

- 1¼ cups gingersnap cookie crumbs (about 22 (2-inch) cookies)
- 2 tablespoons minced crystallized ginger
- 3 tablespoons sugar
- ½ teaspoon ground cinnamon
- ⅓ cup unsalted butter, melted

FILLING

- 1 cup heavy whipping cream
- ¼ cup water
- 1 (¼-oz.) pkg. unflavored gelatin
- 3 eggs
- ¾ cup sugar
- 2 tablespoons cornstarch
- 2 teaspoons ground ginger
- 1 teaspoon ground cinnamon
- ½ teaspoon ground nutmeg
- ¼ teaspoon ground cloves
  Dash salt
- ¾ cup milk
- ¾ cup canned pure pumpkin

TOPPING

- 1 cup heavy whipping cream
- 1 tablespoon sugar

1 Heat oven to 350°F. In medium bowl, stir together cookie crumbs, crystallized ginger, 3 tablespoons sugar and ½ teaspoon cinnamon. Add butter; stir until crumbs are well moistened. Press into bottom and up sides of 9-inch pie pan. Bake 5 to 7 minutes or until fragrant, slightly darker and slightly firm to the touch. Cool completely on wire rack.

2 In medium bowl, beat 1 cup cream at medium-high speed until soft peaks form; refrigerate. Place ¼ cup water in small bowl; add gelatin. Let stand 5 minutes or until gelatin is softened.

3 Meanwhile, in medium saucepan, whisk together eggs, ¾ cup sugar, cornstarch, ginger, 1 teaspoon cinnamon, nutmeg, cloves and salt. Whisk in milk until smooth. Whisk in gelatin mixture. Cook over medium heat, whisking constantly, 5 to 8 minutes or until gelatin is completely dissolved and mixture thickens and comes to a boil. (Mixture should be between 165°F. and 170°F.) Immediately pour into medium bowl. Whisk in pumpkin. Place bowl in large bowl of ice water; whisk constantly 4 to 5 minutes or until mixture is cool. Fold in whipped cream; pour into crust.

4 In medium bowl, beat 1 cup cream and 1 tablespoon sugar at medium-high speed until slightly firm peaks form. Spread over filling. Refrigerate 4 to 6 hours or until set. Remove pie from refrigerator 20 to 30 minutes before serving so it is cool but not cold. Store in refrigerator.

8 servings

PER SERVING: 515 calories, 34 g total fat (20 g saturated fat), 6 g protein, 49.5 g carbohydrate, 185 mg cholesterol, 215 mg sodium, 1.5 g fiber

Carolyn Weil is a food writer and cooking instructor in Berkeley, California.

Rhubarb-Ginger Upside-Down Cake

Seeing Red

Old-fashioned rhubarb grabs the spotlight in sweet *and* savory dishes.

Text and Recipes by Mary Evans

Rhubarb traditionally finds its way into sweet springtime treats, earning it an appropriate nickname, the pieplant. But more recently, cooks are discovering it's equally at home in savory fare, such as salads and main dishes. Adaptable to many treatments, rhubarb can be mysteriously subtle or decidedly tart, depending on how it's prepared.

Perhaps this has helped fuel rhubarb's expanding repertoire. More people can get it. While it used to be found only in the spring and only by those who had access to northern-climate gardens, hothouse varieties have extended the rhubarb season and its availability. Rhubarb lovers couldn't be happier!

Rhubarb-Ginger Upside-Down Cake

Rhubarb cake gets a delightful update with the spicy-sweet addition of crystallized ginger to its caramelized topping. Cake flour provides an extra-light crumb.

- 2 cups chopped rhubarb (1/2 inch)
- 1/4 cup plus 2/3 cup sugar, divided
- 3 tablespoons finely chopped crystallized ginger
- 10 tablespoons unsalted butter, softened, divided
- 1/2 cup packed light brown sugar
- 1 1/3 cups cake flour
- 1 1/4 teaspoons baking powder
- 1/4 teaspoon ground ginger
- 1/4 teaspoon ground coriander
- 1/4 teaspoon salt
- 2 eggs, room temperature
- 1 teaspoon vanilla extract
- 1/4 cup milk

1 Heat oven to 350°F. Spray bottom of 8x8-inch baking pan with nonstick cooking spray; line bottom with parchment paper. Spray sides of pan and paper with nonstick cooking spray.
2 In medium bowl, combine rhubarb, 1/4 cup of the sugar and crystallized ginger; toss to blend.
3 Melt 4 tablespoons of the butter in medium skillet over medium heat. Add brown sugar; cook until sugar is melted. Spread evenly in bottom of pan; top with rhubarb mixture.
4 In medium bowl, stir together flour, baking powder, ground ginger, coriander and salt.
5 In large bowl, beat remaining 6 tablespoons butter at medium speed until smooth. Add remaining 2/3 cup sugar; beat 4 to 5 minutes or until light and fluffy. Add eggs one at a time, beating well after each addition and scraping down sides of bowl several times. Beat in vanilla. Reduce speed to low; beat in half of the flour mixture until combined. Alternately stir in milk and remaining flour mixture in two batches, mixing just until combined. (Stirring in remaining milk and flour mixture instead of using an electric mixer makes this cake extra-tender.)
6 Spread batter over rhubarb, pressing with spatula to remove as much air as possible. Tap pan on counter several times to remove air. Bake 40 to 45 minutes or until cake is golden brown, firm to the touch in center and toothpick inserted in center halfway down comes out clean.
7 Cool on wire rack 10 minutes. Run knife around edges of pan. Invert onto serving platter; carefully remove pan and parchment. Cool completely.
8 servings

PER SERVING: 390 calories, 16 g total fat (9.5 g saturated fat), 4 g protein, 59 g carbohydrate, 90 mg cholesterol, 190 mg sodium, 1 g fiber

Individual Rhubarb Tarts

Almond's heady aroma and rich flavor complement a sweet-tart rhubarb filling. The almond slices add pleasant crunch to each bite.

CRUST
- 1 3/4 cups all-purpose flour
- 1 tablespoon powdered sugar
- 1/4 teaspoon salt
- 10 tablespoons unsalted butter, chilled, cut up
- 1 egg, beaten

FILLING
- 1 1/4 cups chopped rhubarb (1/2 inch)
- 2/3 cup plus 1 tablespoon powdered sugar, divided
- 2 teaspoons all-purpose flour
- 1/3 cup heavy whipping cream
- 1 egg
- 1/8 teaspoon almond extract
- 1/4 cup sliced almonds

1 Place 1 3/4 cups flour, 1 tablespoon powdered sugar and salt in food processor; pulse to combine. Add butter; pulse until mixture resembles coarse crumbs with some pea-sized pieces. Add beaten egg; pulse until dough just begins to form. Shape into flat round; cover and refrigerate 30 minutes. (Dough also can be made by hand using pastry blender.)
2 Meanwhile, heat oven to 425°F. On lightly floured surface, roll dough slightly thicker than 1/8 inch. Cut into 6 (5-inch) circles, re-rolling scraps as needed. Line 6 (4-inch) tart pans with dough; line dough with foil. Place on baking sheet; bake 10 minutes or until crust is dry and set (crust will not be brown). Remove foil; cool on wire rack.
3 Place rhubarb, 2/3 cup of the powdered sugar and 2 teaspoons flour in medium bowl; stir until sugar

and flour completely coat rhubarb. Divide rhubarb mixture evenly among partially baked crusts, spreading with back of spoon to cover bottom. Bake 8 to 10 minutes or until edges of crust begin to brown. Remove from oven. Reduce oven temperature to 350°F.

4 Meanwhile, in same medium bowl, whisk together cream, 1 egg and almond extract. Divide cream mixture evenly among tarts; sprinkle evenly with almonds. Bake at 350°F. for 25 to 30 minutes or until filling is set and crusts are puffed and lightly browned. Cool on wire rack; remove from pans. Sprinkle with remaining 1 tablespoon powdered sugar.

6 servings

PER SERVING: 455 calories, 27.5 g total fat (15 g saturated fat), 7.5 g protein, 46 g carbohydrate, 135 mg cholesterol, 125 mg sodium, 2 g fiber

Spring Greens with Roasted Rhubarb and Peppered Pecans

This salad is a feast for your eyes as well as your appetite. Red, green and orange ingredients meet sour, sweet and spicy flavors. Roasting is an easy method that deepens rhubarb's flavor and contributes to the dish's appeal.

SALAD
- 2 cups sliced rhubarb (1 inch)
- 1 cup pecan halves
- 1 tablespoon extra-virgin olive oil
- 1 tablespoon orange juice
- 5 tablespoons sugar, divided
- 3/4 teaspoon freshly ground mixed or black pepper, divided
- 1/2 teaspoon salt, divided
- 8 cups mixed salad greens

VINAIGRETTE
- 1 tablespoon orange juice
- 1/2 teaspoon Dijon mustard
- 1/4 teaspoon salt
- 3 tablespoons extra-virgin olive oil

GARNISH
- 1/4 cup orange peel strips*

1 Heat oven to 450°F. Place rhubarb in shallow 9-inch glass pie plate. Place pecans in jelly-roll pan or shallow pan.
2 In small bowl, stir together 1 tablespoon oil and 1 tablespoon orange juice; drizzle half of the mixture over rhubarb and half over pecans. Stir each to coat. Arrange rhubarb in single layer.
3 In another small bowl, stir together 3 tablespoons of the sugar, 1/4 teaspoon of the pepper and 1/4 teaspoon of the salt. Sprinkle over rhubarb. In another small bowl, stir together remaining 2 tablespoons sugar, 1/2 teaspoon pepper and 1/4 teaspoon salt. Sprinkle over pecans; stir to combine.
4 Bake pecans and rhubarb 5 minutes. Remove pecans; stir. Return to oven; bake an additional 1 to 2 minutes until pecans are golden brown and bubbly and rhubarb is barely tender when pierced with knife. Turn pecans out onto waxed paper, separating with fork. Cool rhubarb in baking dish on wire rack about 30 minutes. Reserve 2 tablespoons of the rhubarb juices.
5 To make vinaigrette, in another small bowl, whisk together reserved 2 tablespoons rhubarb juices, 1 tablespoon orange juice, Dijon mustard and 1/4 teaspoon salt. Whisk in 3 tablespoons oil.
6 Before serving, toss greens with enough vinaigrette to lightly coat. Arrange on 4 salad plates. Top with roasted rhubarb; sprinkle with pecans and orange peel.
TIP *To make orange peel strips, use zester or vegetable peeler to remove orange peel in thin strips, avoiding bitter white pith beneath peel.

4 servings

PER SERVING: 395 calories, 33.5 g total fat (3.5 g saturated fat), 5 g protein, 25 g carbohydrate, 0 mg cholesterol, 485 mg sodium, 6 g fiber

Roasted Halibut with Rhubarb Beurre Blanc

Rhubarb adds a delicate pink color and tart accent to a classic wine and butter sauce.

Spring Greens with Roasted Rhubarb and Peppered Pecans

- 3/4 cup water
- 1/2 cup finely chopped rhubarb (1/4 inch)
- 1 cup sliced rhubarb (1/2 inch)
- 1/2 cup dry white wine
- 6 (6- to 8-oz.) halibut fillets
- 1 tablespoon olive oil
- 1/2 teaspoon salt
- 1/4 teaspoon white pepper
- 1/2 cup butter, chilled, cut up
  Dash salt

1 Heat oven to 450°F. Place water in medium saucepan; bring to a simmer over medium-low heat. Add 1/2 cup finely chopped rhubarb; simmer 2 to 3 minutes or until crisp-tender. Place in small bowl with slotted spoon; reserve for sauce.
2 Place 1 cup sliced rhubarb in same saucepan with water; increase heat to medium. Cook 3 to 4 minutes or until very tender and breaking apart. Remove from heat; strain through fine mesh strainer, reserving liquid and pressing gently to remove excess moisture. Return rhubarb liquid to saucepan; discard strained pulp. Add wine to saucepan; increase heat to medium-high. Boil 10 to 15 minutes or until reduced to 2 tablespoons.
3 Meanwhile, arrange halibut in single layer in shallow baking pan. Drizzle fish with oil; sprinkle with salt and pepper. Bake halibut 10 to 12 minutes or until fish just begins to flake.
4 When rhubarb liquid is reduced, remove from heat; whisk in butter, 1 to 2 pieces at a time, until butter is melted and sauce is thick and creamy.

(If butter hasn't melted completely, briefly return to low heat but do not leave on heat or sauce will separate.) Stir in reserved 1/2 cup rhubarb and salt. (If rhubarb is very tart, add dash sugar.) Place halibut on individual plates; spoon sauce over halibut.

WINE Try E. Guigal Côtes du Rhône from France, with its ripe red berry fruit and slight earthiness, or Babcock Pinot Noir from Santa Barbara County in California, which is elegant and medium- to full-bodied.

6 servings

PER SERVING: 315 calories, 19.5 g total fat (10.5 g saturated fat), 32.5 g protein, 1 g carbohydrate, 130 mg cholesterol, 485 mg sodium, .5 g fiber

Mustard-Crusted Pork Loin with Rhubarb Compote

Baking the compote is a gentle cooking method that helps the rhubarb retain its shape and infuses the fruit with a spicy sweetness.

COMPOTE
- 3 cups chopped rhubarb (1/2 inch) (about 1 1/4 lb.)
- 1/2 cup chopped dried mixed fruit
- 2/3 cup sugar
- 1/4 teaspoon ground cinnamon
- 1/8 teaspoon ground allspice
- 1/8 teaspoon ground cloves
- 2 tablespoons water

PORK
- 1 (2- to 2 1/4-lb.) single boneless pork loin
- 1 tablespoon olive oil
- 1 tablespoon country Dijon mustard
- 2 teaspoons minced garlic
- 1 tablespoon fennel seeds, crushed*
- 1/2 teaspoon salt
- 1/4 teaspoon freshly ground pepper

1 Heat oven to 400°F. In medium bowl, stir together rhubarb and dried fruit. In small bowl, stir together sugar, cinnamon, allspice and cloves. Add to fruit mixture; stir to evenly coat. Pour into 8x8-inch glass baking dish; sprinkle with water. Cover with foil. Bake 30 minutes or until rhubarb is tender. Remove foil; cool until slightly warm or room temperature.

Guide to Rhubarb

There are many varieties of rhubarb (which is a vegetable, not a fruit), from the greenish pink Victoria to the intensely ruby Crimson Red. Cooks vary in their preferences for field- or hothouse-grown plants, and choice is often determined by what's available in a specific area. All varieties contribute a pleasantly tart taste that needs to be balanced by the addition of a sweetener. For best results, keep the following tips in mind.

Tender stalks The slenderness or plumpness of the stalks is not an indicator of tenderness; instead, look for firm, unblemished stalks without woody ends.

Dangerous leaves Rhubarb leaves should never be eaten because they are toxic. Be sure to discard the leaves before storing and using the stalks.

Brief storage Rhubarb is best used within a few days and should be stored in the refrigerator in a loose plastic bag. Before use, trim the ends and wash the stalks to remove any residual grit.

Pretty in pink To maintain rhubarb's pinkish to red tint, don't peel the stalks, if possible. Stringiness can be an issue, but slicing often takes care of this. If you have to peel the stalks, use them where color is less important or in combination with another reddish fruit, such as strawberries. To keep the color when cooking, don't overcook it. Cook it just until tender and immediately remove it from the heat. And be sure to use nonreactive pans (for example, coated steel, coated aluminum, coated copper or glass) when cooking rhubarb because of its high acidity. Pans made of uncoated aluminum or cast iron will react with the acid in the rhubarb, resulting in discoloration and a metallic taste.

2 With paper towels, pat surface of pork dry. Heat large skillet over medium-high heat until hot. Add oil; heat until hot. Add pork; cook 5 minutes or until browned on all sides. Place in shallow roasting pan.
3 In another small bowl, stir together mustard, garlic, fennel seeds, salt and pepper. Spread over top and sides of roast. Bake 35 to 45 minutes or until internal temperature reaches 145°F. Remove from oven; let stand 10 minutes. Slice; serve with compote.
TIP *Crush fennel seeds using a mortar and pestle, or place in heavy plastic bag and pound with meat mallet.

WINE Pinot Noir or a lighter, fruit-intensive red is an ideal choice. Meridian Pinot Noir from Santa Barbara is a great value, while Rodney Strong Pinot Noir from Sonoma's Russian River Valley has more spice and body.

6 servings

PER SERVING: 395 calories, 14.5 g total fat (4.5 g saturated fat), 35 g protein, 32 g carbohydrate, 95 mg cholesterol, 320 mg sodium, 2 g fiber

Mary Evans is the author of *Bistro Chicken* (Broadway).

Dark and White Chocolate Mousse Tart

Winter White

White chocolate is the key ingredient in decadent party desserts.

Text and Recipes by Elinor Klivans

Whenever you need festive desserts, white chocolate is ready to help celebrate the occasion. White chocolate is the magic ingredient that turns simple home-style sweets into black-tie desserts. A luscious tart rises to the occasion with layers of white and dark chocolate. A yellow cake gets dressed up with a creamy white chocolate frosting and a showering of white chocolate curls. And white chocolate mingles with raspberries, becoming melt-in-your-mouth truffles.

White chocolate is an ideal ingredient for desserts because it has an affinity for pairing with and enhancing other flavors. Raspberries, strawberries, cranberries, lemons and oranges all have a tart quality that balances well with the sweetness of white chocolate. Other good matches are spices—such as cinnamon, nutmeg or cloves—or nuts, such as pistachios, hazelnuts, cashews, macadamias or pecans.

When putting on the ritz, don't forget about white chocolate. It really knows how to party.

Dark and White Chocolate Mousse Tart

Heavy whipping cream, which has a higher fat content than regular whipping cream, is the best choice for producing a firm filling. Make sure you have plenty of time to prepare this dessert because each chocolate cream mixture must be thoroughly chilled before whipping; the dark chocolate mixture will thicken more quickly than the white chocolate one.

FILLING
- 8 oz. white chocolate, finely chopped
- 2½ cups heavy whipping cream, divided
- 2 teaspoons vanilla extract, divided
- 6 oz. semisweet chocolate, finely chopped
- 1 tablespoon Dutch-processed cocoa

CRUST
- 1¼ cups chocolate cookie crumbs
- ⅓ cup unsalted butter, melted

GARNISH
- 1 oz. semisweet chocolate, coarsely chopped

1 Place white chocolate in large bowl. In heavy medium saucepan, heat 1½ cups of the cream over medium heat until hot (about 190°F.). Remove from heat as soon as first bubble appears. Pour over white chocolate. Let stand 1 minute to soften; stir until chocolate is smooth and melted. Stir in 1 teaspoon of the vanilla. Refrigerate 2 to 2½ hours or until cold and slightly thickened.

2 Meanwhile, place 6 oz. semisweet chocolate and cocoa powder in large bowl. In heavy medium saucepan, heat remaining 1 cup cream over medium heat until hot (about 190°F.). Remove from heat as soon as first bubble appears. Pour over chocolate mixture. Let stand 1 minute to soften; stir until mixture is smooth and chocolate is melted. Stir in remaining 1 teaspoon vanilla. Refrigerate 1 hour or until cold and slightly thickened.

3 Meanwhile, make crust. Heat oven to 325°F. Line bottom of 9-inch springform pan with parchment paper. In medium bowl, stir together crumbs and melted butter until crumbs are evenly moistened. Press evenly into bottom and 1 inch up sides of pan. Bake 8 minutes or until crust is set; cool.

4 Beat chilled semisweet chocolate mixture at medium speed just until soft peaks form. Do not overbeat. (The colder the mixture, the less time it will take to beat.) Spread in cooled crust; mixture will thicken as it stands. Refrigerate until white chocolate mixture is ready.

5 Beat chilled white chocolate mixture at medium-high speed just until very soft peaks form. Do not overbeat. Gently spread over semisweet chocolate mixture; mixture will thicken as it stands. Refrigerate.

6 Microwave 1 oz. semisweet chocolate in small microwave-safe bowl 30 to 60 seconds or until chocolate is almost melted. Stir until smooth. Drizzle over white chocolate layer. Freeze 3 to 4 hours or until tart is firm, or overnight. Remove from freezer. Run knife around outside edge; remove sides. Slice; refrigerate until ready to serve. (If tart is too firm to slice directly from freezer, refrigerate 30 minutes before slicing.) (Tart can be made up to 1 week ahead. Cover and freeze.)

WINE A tawny Port is lightly sweet and pairs well with chocolate. Try the nonvintage Lindemans from Australia or the nonvintage Dow's "Boardroom" from Portugal.

12 servings

PER SERVING: 450 calories, 36 g total fat (21.5 g saturated fat), 3.5 g protein, 32 g carbohydrate, 85 mg cholesterol, 105 mg sodium, 1.5 g fiber

Making White Chocolate Curls

It's simple to make white chocolate curls with a thick block of white chocolate and a vegetable peeler. To make a block of white chocolate, melt the chocolate and pour it into a mini loaf pan that has been lined with plastic wrap.

You'll need a block at least 1/2 inch thick (2 ounces of chocolate produces about 1 cup of curls). Let it stand at room temperature until firm. The key to making curls is having the block of chocolate at the right temperature. If the chocolate sticks to the peeler, it's too warm; refrigerate it slightly to cool it. If the chocolate flakes, it's too cold; hold the block of chocolate between the palms of your hands until it warms slightly and softens just enough to feel a bit sticky, or microwave it for 1 to 3 seconds. When the chocolate is at the perfect temperature, the curls will form as the vegetable peeler cuts across the surface.

You can place the freshly made white chocolate curls immediately onto a dessert or freeze them on a lined baking sheet for about 30 minutes to firm them. Chilled chocolate curls can be carefully placed into a rigid container, covered and frozen for up to 2 months. Always, use a wooden skewer to move chocolate curls; your fingers may melt them.

3 Bake, one sheet at a time, 12 to 14 minutes or until edges are light brown and centers are light golden brown. Cool on baking sheet on wire rack 1 minute. Remove from baking sheet; cool completely on wire rack. (Cookies can be stored in airtight container at room temperature for up to 4 days.)

4 To make glaze, place chopped white chocolate in small microwave-safe bowl. Microwave on medium 1 to 1 1/2 minutes or until almost melted; stir until smooth. With fork, drizzle over cookies.

TIPS *Although technically not white chocolate, white baking chips are commonly referred to as white chocolate chips. For best flavor, look for a brand that contains cocoa butter.
**Do not use white baking chips for the glaze. Chips do not melt well or flow easily for drizzling.
About 3 dozen cookies

PER COOKIE: 145 calories, 8.5 g total fat (4.5 g saturated fat), 2 g protein, 17 g carbohydrate, 20 mg cholesterol, 35 mg sodium, .5 g fiber

Cherry, Cashew and White Chocolate Cookies

These cookies lend themselves to a variety of fruits and nuts. Substitute dried cranberries or chopped dried apricots for the cherries, and toasted pine nuts or macadamia nuts for the cashews.

COOKIES
- 1 1/4 cups all-purpose flour
- 1/4 teaspoon baking soda
- 1/4 teaspoon salt
- 3/4 cup unsalted butter, softened
- 1/2 cup sugar
- 1/2 cup packed light brown sugar
- 1 egg
- 1 tablespoon lemon juice
- 1 teaspoon vanilla extract
- 3/4 teaspoon almond extract
- 1 cup cashew halves
- 1 cup white baking chips*
- 3/4 cup dried cherries

GLAZE
- 4 oz. chopped white chocolate**

1 Heat oven to 350°F. Line 3 baking sheets with parchment paper.
2 In medium bowl, stir together flour, baking soda and salt. In large bowl, beat butter, sugar and brown sugar at medium speed 1 minute or until smoothly blended. Beat in egg, lemon juice, vanilla and almond extract 1 minute or until blended. (Mixture may look curdled.) Reduce speed to low; beat in flour mixture just until blended. Stir in cashews, white baking chips and dried cherries. Drop tablespoons of dough 2 inches apart onto baking sheets.

Orange and White Chocolate Layer Cake

An old-fashioned hot-milk cake turns into a spectacular layer cake when enriched with white chocolate and paired with a white chocolate-cream cheese frosting. White chocolate curls top the cake for a final, festive flourish.

CAKE
- 2 cups all-purpose flour
- 2 teaspoons baking powder
- 1/2 teaspoon salt
- 1 cup whole milk
- 1/2 cup unsalted butter, cut up
- 2 oz. white chocolate, chopped
- 4 eggs
- 1 3/4 cups sugar
- 1 teaspoon vanilla extract
- 2 teaspoons finely grated orange peel

FROSTING
- 6 oz. white chocolate, chopped
- 10 oz. cream cheese, softened
- 1/2 cup unsalted butter, softened
- 2 teaspoons vanilla extract
- 1 teaspoon finely grated orange peel

4 to 4½ cups powdered sugar, sifted
GARNISH
White chocolate curls, if desired (see pg. 116)

1 Heat oven to 350°F. Spray bottom and sides of 2 (9x2-inch) round cake pans with nonstick cooking spray. Line bottoms with parchment paper; spray parchment. Flour bottom and sides of pans.

2 In medium bowl, stir together flour, baking powder and salt. In medium saucepan, combine milk, ½ cup butter and 2 oz. white chocolate; heat over medium-low heat until butter and chocolate are melted and mixture is smooth and hot, stirring frequently. (Mixture should be about 150°F.)

3 Meanwhile, in large bowl, beat eggs and sugar at medium speed 3 to 4 minutes or until thick, fluffy and lightened in color. Beat in 1 teaspoon vanilla and 2 teaspoons orange peel. At low speed, beat in flour mixture until blended. Slowly beat in hot milk mixture until smooth. Pour evenly into pans. Bake 30 to 35 minutes or until toothpick inserted in center comes out clean. Cool in pans on wire rack 20 minutes. Run knife around edges of pans to loosen cakes. Invert onto wire rack; remove parchment. Cool completely.

4 To make frosting, fill medium saucepan one-fourth full with water; bring to a simmer over medium heat. Remove from heat. Place 6 oz. white chocolate in medium heatproof bowl; place over saucepan, making sure bowl does not touch water. Stir frequently until chocolate is smooth and melted. Let cool slightly. In large bowl, beat cream cheese and ½ cup butter at medium speed until blended and smooth. Beat in melted white chocolate until blended. Beat in 2 teaspoons vanilla and 1 teaspoon orange peel. At low speed, beat in 4 cups of the powdered sugar, adding additional powdered sugar if needed for spreadable consistency. Beat until blended and smooth.

5 Place 1 cake layer on serving platter or cardboard round; spread top with

Orange and White Chocolate Layer Cake

1 cup of the frosting. Top with second layer. Spread cake sides with thin layer of frosting (a crumb coat). Coat sides with another smooth layer of frosting. Spread remaining frosting over top. Spoon white chocolate curls over top of cake, mounding slightly towards center. (Cake can be made up to 2 days ahead. Cover and refrigerate. Bring to room temperature before serving.)

WINE Quady's nonvintage Orange Muscat Electra is very light and slightly sweet, with a low alcohol content. Another fine choice is a medium-sweet sherry such as the nonvintage Lustau "East India Solera" from Spain.

12 servings

PER SERVING: 760 calories, 35.5 g total fat (21.5 g saturated fat), 8.5 g protein, 104 g carbohydrate, 145 mg cholesterol, 310 mg sodium, .5 g fiber

Cranberry and White Chocolate Spice Cake

Fresh, tart cranberries contrast well with the sweet white chocolate pieces, which melt into this light cake. A combination of oil and sour cream creates a very moist and tender texture. The cake is a good choice for making ahead because the flavor actually improves on the second day.

CAKE
2¾ cups cake flour
2 teaspoons ground cinnamon
1 teaspoon baking powder
½ teaspoon baking soda
½ teaspoon salt
½ teaspoon ground nutmeg
½ teaspoon ground allspice
3 eggs

Raspberry-White Chocolate Truffles

2 cups sugar
1 cup canola oil
1 teaspoon vanilla extract
1 cup sour cream
1½ cups fresh cranberries or frozen unsweetened cranberries, thawed, coarsely chopped
6 oz. white chocolate, chopped (¼- to ½-inch pieces)

GLAZE
2 oz. white chocolate, finely chopped
2 teaspoons shortening

1 Heat oven to 350°F. Generously grease 12-cup Bundt pan with shortening; sprinkle with flour.
2 In medium bowl, stir together flour, cinnamon, baking powder, baking soda, salt, nutmeg and allspice. In large bowl, beat eggs and sugar at medium speed 2 minutes or until fluffy, thick and lightened in color. At low speed, beat in oil and vanilla. Add flour mixture, beating until blended. Beat in sour cream until well mixed. Stir in cranberries and 6 oz. white chocolate. Pour into pan.

3 Bake 60 to 65 minutes or until skewer inserted in center comes out clean or with just a few crumbs attached. Cool in pan on wire rack 15 minutes. Unmold onto wire rack; cool completely.
4 To make glaze, fill medium saucepan half full with water; bring to a simmer over medium heat. Remove from heat. Place 2 oz. white chocolate and shortening in medium heatproof bowl; place over saucepan, making sure bowl does not touch water. Stir frequently until mixture is smooth. Drizzle over cake. Let stand until set. Serve at room temperature. (Cake can be made up to 2 days ahead and stored at room temperature, or up to 1 month ahead and frozen.)
WINE The nonvintage Penfolds "Club Port Reserve" from Adelaide, Australia, is rich with a light sweetness. Baron Herzog Black Muscat from California has delicious berry fruit and is medium-sweet.
12 servings

PER SERVING: 575 calories, 30.5 g total fat (8 g saturated fat), 6 g protein, 72 g carbohydrate, 70 mg cholesterol, 235 mg sodium, 1.5 g fiber

Raspberry-White Chocolate Truffles

As fancy as these truffles look, they're surprisingly easy to prepare. Start making them a day or two in advance so the truffle filling has enough time to firm up; then it will easily roll into balls.

½ to ¾ cup fresh raspberries
¼ cup heavy whipping cream
12 oz. white chocolate, finely chopped
¼ cup unsalted butter, cut up, softened
1 cup sliced almonds, toasted*
Powdered sugar

1 Place raspberries in medium fine-mesh strainer. With back of spoon, press raspberries through strainer into small bowl. Measure and reserve 3 tablespoons of the raspberry puree. Let stand at warm room temperature until ready to use.
2 In heavy medium saucepan, heat cream over medium heat until hot

Working with White Chocolate

White chocolate has a reputation for being finicky and temperamental. These tips will ensure recipe success.

Purchasing The main ingredient in white chocolate is cocoa butter (also called cocoa fat); it gives white chocolate a subtle chocolate flavor and a smooth texture. Products that don't contain cocoa butter are considered white coating, not white chocolate. Unlike brown chocolate, white chocolate has no cocoa liquor (ground up cocoa beans), which allows it to maintain a creamy ivory color.

Melt white chocolate over a pan of hot water that has been removed from the heat.

Until recently, there were no government standards regulating the labeling of white chocolate. Beginning January 1, 2004, however, anything labeled white chocolate must contain at least 20 percent cocoa fat, 14 percent milk solids, 3.5 percent milk fat and not more than 55 percent sugar.

The brand of white chocolate you use in these recipes can affect their outcome. We had good success with Ghirardelli, Lindt and Callebaut.

Melting White chocolate can be tricky to melt. It needs to be melted more slowly and gently than semisweet or milk chocolate; it can easily seize up or harden if exposed to too much heat. For that reason, we recommend turning off the stove or removing the pan from the heat when melting white chocolate.

To melt white chocolate, chop it into 1/4 - to 1/2-inch pieces so it melts evenly, and place it in a nonreactive heatproof bowl (such as Pyrex glass, heatproof ceramic or stainless steel). Bring a medium saucepan one-fourth full of water to a simmer, and then remove the pan from the heat. Place the bowl of chocolate over the saucepan of water, making sure the bottom of the bowl doesn't touch the water. Let the chocolate stand until it begins to melt, then stir it until it's smooth. Remove the bowl from the pan of water, and use the melted white chocolate as directed.

Storing White chocolate should be wrapped tightly in foil, then in plastic wrap, and stored in a cool, dry, odor-free place. (Because white chocolate has a tendency to absorb odors, keep it away from strong-smelling ingredients, such as mint and other herbs.) Stored properly, white chocolate will keep for 6 months. Refrigerating white chocolate is not recommended unless you live in a very warm, humid area.

---

but not boiling; remove from heat. Add chocolate; let stand 1 minute. Stir; return saucepan to low heat. Heat 1 minute or until chocolate is just melted, stirring constantly. Remove from heat. Stir in butter until butter melts and mixture is smooth. Stir in reserved 3 tablespoons raspberry puree. Pour into medium bowl; press plastic wrap directly onto surface. Refrigerate overnight to firm mixture. (Mixture can be made up to 2 days ahead.)

3 Place almonds in small shallow bowl. Roll teaspoon-sized portions of the truffle mixture between palms of hands to form 3/4-inch balls. Roll in sliced almonds, pressing gently onto truffles. Place truffles on baking sheet; cover and refrigerate. Dust lightly with powdered sugar; place truffles in small candy papers before serving. (Truffles can be made up to 2 days ahead. Refrigerate in airtight container.)

TIP *To toast almonds, place on baking sheet; bake at 350°F. for 5 to 10 minutes or until golden brown. Cool completely.

About 3 dozen truffles

PER TRUFFLE: 85 calories, 6.5 g total fat (3 g saturated fat), 1 g protein, 6.5 g carbohydrate, 10 mg cholesterol, 10 mg sodium, .5 g fiber

---

Elinor Klivans is a food writer and cookbook author based in Camden, Maine. Her most recent cookbook is *Fearless Baking* (Simon & Schuster).

Butterscotch-Pineapple Cake

Butterscotch Revival

Butterscotch makes a comeback in these comforting creations.

Text and Recipes by Lisa Saltzman

Open any traditional American cookbook, and you're sure to find at least one butterscotch recipe. Butterscotch has been a part of our food heritage since the early 1900s. Whether it's an old-fashioned butterscotch custard or a creamy butterscotch sauce spooned over a bread pudding, this soothing flavor is popular in restaurants and home kitchens. Perhaps many of us are realizing how much we miss its pure flavor from the days before manufactured pudding mixes and butterscotch chips.

The joy of butterscotch is not only in its luscious texture and rich flavor, but in the ease with which you can make it. Unlike caramel, its elegant cousin, butterscotch requires little experience or expertise. In fact, it's almost foolproof.

As you reacquaint yourself with this old favorite, be prepared for a delicious trip down memory lane ... or a delightful new discovery

Butterscotch-Pineapple Cake

This delicate yellow cake is the perfect backdrop for the rich butterscotch frosting. Use a gentle touch when spreading the frosting, but don't worry if you trap some crumbs in the frosting along the sides. They'll be hidden by a layer of chopped nuts.

FILLING
- 1 (8-oz.) can crushed unsweetened pineapple in juice
- 3 tablespoons sugar
- 1/2 teaspoon vanilla extract

CAKE
- 10 tablespoons unsalted butter, softened
- 3/4 cup sugar
- 3 egg yolks
- 1 1/2 teaspoons vanilla extract
- 1 1/2 cups sifted cake flour
- 3/4 teaspoon baking powder
- 1/4 teaspoon baking soda
- 1/4 teaspoon salt
- 1/2 cup buttermilk

FROSTING
- 3/4 cup unsalted butter, cut up
- 3/4 cup packed light brown sugar
- 3 tablespoons whole milk
- 2 cups powdered sugar
- 1 1/2 teaspoons vanilla extract

GARNISH
- 2/3 cup finely chopped pecans

1 To make filling, drain pineapple in sieve over medium bowl 10 minutes, reserving 1/4 cup of the juice. Place pineapple, reserved pineapple juice and 3 tablespoons sugar in medium saucepan. Bring to a gentle boil over medium-low heat; cook 4 to 6 minutes, stirring occasionally, or until liquid is slightly thickened. Stir in 1/2 teaspoon vanilla. Place in small bowl; refrigerate to cool.

2 Heat oven to 350°F. Grease and flour 2 (8x1 1/2-inch) round cake pans. Line bottoms with parchment paper.

3 In large bowl, beat 10 tablespoons butter and 3/4 cup sugar at medium-high speed 7 to 8 minutes or until light and fluffy. In small bowl, whisk together egg yolks and 1 1/2 teaspoons vanilla. Add to butter mixture in two parts, beating well after each addition. In medium bowl, stir together cake flour, baking powder, baking soda and salt. Beat into butter mixture at low speed alternately with buttermilk, beginning and ending with flour mixture. Divide batter evenly into pans, smoothing with spatula.*

4 Bake 15 to 20 minutes or until golden brown and centers spring back when gently pressed. Cool on wire racks 10 minutes. Invert cakes onto wire racks; cool completely.

5 Meanwhile, melt 3/4 cup butter in medium saucepan over medium heat. Add brown sugar; cook 2 to 3 minutes, stirring occasionally, or until mixture begins to come together. (Brown sugar and butter will appear separated until mixture gets hot enough.) Stir in milk; bring to a boil, stirring constantly. Pour into medium bowl; cool 30 minutes or until room temperature. Once mixture is cool, sift in powdered sugar 1/2 cup at a time, whisking well after each addition. Whisk in 1 1/2 teaspoons vanilla.

6 To assemble, place 1 cake layer on cardboard round or cake platter. If filling is juicy, brush excess juice over bottom cake layer. Spread one-third of the frosting over bottom layer; top with filling. Place top layer on filling, pressing gently to allow cake and filling to come together. Frost top and sides of cake with remaining frosting. Holding cake in one hand, gently press chopped pecans into sides of cake using other hand, allowing extra pecans to fall onto sheet pan. Serve at room temperature.

TIP *To divide batter evenly between 2 cake pans, weigh batter on scale and divide by two. Or, using 1/2 cup measuring cup, add 1/2 cup batter to

Applying Nuts

To decorate the side of Butterscotch-Pineapple Cake with nuts, start by building the cake on a cardboard round or serving plate. Hold the cake in one hand so you can easily rotate it as you gently press the nuts onto the cake's side with your other hand.

first pan, then to second, continuing until all batter is used.

WINE A delicate port is a delicious match for this cake. Try either the nonvintage Yalumba Clocktower from Australia or the nonvintage Sandeman Founders Reserve. Both are elegant and not overly sweet.

12 servings

PER SERVING: 505 calories, 27.5 g total fat (14 g saturated fat), 3 g protein, 64.5 g carbohydrate, 110 mg cholesterol, 125 mg sodium, 1 g fiber

Butterscotch-Pear Bread Pudding

Bread puddings vary, depending on the type of bread used. For this pudding, try to find a dense, fresh-baked white bread, not an airy, fluffy one. For a denser pudding, use a hearty Italian loaf; for a lighter one, use a crumpet-style bread.

- ¾ cup packed light brown sugar
- ½ cup unsalted butter, cut up
- 2 eggs
- 1 egg yolk
- 3 cups whole milk
- 1 cup whipping cream

- 2 teaspoons vanilla extract
- 1 teaspoon ground nutmeg
- 8 cups (½ lb.) cubed dense white bread (¾ inch), divided
- 3 ripe medium Bartlett pears, peeled, cubed (¾ inch)
- 1 tablespoon melted butter
- 1 tablespoon sugar
  Butterscotch Sauce
  (recipe follows)

1 Place brown sugar and ½ cup butter in medium saucepan. Cook over medium heat, stirring constantly, 2 to 3 minutes or until smooth. Remove from heat. In large bowl, whisk together eggs, egg yolk, milk, cream, vanilla and nutmeg. Whisk in brown sugar mixture until smooth. Add 6 cups of the bread cubes, pressing down gently to moisten bread. Let stand 30 minutes.

2 Heat oven to 325°F. Butter 3-quart glass or ceramic baking dish. Pour half of the bread-custard mixture into dish. Arrange pears over mixture; pour in remaining bread-custard mixture. Spread remaining 2 cups bread cubes evenly over pudding, pressing down slightly to moisten. Brush top bread cubes with melted butter; sprinkle with sugar.

3 Bake 1 hour 5 minutes to 1 hour 10 minutes or until top is rich golden brown and center is set. Cool on wire rack 30 minutes. Serve warm with warm Butterscotch Sauce.

12 servings

PER SERVING: 440 calories, 24 g total fat (14 g saturated fat), 6 g protein, 53 g carbohydrate, 120 mg cholesterol, 190 mg sodium, 1.5 g fiber

Butterscotch Sauce

- ¼ cup unsalted butter, cut up
- ⅔ cup packed light brown sugar
- 1 tablespoon water
- ⅓ cup light corn syrup
- 3 tablespoons whipping cream

Melt butter in medium saucepan over medium heat. Add brown sugar, water and corn syrup. Bring to a boil; boil 2 minutes, whisking occasionally. Remove from heat; whisk in cream. Serve warm.

Butterscotch-Macadamia Nut Brownies

These dense, rich and chewy brownies are loaded with butterscotch flavor. If you can't find unsalted macadamia nuts, rinse salted nuts and bake them at 350°F. for 10 minutes to dry them out.

- 1½ cups unsalted butter, cut up, softened
- 3 cups packed dark brown sugar
- 4 eggs
- 1 tablespoon vanilla extract
- 3 cups all-purpose flour
- 1½ teaspoons baking powder
- 1½ cups unsalted macadamia nuts, coarsely chopped
- 1 cup unsweetened finely shredded coconut

1 Heat oven to 350°F. Grease 13x9-inch pan.

2 In large bowl, beat butter and brown sugar at medium speed 2 to 3 minutes or until well blended. Add eggs one at a time, beating well after each addition. Beat in vanilla.

3 In another large bowl, stir together flour and baking powder. Beat into butter mixture at low speed just until blended. Stir in nuts and coconut.

4 Spread batter evenly in pan. Bake 40 to 45 minutes or until toothpick inserted in center comes out clean. Cool completely on wire rack.

24 bars

PER BAR: 360 calories, 21 g total fat (10.5 g saturated fat), 3.5 g protein, 41 g carbohydrate, 65 mg cholesterol, 55 mg sodium, 2 g fiber

Butterscotch Pots de Crème

Be careful when adding the hot brown sugar mixture to the egg yolks. Whisk it in slowly, a little at a time, to gently raise the temperature of the yolks. Adding a hot liquid too quickly can curdle the yolks, giving the custard a broken appearance and texture instead of being smooth and creamy.

- ½ cup unsalted butter, cut up
- 1 cup packed brown sugar
- 3 cups half-and-half

6 egg yolks
1½ teaspoons vanilla extract
1 oz. white chocolate, chopped
1 oz. semisweet chocolate,
  chopped

1 Heat oven to 300°F. Place 8 (6-oz.) ramekins in baking pan. Melt butter in medium saucepan over medium heat. Add brown sugar; whisk 2 to 3 minutes or until combined. Remove from heat; slowly whisk in half-and-half until blended. Return to heat; whisk until mixture is hot but not steaming, and light brown. Remove from heat.

2 In medium bowl, whisk egg yolks. Slowly whisk in hot brown sugar mixture. Whisk in vanilla. Strain through fine strainer into liquid measuring cup.

3 Pour custard into ramekins. Add enough boiling water to roasting pan to come halfway up sides of ramekins. Cover pan securely with foil. Bake 35 to 40 minutes or until custards are set but still quivery like gelatin.

4 With tongs, remove ramekins from hot water; cool on wire rack 45 minutes. Refrigerate at least 2 hours or overnight.

5 To decorate custards, place white chocolate and semisweet chocolate in separate resealable freezer bags; seal bags. Bring medium saucepan of water to a boil. Remove from heat; let stand several minutes. Place bags with chocolate in water 1 to 2 minutes or until melted, squeezing chocolate occasionally to melt thoroughly. Once melted, remove from water; let stand 5 minutes to cool slightly.

6 Snip tiny corner off each bag; pipe decorative lines, swirls or designs directly onto custard surfaces. Or pipe decorative designs (stars, spirals, etc.) onto piece of parchment paper. Let stand until cool and set. Remove from parchment; place on custards. Serve custards cold.

BEER/WINE Choose a slightly sweet beer, such as the Mendocino Brewing Company Red Tail Ale, which is rich enough for this dish. For wine, try the nonvintage Lustau "East India Solera"

Butterscotch Pots de Crème

Butterscotch Meringue Pie

Sherry from Spain, with its delicate sweetness.

8 servings

PER SERVING: 405 calories, 28 g total fat (16 g saturated fat), 5.5 g protein, 35.5 g carbohydrate, 225 mg cholesterol, 60 mg sodium, 0 g fiber

Butterscotch Meringue Pie

A variation on an old classic, this meringue uses brown sugar instead of white. The result is a meringue that is still light and delicious, but less sweet. It marries beautifully with the sweetness of the butterscotch filling.

CRUST
- 1½ cups all-purpose flour
- 1 tablespoon sugar
- ⅛ teaspoon salt
- ¾ cup unsalted butter, chilled, cut up
- 2 to 3 tablespoons ice water

Decorative Meringue

You can make decorative meringue peaks like the ones shown on Butterscotch Meringue Pie using a small spoon. Dip the back of the spoon into the meringue and pull it upward to form a spiky peak.

FILLING
- ¼ cup unsalted butter, cut up
- 1 cup packed brown sugar
- 1¼ cups whole milk, divided
- ½ cup heavy whipping cream
- 1 egg
- 1 egg yolk
- 3 tablespoons cornstarch
  Dash salt
- 1½ teaspoons vanilla extract

MERINGUE
- ⅓ cup water
- 1 tablespoon cornstarch
- 4 egg whites
- ½ cup packed brown sugar
- ½ teaspoon cream of tartar

1 In large bowl, stir together flour, sugar and ⅛ teaspoon salt. With pastry blender or 2 knives, cut in ¾ cup butter until mixture resembles coarse crumbs with some pea-sized pieces. Add 2 tablespoons of the water; stir until dough starts to form, adding additional water 1 teaspoon at a time, if needed. Shape into flat round; cover. Refrigerate at least 20 minutes.

2 On lightly floured surface, roll dough into ⅛-inch-thick round (12 to 13 inches across). Fold dough in half; transfer to 9-inch pie plate. Gently ease dough into plate, without stretching. Trim to ½ inch beyond edge of plate. Turn crust under itself, even with edge of pan. Flute edges. Freeze 20 to 30 minutes or until firm.

3 Meanwhile, heat oven to 375°F. Cover pie crust with foil. Fill with pie weights, beans or rice. Bake 25 minutes. Remove foil and weights; bake an additional 15 to 20 minutes or until crust is golden brown. Cool on wire rack. Reduce oven temperature to 350°F.

4 Melt ¼ cup butter in medium saucepan over medium heat. Add 1 cup brown sugar; cook and stir 3 minutes or until sugar is melted and mixture is smooth. Whisk in ¾ cup of the milk and cream. Cook, whisking constantly, until mixture comes to a boil. Remove from heat.

5 In medium bowl, whisk together egg, egg yolk and remaining ½ cup milk. Whisk in 3 tablespoons cornstarch and dash salt. Slowly whisk in hot sugar mixture. Pour into same saucepan. Cook over medium-low heat, stirring constantly, 5 minutes or until thick. Strain into medium bowl; stir in vanilla. Cover to keep warm.

6 To make meringue, in small saucepan, combine ⅓ cup water and 1 tablespoon cornstarch; mix well. Bring to boil over medium heat. Boil 30 seconds, stirring constantly. Turn off heat; cover to keep warm.

7 In large heatproof bowl, whisk together egg whites and ½ cup brown sugar. Place over pan of simmering water (bowl should not touch water); whisk constantly 1 to 2 minutes or until sugar has dissolved. (To test, remove bowl from heat and rub small amount of mixture between your fingers. It should feel smooth and silky, without any graininess.) Remove from heat. Add cream of tartar; with electric mixer, beat at medium speed until soft peaks form. With mixer running, add warm cornstarch mixture. Increase speed to medium-high; beat 2 to 3 minutes or until meringue is shiny and stiff peaks form.

8 Heat filling until hot; pour into crust. Working quickly, spread meringue evenly over hot filling, making sure meringue completely covers filling and touches crust on all edges. Use spoon to make decorative finish. Bake at 350°F. for 13 to 15 minutes or until meringue is golden brown. Cool on wire rack 2 hours. Refrigerate. (Pie can be made up to 4 hours ahead. Refrigerate.)

WINE This butterscotch offering needs a rich dessert wine. The nonvintage Barbadillo Oloroso Sherry from Spain is a full-flavored and moderately sweet wine. For an especially memorable pairing, try Castello di Brolio Vin Santo, Tuscany's most famous dessert wine. It has outstanding caramel and nut flavors.

8 servings

PER SERVING: 555 calories, 30.5 g total fat (18.5 g saturated fat), 7 g protein, 65 g carbohydrate, 135 mg cholesterol, 150 mg sodium, .5 g fiber

Lisa Saltzman is a cooking school instructor and former pastry chef living in Eugene, Oregon.

Making the Best Butterscotch

Butterscotch is as basic as it comes, yet it's so delicious. It is made with butter and brown sugar and is often flavored with vanilla. These ingredients are gently cooked until they become smooth and creamy. Once the mixture is made, it can be used in a wide variety of desserts. For perfect butterscotch, follow these tips.

Which brown sugar? Whether you use light or dark brown sugar is a matter of personal taste. It's the molasses in brown sugar that determines how rich the flavor of your butterscotch will be; dark brown sugar provides a more pronounced flavor and a deeper color.

Gentle cooking When making the butterscotch base, melt the butter in a saucepan over medium-low heat. Whisk in the brown sugar, and cook the mixture over medium-low to medium heat for 2 to 3 minutes. Don't be alarmed if the mixture looks separated. After a minute or so, it will boil gently. As you stir, it will come together to form a smooth sauce.

At first the mixture will look separated…

…but it will pull together into a smooth sauce.

Overheating To avoid overheating the butterscotch mixture, the heat should be no higher than medium. If the mixture is overheated or cooked too long, the milk or cream may curdle or harden into little pieces when added to it.

Simplified sauce A traditional butterscotch sauce recipe requires you to use a

The milk or cream may curdle if overheated.

candy thermometer to monitor its process. For a much simpler yet still delicious sauce, add corn syrup and a small amount of water to the butterscotch base (see Butterscotch Sauce, which accompanies Butterscotch-Pear Bread Pudding). Once the mixture has simmered gently for several minutes, add the cream. To reheat the sauce, either microwave it on low several minutes, or heat it in a bowl or jar set over a pan of simmering water.

DESSERTS

Chocolate-Mint Cheesecake

Doubly Decadent Cheesecakes

An American favorite gets a second layer of flavor.

Text and Recipes by Elinor Klivans

It's no surprise that cheesecake often tops lists of favorite desserts. Rich and elegant, sweet and creamy, it's exactly what many people crave when indulging in an after-dinner treat. And while cheesecakes have a well-deserved reputation for sophistication, they're a boon for the cook because they're easy to put together and must be made ahead.

For many years, I baked cheesecakes for a restaurant and was constantly developing new ideas. Layered cheesecakes were my favorite creations. They take the dessert to the limit, providing two layers of flavor, while using the same familiar techniques as regular cheesecakes. All that's needed to produce these stunning desserts is a simple shortcut—flavoring one batch of batter two ways. And because the top layer is added during the last half of baking, it seldom overcooks, thus avoiding unsightly cracks as it cools.

Whether you want to spoil your guests or yourself, here are five doubly good reasons to pull out your springform pan.

Chocolate-Mint Cheesecake

Chocolate and peppermint combine to create a decadent version of the after-dinner mint. Sour cream imbues this cheesecake with an exceptionally light and creamy texture.

CRUST
- 1 (9-oz.) box chocolate cookie crumbs (2 cups)
- 6 tablespoons unsalted butter, melted

FILLING
- 6 oz. semisweet chocolate, chopped
- 3 (8-oz.) pkg. cream cheese, softened
- 1 cup sugar
- 2 tablespoons all-purpose flour
- 4 eggs, room temperature
- 1 cup sour cream
- 2 teaspoons vanilla extract
- 1 teaspoon peppermint extract

GLAZE
- 6 oz. semisweet chocolate, finely chopped
- 1/3 cup whipping cream
- 2 tablespoons unsalted butter, cut up
- 1 tablespoon light corn syrup
- 1/2 teaspoon peppermint extract

1 Heat oven to 350°F. Wrap bottom and sides of 9-inch springform pan with wide heavy-duty foil. In medium bowl, stir together cookie crumbs and melted butter until crumbs are evenly moistened. Press evenly into bottom and 1 inch up sides of pan. Bake 6 to 8 minutes or until set; cool on wire rack.

2 Place 6 oz. chopped chocolate in medium heatproof bowl; place over saucepan of barely simmering water (do not let bowl touch water). Stir frequently until chocolate is smooth and melted; remove bowl from saucepan.

3 In large bowl, beat cream cheese and sugar at low speed until smooth. Beat in flour. Beat in 2 of the eggs just until combined; repeat with remaining 2 eggs. Scrape down sides of bowl. Beat in sour cream and vanilla just until blended.

4 Reserve 2 cups batter in another medium bowl; stir in 1 teaspoon peppermint extract.

5 Stir melted chocolate into batter in large bowl until completely blended; pour into crust. Place pan in large shallow roasting or broiler pan. Fill with enough hot tap water to come halfway up sides of springform pan.

6 Bake 35 minutes. Carefully slide out oven rack several inches. Pour reserved peppermint batter evenly over cheesecake. Bake 25 minutes or until edges are puffed and top is dry to the touch. Center should move slightly when pan is tapped but should not ripple as if liquid. Remove cake from water bath; remove foil. Place on wire rack; cool to room temperature, about 2 hours.

7 Meanwhile, place 6 oz. finely chopped chocolate in another large bowl. Place cream, 2 tablespoons butter and corn syrup in heavy medium saucepan; heat over medium heat 2 to 3 minutes or until hot (temperature will be about 190°F.). Remove saucepan from heat as soon as first bubble appears; pour over chocolate. Let stand 1 minute to soften; stir until mixture is smooth and chocolate is melted. Stir in 1/2 teaspoon peppermint extract. Cool to room temperature, about 1 hour. Pour glaze over cooled cheesecake in pan, spreading evenly over top; refrigerate at least 6 hours before serving. (Cheesecake can be made up to 3 days ahead. Cover and refrigerate.) Store in refrigerator.

12 servings

PER SERVING: 655 calories, 46.5 g total fat (27.5 g saturated fat), 10 g protein, 55 g carbohydrate, 175 mg cholesterol, 330 mg sodium, 2.5 g fiber

Lemon-Raspberry Cheesecake

eggs just until combined; repeat with remaining 2 eggs. Scrape down sides of bowl. Beat in cream, vanilla and almond extract just until blended.

4 Reserve 2 1/2 cups batter in medium bowl; stir in lemon juice and 2 teaspoons lemon peel.

5 Stir 1/2 cup raspberry puree into batter in large bowl until completely blended; pour into crust. Place pan in large shallow roasting or broiler pan. Fill with enough hot tap water to come halfway up sides of springform pan.

6 Bake 35 minutes. Carefully slide out oven rack several inches. Pour reserved lemon batter evenly over cheesecake. Bake 25 minutes or until edges are puffed and top is dry to the touch. Center should move slightly when pan is tapped but should not ripple as if liquid. Remove cake from water bath; remove foil. Place on wire rack; cool to room temperature, about 2 hours. Refrigerate at least 6 hours before serving. (Cheesecake can be made to this point up to 3 days ahead. Cover and refrigerate.) Arrange 1/2 cup raspberries over top just before serving. Store in refrigerator.

12 servings

PER SERVING: 520 calories, 37 g total fat (22.5 g saturated fat), 9.5 g protein, 38.5 g carbohydrate, 180 mg cholesterol, 245 mg sodium, 1 g fiber

Lemon-Raspberry Cheesecake

The pastel colors of raspberry and lemon layers make this cheesecake a gorgeous centerpiece for a spring celebration.

CRUST
1 1/4 cups all-purpose flour
1 tablespoon sugar
1 teaspoon grated lemon peel
1/2 cup unsalted butter, cut up, softened

FILLING
1 1/2 cups fresh raspberries or frozen unsweetened raspberries, thawed
4 (8-oz.) pkg. cream cheese, softened
1 1/3 cups sugar
2 tablespoons all-purpose flour
4 eggs, room temperature
2 tablespoons heavy whipping cream
2 teaspoons vanilla extract
1/2 teaspoon almond extract

2 tablespoons fresh lemon juice
2 teaspoons grated lemon peel
GARNISH
1/2 cup fresh raspberries, if desired

1 Heat oven to 325°F. Wrap bottom and sides of 9-inch springform pan with wide heavy-duty foil. In large bowl, stir together 1 1/4 cups flour, 1 tablespoon sugar and 1 teaspoon lemon peel. Add butter; beat at low speed until pea-sized crumbs form. Press mixture evenly into bottom and 1 inch up sides of pan. Bake 20 minutes or until edges are slightly brown; cool on wire rack.

2 Place 1 1/2 cups raspberries in food processor or blender; process until pureed. Strain into small bowl. Reserve 1/2 cup puree; save remaining puree for another use, if desired.

3 In another large bowl, beat cream cheese and 1 1/3 cups sugar at low speed until smooth. Beat in 2 tablespoons flour. Beat in 2 of the

Cappuccino Cheesecake

Skip your after-dinner coffee and indulge in a piece of this coffee-and-cinnamon-spiked cheesecake instead. It relies on creamy Italian mascarpone cheese for its smooth texture. Look for chocolate cookie crumbs in the same aisle as graham cracker crumbs.

CRUST
2 cups chocolate cookie crumbs
6 tablespoons unsalted butter, melted
FILLING
3 (8-oz.) pkg. cream cheese, softened
8 oz. mascarpone cheese*
1 1/4 cups sugar
2 tablespoons all-purpose flour

Tips for Baking the Perfect Cheesecake

While making a cheesecake isn't complicated, it is important to use the correct technique. These tips will help ensure perfect versions of this creamy dessert.

Bring cream cheese and eggs to room temperature. Thoroughly softening cream cheese eliminates the problems caused by cold cream cheese: white lumps in the batter and baked filling. Likewise, room-temperature eggs incorporate more smoothly into the batter.

Mix gently and at low speed. The purpose of the mixing process is only to blend the ingredients smoothly. Vigorous beating, which introduces a lot of air, causes cheesecake batter to expand during baking and then deflate. This can lead to cracks as it cools.

Use a water bath. A cheesecake filling is actually a custard, and like a custard, it works best when baked in the gentle heat of a water bath. The water bath protects the eggs in the cheesecake from the direct heat of the oven and prevents curdling. It also provides slow, even heat and moisture that keeps the cheesecake from becoming overcooked and dry. To make sure that water won't seep into

Use a single sheet of foil with no seams to wrap the pan.

Baking the cheesecake in a water bath helps prevent it from overcooking.

the springform pan, waterproof it by wrapping it with heavy-duty foil. Use a single sheet of wide foil so the pan is totally covered without any seams. Make sure there are no tears or tiny holes that would allow water to get in.

Halfway through baking, carefully pour the second layer over the cheesecake.

Add the second layer carefully. When making layered cheesecakes, make sure to bake the bottom layer for the amount of time indicated in the recipe to ensure that it's firm enough to have another layer poured over it without collapsing. To add a second layer, carefully and slowly pour the batter over the cheesecake. Put darker-colored layers or heavier chocolate ones on the bottom.

Don't overbake. Cheesecakes are done when the edges are slightly puffed and the top is dry to the touch. The edges should look firm and may have some tiny cracks, which will disappear as the cheesecake cools. The center of the cake should move slightly when the pan is tapped, but it shouldn't ripple as if liquid. Although cheesecakes are soft when warm and freshly baked, they become firm as they cool and even firmer after being refrigerated.

If necessary, cover the top of the cheesecake loosely with paper towels to protect it from drafts as it cools (do not touch the top of the cheesecake). The paper towels allow steam to escape so that moisture doesn't collect on top of the warm cheesecake. Cheesecakes should be completely cooled to room temperature before being refrigerated (about two hours).

Serve and store properly. Cheesecakes actually taste better the day after they're baked because the flavors have had a chance to develop. Once the cheesecake is thoroughly chilled, wrap it in plastic wrap; it can be refrigerated up to one week. To serve, use a small, sharp knife to loosen the cake from the sides of the pan, and then remove the sides. To cut neat slices, use a large, sharp knife and carefully wipe it clean after cutting each piece. For the creamiest texture and fullest flavor, bring cheesecakes to cool room temperature before serving.

dry to the touch. Center should move slightly when pan is tapped but should not ripple as if liquid. Remove cake from water bath; remove foil. Place on wire rack; cool to room temperature, about 2 hours. Sprinkle lightly with ground cinnamon. Refrigerate at least 6 hours before serving. (Cheesecake can be made up to 3 days ahead. Cover and refrigerate.) Store in refrigerator.

TIP *Mascarpone cheese is a double- or triple-cream cheese from Italy. Look for it in the dairy section of the supermarket or in Italian markets. If unavailable, substitute 1 (8-oz.) pkg. cream cheese.

12 servings

PER SERVING: 535 calories, 38.5 g total fat (22.5 g saturated fat), 9.5 g protein, 40 g carbohydrate, 175 mg cholesterol, 370 mg sodium, 1 g fiber

Strawberry Swirl Cheesecake

As if one layer of strawberry cheesecake isn't enough, this luscious dessert has a second layer of vanilla cheesecake topped with strawberry puree. Swirl the puree into the vanilla batter carefully so you don't cut into the bottom layer of the cheesecake.

CRUST
- 1 (10-oz.) pkg. shortbread cookies
- ¼ cup unsalted butter, melted

FILLING
- 3 cups fresh strawberries
- 4 (8-oz.) pkg. cream cheese, softened
- 1⅓ cups sugar
- 2 tablespoons all-purpose flour
- 4 eggs, room temperature
- 2 tablespoons heavy whipping cream
- 1 tablespoon fresh lemon juice
- 2 teaspoons vanilla extract

1 Heat oven to 325°F. Wrap bottom and sides of 9-inch springform pan with wide heavy-duty foil. Place cookies in food processor; process until finely ground. There should be 2¼ cups. (Or place cookies in resealable plastic bag; crush with rolling pin.) In medium bowl, stir

Strawberry Swirl Cheesecake

- 4 eggs, room temperature
- 2 teaspoons vanilla extract
- 1 tablespoon instant coffee granules
- 3 tablespoons heavy whipping cream, divided
- 2 teaspoons ground cinnamon plus extra for sprinkling over top

1 Heat oven to 325°F. Wrap bottom and sides of 9-inch springform pan with wide heavy-duty foil. In medium bowl, stir together cookie crumbs and melted butter until crumbs are evenly moistened. Press evenly into bottom and 1 inch up sides of pan. Bake 8 minutes or until set; cool on wire rack.

2 In large bowl, beat cream cheese, mascarpone cheese and sugar at low speed 2 minutes or until

smooth. Beat in flour. Beat in 2 of the eggs just until combined; repeat with remaining 2 eggs. Scrape down sides of bowl. Beat in vanilla just until blended.

3 Reserve 2 cups batter in another medium bowl. In small bowl, dissolve coffee in 2 tablespoons of the cream; stir into reserved batter.

4 Stir remaining 1 tablespoon cream and 2 teaspoons cinnamon into batter in large bowl until completely blended; pour into crust. Place pan in large shallow roasting or broiler pan. Fill with enough hot tap water to come halfway up sides of springform pan.

5 Bake 40 minutes. Carefully slide out oven rack several inches. Pour reserved coffee batter evenly over cheesecake. Bake 20 minutes or until edges are slightly puffed and top is

together cookie crumbs and melted butter until crumbs are evenly moistened. Press evenly into bottom and 1 inch up sides of pan. Bake 8 minutes or until set; cool on wire rack.

2 Place strawberries in food processor or blender; process until pureed. Strain through fine mesh strainer into small bowl. Reserve 1 cup puree; save remaining puree for another use, if desired.

3 In large bowl, beat cream cheese and sugar at low speed until smooth. Beat in flour. Beat in 2 of the eggs just until combined; repeat with remaining 2 eggs. Scrape bowl. Beat in cream, lemon juice and vanilla just until blended.

4 Reserve 2 1/2 cups batter in another medium bowl. Stir 3/4 cup of the strawberry puree into batter in large bowl until completely blended; pour into crust. Place pan in large shallow roasting or broiler pan. Fill with enough hot tap water to come halfway up sides of springform pan.

5 Bake 35 minutes. Carefully slide out oven rack several inches. Pour reserved vanilla batter evenly over cheesecake. Drizzle remaining 1/4 cup strawberry puree over top. Pull tip of knife lightly through top of vanilla batter to swirl strawberry puree.* Bake 20 minutes or until edges are puffed and top is dry to the touch. (Strawberry swirl may be moist.) Center should move slightly when pan is tapped but should not ripple as if liquid. Remove cake from water bath; remove foil. Place on wire rack; cool to room temperature, about 2 hours. Refrigerate at least 6 hours before serving. (Cheesecake can be made up to 3 days ahead. Cover and refrigerate.) Store in refrigerator.

TIP *Cheesecake may crack slightly where the strawberry puree meets the vanilla batter. Carefully running the knife through the very top only when swirling will help this problem.

12 servings

PER SERVING: 550 calories, 38.5 g total fat (21.5 g saturated fat), 9.5 g protein, 42.5 g carbohydrate, 170 mg cholesterol, 355 mg sodium, 1 g fiber

Lime and Pistachio Praline Cheesecake

This dessert's creaminess is nicely balanced by the crunch of praline that graces the top. In addition to being used as a garnish, the praline is ground into a powder and added to the crust for more pistachio flavor.

PISTACHIO PRALINE
  3/4 cup sugar
  1 1/2 tablespoons water
  1 tablespoon light corn syrup
  3/4 cup pistachios*
CRUST
  1 1/4 cups all-purpose flour
  1 tablespoon sugar
  1/2 cup unsalted butter, chilled, cut up
FILLING
  4 (8-oz.) pkg. cream cheese, softened
  1 1/3 cups sugar
  2 tablespoons all-purpose flour
  4 eggs, room temperature
  2 tablespoons heavy whipping cream
  2 teaspoons vanilla extract
  1 teaspoon almond extract
  1/4 cup fresh lime juice
  1 teaspoon finely grated lime peel

1 Lightly oil baking sheet. Place 3/4 cup sugar, water and corn syrup in medium saucepan; cook over medium-high heat, stirring just until sugar is dissolved. Bring to a boil; boil until syrup begins to turn rich golden brown, brushing sides of pan occasionally with water but not stirring. Remove from heat; stir in pistachios. Immediately spread onto baking sheet; cool completely until hard. Break praline into pieces; coarsely crush with meat mallet. Reserve 1/2 cup crushed praline for garnish. Pulse remaining praline in food processor until finely ground. Reserve 1/3 cup of the ground praline for crust and 1/2 cup for filling.

2 Heat oven to 350°F. Wrap bottom and sides of 9-inch springform pan with wide heavy-duty foil. Spray bottom of pan with nonstick cooking spray. Place 1 1/4 cups flour, 1 tablespoon sugar and 1/3 cup

ground pistachio praline in large bowl or food processor; stir together or pulse to blend. Add butter; beat at low speed or pulse in food processor until pea-sized crumbs form. Press mixture evenly into bottom and 1 inch up sides of pan. Bake 20 minutes or until edges are slightly brown; cool on wire rack.

3 In another large bowl, beat cream cheese and 1 1/3 cups sugar at low speed until smooth. Beat in 2 tablespoons flour. Beat in 2 of the eggs just until combined; repeat with remaining 2 eggs. Scrape down sides of bowl. Beat in cream, vanilla and almond extract just until blended.

4 Reserve 2 cups batter in medium bowl; stir in 1/2 cup ground pistachio praline.

5 Stir lime juice and lime peel into batter in large bowl until completely blended; pour into crust. Place pan in large shallow roasting or broiler pan. Fill with enough hot tap water to come halfway up sides of springform pan.

6 Bake 40 minutes. Carefully slide out oven rack several inches. Pour reserved praline batter evenly over cheesecake. Bake 20 minutes or until edges are puffed and top is dry to the touch. Center should move slightly when pan is tapped but should not ripple as if liquid. Remove cake from water bath; remove foil. Place on wire rack; cool to room temperature, about 2 hours. Refrigerate at least 6 hours before serving. (Cheesecake can be made to this point up to 3 days ahead. Cover and refrigerate.) Sprinkle with reserved 1/2 cup crushed praline just before serving. Store in refrigerator.

TIP *If available, use raw pistachios because they have a bright-green color. If you can't find them, use roasted, salted pistachios.

12 servings

PER SERVING: 610 calories, 40.5 g total fat (23 g saturated fat), 11 g protein, 53 g carbohydrate, 180 mg cholesterol, 250 mg sodium, 1 g fiber

Elinor Klivans is a food writer and cookbook author based in Camden, Maine. Her most recent cookbook is *Fearless Baking* (Simon & Schuster).

Banana-Toffee Cream Pie

Diner Divas

Decadent updates make these restaurant classics even more appealing.

Recipes by Elinor Klivans

Billows of whipped cream, pools of hot fudge, blankets of creamy frosting. These mouthwatering qualities belong to the divas of diner desserts, yummy treats that set the American standard for sweet comfort. We picked four favorites and added some tasty twists to make them even more delectable. There's a carrot cake that reaches for the sky, and an ice cream pie that tastes like a turtle sundae. Toffee tops a banana cream pie, while coffee lends deep flavor to a chocolate cake. Choosing won't be easy, but you'll be deliciously rewarded no matter which one you make.

Banana-Toffee Cream Pie

Crushed toffee candy bars in the graham cracker crust and the whipped cream topping add a sweet crunch to this updated classic dessert. Make sure you chill the filling for at least 4 hours or as long as overnight. Sprinkle the toffee on the pie just before serving so it remains crisp.

FILLING
- 1¾ cups whole milk
- ¾ cup sugar
- ¼ cup all-purpose flour
- 6 egg yolks
- 1 teaspoon vanilla extract
- 2 cups thinly sliced bananas (about 3 small bananas)

CRUST
- 1¼ cups graham cracker crumbs
- 2 (1.4-oz.) toffee candy bars (such as Heath bars), finely chopped
- 6 tablespoons unsalted butter, melted

TOPPING
- 1½ cups heavy whipping cream, chilled
- 2 tablespoons powdered sugar
- 1 teaspoon vanilla extract
- 3 (1.4-oz.) toffee candy bars, coarsely chopped

1 In medium saucepan, bring milk to a simmer over medium heat. Meanwhile, in medium bowl, whisk sugar, flour and egg yolks until smooth. Slowly pour hot milk into egg yolk mixture, whisking constantly. Return mixture to saucepan; cook 5 minutes or until mixture thickens and boils, stirring constantly. Remove from heat; stir in 1 teaspoon vanilla. Strain into medium bowl; press plastic wrap directly onto surface. Refrigerate until cold, at least 4 hours or overnight.
2 Meanwhile, heat oven to 375°F. In medium bowl, stir together graham cracker crumbs and 2 finely chopped candy bars. Stir in butter until crumbs are moistened. Press evenly into bottom and up sides of ungreased 9-inch pie plate. Bake 6 to 8 minutes or until set. Cool. (Crust can be made up to 1 day ahead. Cover and store at room temperature.)
3 Spread generous ½ cup filling over crust; top with banana slices. Cover with remaining filling.
4 In medium bowl, beat cream, powdered sugar and 1 teaspoon vanilla at medium-high speed until firm peaks form. Spread over filling. Refrigerate up to 6 hours. Let stand at room temperature 10 to 15 minutes before serving. Sprinkle with 3 coarsely chopped candy bars; cut with hot dry knife (run knife under hot water and dry). Refrigerate leftovers.
WINE Try a lightly sweet sherry, such as the nonvintage Lustau "Los Arcos" Amontillado Sherry from Spain, or the slightly sweeter nonvintage Barbadillo Oloroso Sherry.
8 servings

PER SERVING: 595 calories, 37.5 g total fat (22 g saturated fat), 6.5 g protein, 60.5 g carbohydrate, 265 mg cholesterol, 170 mg sodium, 1 g fiber

Caramel Turtle Ice Cream Pie

This rich ice cream pie has the perfect proportions of caramel, pecans, ice cream and chocolate. To remove the sides of the springform pan, dip a dish towel in hot water, wring it out and wrap the hot towel around the sides for 15 seconds.

CRUST
- 1¾ cups graham cracker crumbs
- 6 tablespoons unsalted butter, melted

CARAMEL SAUCE
- ½ cup heavy whipping cream
- 2 tablespoons butter
- ¾ cup packed light brown sugar
- 2 tablespoons corn syrup
- 1 teaspoon vanilla extract
- 1¼ cups coarsely chopped pecans

MILK CHOCOLATE
- 6 oz. milk chocolate, chopped
- 1 tablespoon canola oil
- 3 pints vanilla ice cream, softened*

HOT CHOCOLATE SAUCE
- 8 oz. semisweet chocolate, chopped
- 1¼ cups whipping cream

1 Heat oven to 325°F. Butter 9-inch springform pan. In medium bowl, stir together all crust ingredients until crumbs are evenly moistened. Press evenly into bottom and 1 inch up sides of pan. Bake 6 minutes; cool.

2 In heavy medium saucepan, heat cream, 2 tablespoons butter, brown sugar and corn syrup over medium heat until sugar is dissolved. Increase heat to medium-high; bring to a boil. Boil 2 minutes, stirring occasionally. Remove from heat; stir in vanilla. Cool completely at room temperature or in refrigerator, stirring occasionally.

3 Meanwhile, put milk chocolate and oil in small heatproof bowl; place over saucepan of barely simmering water. Heat, stirring frequently, until chocolate is smooth and melted. Remove bowl from saucepan; cool to room temperature.

4 Drizzle 1/4 cup cooled caramel sauce over crust; stir pecans into remainder of sauce. Spread 1 1/2 pints ice cream in bottom of crust. Drizzle half of the caramel-pecan sauce over ice cream; drizzle half of the chocolate mixture over caramel-pecan sauce. Top with remaining 1 1/2 pints ice cream. Drizzle with remaining caramel-pecan sauce and chocolate. Freeze 2 hours or until firm. (Pie can be made up to 5 days ahead. Cover and freeze.)

5 To make hot chocolate sauce, place semisweet chocolate and cream in medium saucepan. Heat over medium-low heat 5 minutes or until chocolate is melted, stirring constantly. (Sauce can be made up to 5 days ahead. Cover and refrigerate.) To serve pie, remove sides of springform pan; cut pie into slices. Serve with warm hot chocolate sauce. Store in freezer.

TIP *To soften ice cream, place in refrigerator 20 minutes or until spreadable.

WINE Select a tawny port that isn't too sweet. Two nice options are the nonvintage Yalumba Clocktower from Australia or the nonvintage

Dow's Boardroom from Portugal.
12 servings

PER SERVING: 675 calories, 47.5 g total fat (23.5 g saturated fat), 6.5 g protein, 64 g carbohydrate, 95 mg cholesterol, 160 mg sodium, 3 g fiber

Outrageous Carrot Cake

This lavish cake boasts three layers loaded with carrots, pineapple, coconut and walnuts. It's filled and crowned with a cream cheese frosting. While cake layers are often created by slicing a single layer horizontally, the fruit and nuts in this cake make that difficult, so the batter is baked in three pans.

CAKE
- 3 cups all-purpose flour
- 2 teaspoons baking soda
- 1 teaspoon salt
- 1 tablespoon plus 1 teaspoon ground cinnamon
- 6 eggs
- 2 1/2 cups sugar
- 1 1/2 cups canola oil
- 2 1/2 cups finely grated carrots (about 6 carrots)
- 2 (8-oz.) cans crushed pineapple in juice, well drained*
- 1 cup shredded sweetened coconut
- 1 cup finely chopped walnuts

FROSTING
- 12 oz. cream cheese, softened
- 1 cup unsalted butter, softened
- 2 teaspoons vanilla extract
- 6 cups powdered sugar
- 1 1/2 cups finely chopped walnuts, if desired

1 Evenly space 2 baking racks in oven. Heat oven to 350°F. Spray bottom and sides of 3 (9x2-inch) round cake pans with nonstick cooking spray. Line bottoms with parchment paper; spray parchment with nonstick cooking spray.

2 Sift flour, baking soda, salt and cinnamon into medium bowl.

3 In large bowl, beat eggs and sugar at medium speed 1 to 3 minutes or until thickened and slightly lighter in color. Beat in oil at low speed. Stir in flour mixture until blended. Stir in carrots, pineapple, coconut and 1 cup

Outrageous Carrot Cake

walnuts until blended. Divide batter evenly among pans. Bake 25 minutes; turn and reverse cake pans. Bake an additional 10 minutes or until toothpick inserted in center comes out clean and cake pulls slightly away from sides of pan. Cool in pans on wire rack 15 minutes. Invert onto wire rack; remove parchment. Cool completely.

4 To make frosting, beat cream cheese and butter in large bowl at medium speed 3 minutes or until blended and smooth. Beat in vanilla. Add powdered sugar; beat at low speed 1 minute or until blended and smooth.

5 Place 1 cake layer on serving platter or cardboard round; spread with 1 cup frosting. Repeat. Top with remaining cake layer; spread top and sides with thin layer of frosting. Coat sides with another smooth layer of frosting; spread remaining frosting on top. Press 1 1/2 cups walnuts onto sides of cake. (Cake can be made up to 2 days ahead and refrigerated, or 3 weeks ahead and frozen. To freeze, place cake in freezer until frosting is firm; wrap in plastic wrap, then heavy-duty foil. To defrost, place in refrigerator overnight; remove wrapping. Serve at room temperature.) Refrigerate leftovers.

TIP *If pineapple has any large pieces, finely chop.

WINE Quady dessert wines are perfect for this cake. Try the nonvintage Electra ($10), which has orange flavors and only 4 percent alcohol, or the 2001 Essencia, a richer and sweeter dessert wine with lush orange peel flavors ($18).

20 servings

PER SERVING: 755 calories, 45 g total fat (13.5 g saturated fat), 8 g protein, 84.5 g carbohydrate, 105 mg cholesterol, 330 mg sodium, 2.5 g fiber

Totally Chocolate Layer Cake

This moist chocolate cake with a fine, delicate crumb is made with unsweetened chocolate and cocoa. To slice each layer in half, use a serrated knife and, with a sawing motion, make a 1-inch-deep horizontal cut around the middle of each layer. Use this cut to guide the knife as you slice from one side through to the other.

CAKE
- 2 oz. unsweetened chocolate, chopped
- 2 cups cake flour
- 1/4 cup unsweetened Dutch-processed cocoa
- 1 teaspoon baking powder
- 1 teaspoon baking soda
- 1/2 teaspoon salt
- 3/4 cup unsalted butter, cut up, softened
- 1 3/4 cups sugar
- 3 eggs
- 2 teaspoons vanilla extract
- 1 cup sour cream
- 1 cup strong coffee

FROSTING
- 6 oz. unsweetened chocolate, chopped
- 5 cups powdered sugar
- 3 tablespoons unsweetened Dutch-processed cocoa
- 1 1/2 cups unsalted butter, cut up, softened
- 2 teaspoons vanilla extract
- 1/2 cup heavy whipping cream, room temperature

1 Heat oven to 350°F. Spray bottom and sides of 2 (9x2-inch) round cake pans with nonstick cooking spray. Line bottoms with parchment paper; spray parchment with nonstick cooking spray.

2 Place 2 oz. chocolate in small heatproof bowl; place over small saucepan of barely simmering water. Stir frequently until chocolate is smooth and melted. Remove bowl from saucepan; cool slightly.

3 Sift cake flour, 1/4 cup cocoa powder, baking powder, baking soda and salt into medium bowl. In large bowl, beat 3/4 cup butter and 1 3/4 cups sugar at medium speed 2 minutes or until light and fluffy. Stir in melted chocolate until combined. Add eggs one at a time, beating well after each addition. Beat in 2 teaspoons vanilla and sour cream at low speed until combined. Add flour mixture in 3 parts alternating with coffee, beginning and ending with flour mixture; beat just until incorporated. Pour into pans, smoothing top with spatula.

4 Bake 35 to 40 minutes or until top springs back when gently pressed and toothpick inserted in center comes out clean. (Cake may crack slightly during baking.) Cool in pans on wire rack 15 minutes. Invert onto wire rack; remove parchment. Cool completely.

5 To make frosting, place 6 oz. chocolate in small heatproof bowl; place over small saucepan of barely simmering water. Stir frequently until chocolate is smooth and melted. Remove bowl from saucepan; cool slightly. In large bowl, sift together powdered sugar and 3 tablespoons cocoa powder. In another large bowl, beat 1 1/2 cups butter at medium speed until smooth. Add sugar mixture; beat at low speed until blended and smooth. Beat in melted chocolate. Add 2 teaspoons vanilla and whipping cream; beat 2 minutes or until fluffy, smooth and lighter in color.

6 Cut each cake in half horizontally. Place 1 cake layer on platter or cardboard round. Spread generous 3/4 cup frosting over top. Repeat with 2 more cake layers and frosting. Top with fourth cake layer. Spread top and sides with thin layer of frosting. Coat sides with another smooth layer of frosting; spread remaining frosting on top, swirling decoratively. (Cake can be made up to 2 days ahead and refrigerated, or 3 weeks ahead and frozen. To freeze, place cake in freezer until frosting is firm; wrap in plastic wrap, then heavy-duty foil. To defrost, place in refrigerator overnight; remove wrapping. Serve at room temperature.)

WINE Port and chocolate are a great match. Select the nonvintage Ficklin Tinta from California or the nonvintage Quinta do Noval Tawny from Portugal.

12 servings

PER SERVING: 895 calories, 54.5 g total fat (33 g saturated fat), 7 g protein, 105.5 g carbohydrate, 170 mg cholesterol, 280 mg sodium, 4.5 g fiber

Elinor Klivans is a food writer and cookbook author based in Camden, Maine. Her most recent cookbook is *Fearless Baking* (Simon & Schuster).

Test Kitchen Tips

These luscious desserts are relatively easy to make. The following tips from the test kitchen staff will help ensure success.

Banana-Toffee Cream Pie You may be tempted to spray the pie plate with nonstick cooking spray to make it easier to remove each piece, but don't do it. We found that spraying made it more difficult to remove the pie.

Caramel Turtle Ice Cream Pie Use good-quality ice cream for this recipe; it's denser and less airy than inexpensive brands. Make sure your freezer is set to a very cold temperature to properly set the filling in the pie. Before serving, remove the pie from the freezer and cut it into 12 pieces. Return the pie to the freezer until you're ready to serve it, then place each piece on a plate. This reduces the amount of time the ice cream spends out of the freezer.

Outrageous Carrot Cake We found some cans of crushed pineapple contained fairly large pineapple pieces. If this is the case, chop them finely before adding to the batter or the cake will be very difficult to slice. When baking three cake pans at once, remember to exchange the pans on the top rack with those on the bottom rack, or rotate the pans so that those in the front are moved to the back. This allows the cakes to rise more evenly during baking.

Totally Chocolate Layer Cake When recipes such as this one call for adding dry and wet ingredients alternately, begin and end with the dry ingredients. Start by adding one-third of the dry ingredients and beating the mixture at low speed until most of the dry ingredients are absorbed. Then pour in half of the liquid ingredients and beat only until the liquid is absorbed. Continue by adding one-third of the dry mixture and beating, and then adding the remaining liquid and beating. Finish with the final addition of the dry ingredients. This sequence allows you to add ingredients in amounts that can be absorbed quickly without overbeating.

Nectarine Pandowdy

American Fruit Classics

Rich fruit bounty shines in these familiar favorites.

Text and Recipes by Bruce Weinstein and Mark Scarbrough

Strawberries, nectarines, berries and cherries—the season's fruits are as much a part of summer traditions as a day at the beach. While there are plenty of ways to enjoy them, for simple dishes that showcase their luscious nature, let tradition rule.

We turned to four American classic desserts and tweaked them just a bit to heighten their appeal. Ginger brightens a strawberry crisp. Almonds add subtle notes to a cobbler. Sourdough bread boosts a berry brown betty. Nectarines give a pandowdy a place in the sun.

These homey desserts fit right in with the relaxed pace we seek these days, whether you're at home or at the beach. And with fruits available year-round, you can enjoy the taste of summer any time of year.

Nectarine Pandowdy

Be sure the nectarines are ripe but only slightly soft. To ripen them, leave them on the counter for a few days. Or, to speed the process, place them in a paper bag with an apple. Leave the bag on the counter for a day or two.

CRUST
- 1 1/2 cups all-purpose flour
- 1 tablespoon sugar
- 1/4 teaspoon salt
- 1/2 cup unsalted butter, chilled, cut up
- 4 to 6 tablespoons cold water

FILLING
- 8 cups sliced (generous 1/2 inch) unpeeled nectarines (about 3 1/2 lb.)
- 3/4 cup packed light brown sugar
- 3 tablespoons all-purpose flour
- 2 teaspoons grated lemon peel
- 1 teaspoon grated nutmeg
- 1 teaspoon lemon juice
- 1 teaspoon vanilla extract
- 2 tablespoons sugar
- 1/2 teaspoon ground cinnamon

1 In large bowl, stir together 1 1/2 cups flour, 1 tablespoon sugar and salt. With pastry blender or 2 knives, cut in butter until mixture resembles coarse crumbs with some pea-sized pieces. Add 4 tablespoons of the water; stir until dough begins to form, adding additional water 1 teaspoon at a time, if necessary. Shape into flat round; cover. Refrigerate 30 minutes or until chilled.

2 Meanwhile, heat oven to 375°F. Butter 13x9-inch glass baking dish. In another large bowl, toss together nectarines, brown sugar, 3 tablespoons flour, lemon peel, nutmeg, lemon juice and vanilla; spread evenly in baking dish.

3 On lightly floured surface, roll dough into 13x9-inch rectangle. Place over fruit in baking dish. Crimp or fold under edges to fit inside dish; do not seal crust against pan's edges. In small bowl, stir together 2 tablespoons sugar and cinnamon; sprinkle over crust.

4 Bake 40 minutes or until crust is light brown. Remove from oven. With knife, cut crust into 12 squares. Using spatula, gently press crust into filling. Bake an additional 5 minutes or until golden brown and bubbly. Cool 20 to 30 minutes; serve warm or at room temperature.

12 servings

PER SERVING: 245 calories, 8.5 g total fat (5 g saturated fat), 3 g protein, 41 g carbohydrate, 20 mg cholesterol, 55 mg sodium, 2 g fiber

Four-Berry Sourdough Brown Betty

Apples may be the traditional fruit for a brown betty, but a melange of fresh berries lends a summery twist to this classic dessert. Serve it with vanilla ice cream, sweetened heavy cream or fat-free yogurt.

- 1 1/2 lb. sourdough bread
- 3/4 cup unsalted butter, melted
- 1 1/2 cups plus 2 tablespoons sugar, divided
- 3/4 teaspoon grated nutmeg
- 3 cups thinly sliced fresh strawberries
- 2 cups fresh blackberries
- 2 cups fresh blueberries
- 2 cups fresh raspberries
- 2 teaspoons finely grated lemon peel
- 1/4 teaspoon salt

1 Heat oven to 375°F. Butter 13x9-inch glass baking dish.

2 Remove and discard crusts from bread; cut bread into 1-inch cubes. Place in food processor; process until finely ground. Measure out 6 cups crumbs (reserve any remaining crumbs for another use). In large bowl, stir together bread crumbs, melted butter, 1/4 cup of the sugar and nutmeg until crumbs are well moistened.

3 In another large bowl, stir together 1 1/4 cups of the sugar, strawberries, blackberries, blueberries, raspberries, lemon peel and salt.

4 Spread one-third of the bread crumb mixture over bottom of dish; top with half of the berry

What's In a Name?

Treats for the well-heeled have well-documented roots. But cobblers and pandowdies, homey desserts without pedigrees, have less certain beginnings. Unleavened (at least not dramatically so), they didn't require a bread oven, so they gained countrywide appeal because they could be made fireside. Even in colonial times, quicker and simpler was better for the home cook.

Brown Betty Some claim a betty is a homespun answer to a charlotte, a fancy bread-lined molded dessert. Both are made with bread, but a charlotte was made with fresh bread, an extravagance in colonial times. A brown betty, on the other hand, was made with bread crumbs, a frugal way to finish off yesterday's loaf. It was originally a pudding, a dish to be served alongside a roast, so it was less sweet than today's versions. As fruit lost its side dish appeal, the brown betty slowly switched places, from main course to dessert.

Cobbler Food scholars rely on a dish's name to provide clues to its origin—an inexact science at best. For years, they said a cobbler was made quickly from disparate parts cobbled together. But, as several food historians have noted, a cobbler was an alcoholic punch popular in colonial times. It was made with rum, fruit juices and sugar. It's believed to have developed into a dessert by adding fresh fruit to leftover punch and baking it under a sugary crust.

Crisp Of all the classic desserts mentioned here, this one's origins are the most obscure. To crispen a vegetable is, in some sense, to return it to its original texture. So some experts theorize that a crisp is a way to freshen fruit past its prime. Today, a crisp is identified by its topping: usually oats and sugar, as opposed to the biscuit topping in cobblers and pandowdies.

Pandowdy It's a strange name, indeed, but one with a fine American twang. Most experts believe a pandowdy is so-named because of its dowdy appearance: The crust is cracked as it bakes, allowing the filling to come through. The original pandowdy was most likely made with a cream custard; later, cream was simply poured over the dish when served.

mixture. Repeat layers, spreading remaining one-third bread crumb mixture evenly over top layer of berries. Sprinkle with remaining 2 tablespoons sugar.

5 Bake 40 to 45 minutes or until topping is golden brown and filling is bubbly. Let stand 30 minutes; serve warm or at room temperature.

8 servings

PER SERVING: 500 calories, 19.5 g total fat (11 g saturated fat), 5 g protein, 79.5 g carbohydrate, 45 mg cholesterol, 325 mg sodium, 7.5 g fiber

Fresh Cherry Cobbler with Almond Biscuit Topping

The best sweet cherries for this dish are Bing (dark red) or Tartarian (purple). The cherries should be firm but not hard. It's easiest to remove the pits with a cherry pitter. If you need to remove pits by hand, cut down from the stem, along the fruit's natural planes, rather than around the middle. Take out the pit with your fingers rather than squeezing it out.

FILLING

- 6 cups pitted fresh cherries (about 3 lb. unpitted)
- 1/3 cup sugar
- 3 tablespoons honey
- 1 teaspoon lemon juice
- 1/2 teaspoon vanilla extract
- 2 tablespoons all-purpose flour
- 1/4 teaspoon salt

TOPPING

- 1 cup plus 2 tablespoons all-purpose flour
- 1 cup toasted sliced almonds, ground*
- 1/4 cup sugar
- 2 teaspoons baking soda
- 1/2 teaspoon salt
- 1/4 cup unsalted butter, melted
- 1/2 cup buttermilk
- 1/8 teaspoon almond extract

1 Heat oven to 400°F. Butter 13x9-inch glass baking dish.

2 In large bowl, stir together cherries, 1/3 cup sugar, honey, lemon juice and vanilla. Stir in 2 tablespoons flour and 1/4 teaspoon salt. Spoon mixture evenly into baking dish; bake 10 minutes. Remove from oven; reduce oven temperature to 350°F.

3 Meanwhile, in medium bowl, stir together 1 cup plus 2 tablespoons flour, ground almonds, 1/4 cup sugar, baking soda and 1/2 teaspoon salt. Stir in melted butter until mixture is crumbly. Stir in buttermilk and almond extract until combined.

4 Drop tablespoonfuls of dough in cobblestone pattern over hot cherry filling. Return cobbler to oven. Bake at 350°F. for 25 to 30 minutes or until topping is golden brown and filling is bubbly. Let stand 30 minutes; serve warm.

TIP *To toast almonds, place on baking sheet; bake at 375°F. for 5 minutes or until golden brown. Cool; pulse in food processor until finely ground.

8 servings

PER SERVING: 390 calories, 14 g total fat (4.5 g saturated fat), 7 g protein, 64.5 g carbohydrate, 15 mg cholesterol, 550 mg sodium, 5.5 g fiber

Strawberry-Rhubarb Crisp with Ginger-Oat Crust

Strawberry-Rhubarb Crisp with Ginger-Oat Crust

Ginger adds a pleasing, spicy dimension to the classic combination of strawberries and rhubarb. Look for crisp, brightly colored stalks of rhubarb.

1 1/2 cups sugar
  1 cup plus 3 tablespoons all-purpose flour, divided
  1 tablespoon cornstarch
  1/2 teaspoon salt, divided
  4 cups halved fresh strawberries (quartered if very large)
  4 cups sliced (1/2 inch) fresh rhubarb

  1 tablespoon lemon juice
  1 cup old-fashioned rolled oats (not quick-cooking)
  3/4 cup finely chopped walnuts
  1/2 cup packed light brown sugar
  1/3 cup chopped crystallized ginger
  1/4 teaspoon ground ginger
  1/2 cup unsalted butter, melted
     Powdered sugar

1 Heat oven to 375°F. In large bowl, stir together sugar, 3 tablespoons of the flour, cornstarch and 1/4 teaspoon of the salt until blended. Add strawberries, rhubarb and lemon juice; toss to coat. Place in 13x9-inch glass baking dish.

2 In medium bowl, stir together remaining 1 cup flour, oats, walnuts, brown sugar, crystallized ginger, ground ginger and remaining 1/4 teaspoon salt until combined. Stir in melted butter until moistened; sprinkle over fruit.

3 Bake 40 to 45 minutes or until topping is golden brown and fruit is bubbly. Cool 20 to 30 minutes; serve warm. Sprinkle with powdered sugar right before serving.

12 servings

PER SERVING: 355 calories, 13 g total fat (5.5 g saturated fat), 4 g protein, 59 g carbohydrate, 20 mg cholesterol, 115 mg sodium, 3.5 g fiber

---

Bruce Weinstein and Mark Scarbrough are food writers based in New York City. Their most recent cookbook is *The Ultimate Potato Book* (Morrow).

Peanut Brittle-Hot Fudge Sundae Squares

Sweet Relief

Cool desserts relieve the heat any time.

Text and Recipes by Melanie Barnard

Delightfully creamy and billowy, five chilled desserts offer refreshing respite to long, hot days. From an old-fashioned mousse cake to a blushing pink chiffon tart to the ultimate fudge sundae, all meet summertime (or anytime) treat criteria—high on pleasure and low on work.

With no baking required, aside from making a simple cookie crumb crust, and nothing more difficult than whipping cream, these recipes are astoundingly easy and impressive. Prepare them in the morning; then let them sit in the refrigerator until after dinner, when you're ready to serve dessert.

These are so cool, you'll want to make every single one.

Peanut Brittle-Hot Fudge Sundae Squares

This recipe is an excellent way to make hot fudge sundaes for a crowd. Start the dessert at least nine hours before you plan to serve it, to give the layers time to set.

CRUST
12 oz. peanut butter sandwich cookies (about 24 cookies)
6 tablespoons unsalted butter, melted

FILLING
12 oz. purchased peanut brittle*
1/2 gallon vanilla ice cream, slightly softened**

SAUCE
1/3 cup sugar
1/3 cup packed light brown sugar
1/2 cup unsweetened cocoa
3/4 cup heavy whipping cream
1/3 cup light corn syrup
Dash salt
1/2 oz. unsweetened chocolate, chopped
5 tablespoons unsalted butter
1 1/2 teaspoons vanilla extract

GARNISH
1/2 cup roasted peanuts (preferably small)
16 pieces peanut brittle

1 Heat oven to 350°F. Place cookies in food processor; process until finely crushed. (You should have about 3 cups.) Add 6 tablespoons melted butter; process until combined. Press into bottom of 13x9-inch baking pan. Bake 8 to 10 minutes or until fragrant and slightly darker. Cool completely on wire rack. (Crust can be made up to 1 day ahead. Cover and store at room temperature.)

2 Place 12 oz. peanut brittle in food processor; process until coarsely crushed. Spoon ice cream into large bowl; stir in crushed peanut brittle. Spoon ice cream into crust, spreading carefully to cover and smooth top. Cover with foil; freeze at least 6 hours or up to 12 hours, until firm.

3 Meanwhile, in medium saucepan, stir together sugar, brown sugar, cocoa, cream, corn syrup and salt. Bring to a boil over medium heat, stirring constantly; cook until sugars are dissolved. Reduce heat to medium-low; simmer 5 minutes, stirring frequently. Remove pan from heat; stir in chocolate, 5 tablespoons butter and vanilla until smooth. Cool completely. (Sauce can be made up to 5 days ahead. Cover and refrigerate. Bring to room temperature or rewarm slightly before spreading on dessert.)

4 Spread ice cream with 1 cup of the fudge sauce; sprinkle with peanuts. Cover; freeze at least 2 hours or up to 8 hours, until set.

5 To serve, warm remaining fudge sauce (you should have about 1 cup). Cut dessert into squares; place on individual serving plates. Garnish each serving with 1 piece peanut brittle; drizzle with sauce.

TIPS *If peanut brittle is difficult to find, substitute 1 cup toffee bits and 1 1/2 cups coarsely chopped peanuts for the peanut brittle in the ice cream filling.
**To easily soften ice cream, cut into fourths. Place in 13x9-inch baking pan; refrigerate 15 to 20 minutes or until ice cream is slightly softened.

16 servings

PER SERVING: 525 calories, 32 g total fat (15 g saturated fat), 8 g protein, 57 g carbohydrate, 65 mg cholesterol, 210 mg sodium, 3 g fiber

Coffee-Praline Ice Box Cheesecake

This no-bake cheesecake is light and billowy, yet it's as rich and silky smooth as its long-baked counterpart. It's like having an iced praline café au lait for dessert, only better. To save time, you can substitute sugared nuts or purchased praline candy for the homemade praline.

PRALINE
2 tablespoons unsalted butter
1/4 cup packed light brown sugar
1 tablespoon light corn syrup
1/2 teaspoon ground cinnamon
1 1/2 cups pecan halves or pieces

CRUST
7 oz. pecan shortbread cookies (about 14 cookies)

3 tablespoons unsalted butter, melted

½ teaspoon vanilla extract

½ teaspoon ground cinnamon

FILLING

⅔ cup packed light brown sugar, divided

3 tablespoons instant espresso coffee powder or coffee granules

1 (¼-oz.) pkg. unflavored gelatin

¾ cup hot water

2 tablespoons Kahlúa (coffee-flavored liqueur) or strong coffee

1 teaspoon vanilla extract

2 (8-oz.) pkg. cream cheese, softened

1 cup heavy whipping cream

1 Line small baking sheet with foil. Heat 2 tablespoons butter, brown sugar, corn syrup and ½ teaspoon cinnamon in small saucepan over medium heat until butter is melted and mixture is smooth and bubbly. Cover and cook 1 minute. Add pecans. Increase heat to medium-high; cook, uncovered, 3 to 5 minutes or until pecans are fragrant and syrup is dark gold, stirring constantly. Immediately pour mixture onto baking sheet, quickly spreading thinly. Cool at least 15 minutes. Remove from foil; break into pieces. (Praline can be made up to 3 days ahead. Cover and store at room temperature.)

2 Heat oven to 350°F. Place cookies in food processor; process until finely crushed. (You should have about 1½ cups.) Add 3 tablespoons butter, ½ teaspoon vanilla and ½ teaspoon cinnamon; process to combine. Press in bottom of 9-inch square pan. Bake 8 to 10 minutes or until fragrant and slightly darker. Cool completely. (Crust can be made up to 1 day ahead. Cover and store at room temperature.)

3 In small bowl, stir together ⅓ cup of the brown sugar, coffee granules and gelatin. Add hot water, stirring until brown sugar, coffee granules and gelatin are dissolved. Stir in Kahlúa and

1 teaspoon vanilla. Refrigerate, stirring frequently, 30 to 45 minutes or until chilled and mixture begins to thicken.

4 In large bowl, beat cream cheese and remaining ⅓ cup brown sugar at medium speed until light and fluffy. Slowly add gelatin mixture; beat until blended. In medium bowl, beat cream at medium-high speed until soft peaks form. Fold whipped cream into cream cheese mixture. Pour over crust. Refrigerate at least 3 hours or up to 24 hours, until firm.

5 Cut into 16 squares. Sprinkle each square with some of the pralines. Store in refrigerator.

16 servings

PER SERVING: 365 calories, 28 g total fat (12.5 g saturated fat), 4.5 g protein, 26 g carbohydrate, 60 mg cholesterol, 150 mg sodium, 1 g fiber

Black-Bottom Raspberry Tart

This dessert seems so decadent, with its layers of chocolate and raspberry cream, that you'll be surprised to find it's not overly sweet. Although you can use frozen raspberries for the filling, you'll want to find the ripest, reddest, most fragrant fresh berries to decorate the top.

CRUST

⅓ cup sliced almonds

1 cup graham cracker crumbs

2 tablespoons sugar

¼ cup unsalted butter, melted

½ teaspoon almond extract

CHOCOLATE FILLING

8 oz. semisweet chocolate, coarsely chopped

½ cup heavy whipping cream

1½ tablespoons raspberry liqueur or syrup

RASPBERRY FILLING

1 (10-oz.) pkg. frozen sweetened raspberries, thawed

1 tablespoon raspberry liqueur or syrup

1½ teaspoons unflavored gelatin

2 cups heavy whipping cream

2 tablespoons sugar

GARNISH

1 cup fresh raspberries

1 Heat oven to 350°F. Place almonds in food processor; pulse until finely ground. Add graham cracker crumbs and 2 tablespoons sugar; pulse to combine. Add butter and almond extract; pulse to combine. Press in bottom and up sides of 10-inch tart pan with removable bottom. Bake 8 to 10 minutes or until fragrant and slightly darker. Cool completely on wire rack. (Crust can be made up to 1 day ahead. Cover and store at room temperature.)

2 Place all chocolate filling ingredients in small saucepan. Heat over medium-low heat until chocolate is melted, stirring occasionally. Stir

Black-Bottom Raspberry Tart

until blended. Pour into crust; refrigerate while making raspberry filling. (Tart can be made to this point up to 1 day ahead. Cover and refrigerate.)

3 Place thawed raspberries in food processor; process until pureed. Press through strainer into medium saucepan; discard seeds. Stir in 1 tablespoon liqueur. Sprinkle gelatin over raspberry mixture; let stand 2 minutes or until gelatin softens. Cook and stir over medium heat 2 to 3 minutes or until mixture is warm and gelatin is dissolved. Pour into medium bowl; place bowl in larger bowl of ice water. Stir 8 to 10 minutes or

until mixture is cool and begins to jell.

4 In medium bowl, whip 2 cups cream and 2 tablespoons sugar at medium-high speed until soft peaks form. Fold in raspberry mixture until no streaks of white remain; spread in crust over chocolate. Place raspberries on top. Cover; refrigerate at least 2 hours or up to 12 hours. Store in refrigerator.

8 servings

PER SERVING: 550 calories, 40.5 g total fat (23.5 g saturated fat), 5 g protein, 47.5 g carbohydrate, 100 mg cholesterol, 90 mg sodium, 4 g fiber

Key Lime-Coconut Mousse Pie

If you can't find Key limes, don't worry. This pie is just as tart and delicious with Persian limes, the most common variety in markets. When you grate the peel, be sure to get only the colored part; the white pith underneath can be bitter. For a flavor twist, substitute fresh lemon juice for the lime juice.

CRUST
10 oz. soft coconut macaroons (about 12 cookies)*
GARNISH
3 tablespoons sweetened shredded coconut

Chocolate Malted Mousse Cake

FILLING

3 eggs
4 egg yolks
1 1/4 cups sugar
Dash salt
1/2 cup fresh Key lime juice (about 15 Key limes)
1 1/2 tablespoons grated lime peel

1/4 cup unsalted butter, cut up
1 cup heavy whipping cream

1 Heat oven to 350°F. Spray 9-inch pie plate with nonstick cooking spray. Place macaroons in food processor; process until finely crushed. (You should have about 1 1/2 cups.) Gently

press into bottom and up sides of pie plate. Bake 10 to 12 minutes or until golden and fragrant. Cool completely on wire rack. (Crust can be prepared up to 1 day ahead. Cover and store at room temperature.)

2 Meanwhile, spread coconut on small baking sheet. Bake 6 to 8

Add butter. Cook over medium-low heat, stirring almost constantly, 8 to 12 minutes or until mixture is smooth and thick enough to coat back of spoon. (Mixture should reach 165°F.) Pour lime filling into medium bowl; cover and refrigerate at least 3 hours or up to 24 hours, until chilled.

4 In another medium bowl, beat cream at medium-high speed until stiff peaks form; fold into lime filling until no streaks of white remain. Spoon filling into crust; sprinkle with toasted coconut. Refrigerate at least 1 hour or until firm. Store in refrigerator up to 12 hours.

TIP *Look for soft coconut macaroon cookies, often sold in bakeries. Archway brand has a soft macaroon in its grocery line. Dry, crisp macaroon cookies will not hold together for this crust.

8 servings

PER SERVING: 475 calories, 26 g total fat (17 g saturated fat), 6 g protein, 57 g carbohydrate, 235 mg cholesterol, 205 mg sodium, 1 g fiber

Chocolate Malted Mousse Cake

Chocoholics will love this dessert. The combination of malted milk powder and chocolate-covered malted milk balls gives this mousse cake the old-fashioned flavor of a chocolate malted milk shake.

CRUST
- 1¼ cups chocolate wafer cookie crumbs
- 5 oz. chocolate-covered malted milk balls (about 1½ cups)
- ⅓ cup unsalted butter, melted

FILLING
- 8 oz. milk chocolate, coarsely chopped
- 6 oz. bittersweet or semisweet chocolate, coarsely chopped
- 2½ cups heavy whipping cream, divided
- ⅓ cup malted milk powder
- 1 teaspoon vanilla extract

GARNISH
- 12 chocolate-covered malted milk balls

1 Heat oven to 350°F. Place cookie crumbs in medium bowl. Place 5 oz. malted milk balls in food processor; pulse until finely crushed. (You should have about 1 cup.) Add ½ cup of the crushed malted milk balls to cookie crumbs. Reserve remaining ½ cup for filling.

2 Stir butter into crumb mixture. Press into bottom and ½ inch up sides of 9-inch springform pan with removable bottom. Bake 8 to 10 minutes or until fragrant and firm. Cool completely on wire rack. (Crust can be made up to 1 day ahead. Cover and store at room temperature.)

3 Gently melt milk chocolate and bittersweet chocolate in medium bowl set over saucepan of simmering water (bowl should not touch water). In small bowl, stir together ½ cup of the cream, malted milk powder and vanilla until powder is dissolved. Stir into chocolate mixture until smooth; cool to room temperature.

4 In large mixing bowl, beat remaining 2 cups cream at medium-high speed until stiff peaks form. Stir about 1 cup of the whipped cream into chocolate mixture; fold chocolate mixture into remaining whipped cream until blended. Fold in reserved ½ cup crushed malted milk balls. Spoon mousse into crust, smoothing top. Refrigerate until firm, at least 3 hours. (Cake can be made up to 2 days ahead. Cover and refrigerate.)

5 To serve, run thin knife around side of pan to separate mousse from pan; remove sides of pan. Cut cake into wedges, wiping knife on damp cloth between cuts; top each piece with chocolate-covered malted milk ball. Store in refrigerator.

12 servings

PER SERVING: 495 calories, 37 g total fat (22 g saturated fat), 5 g protein, 41 g carbohydrate, 75 mg cholesterol, 150 mg sodium, 3 g fiber

Melanie Barnard is a food writer and cookbook author based in New Canaan, Connecticut.

minutes, stirring frequently, or until golden and toasted. Cool completely. (Coconut can be made up to 1 day ahead. Cover and store at room temperature.)

3 In heavy medium saucepan, whisk eggs, egg yolks, sugar and salt until thick. Whisk in lime juice and peel.

Apple Cake with Maple-Walnut Glaze

The Sticky Side of Sweet

Fall desserts take a luscious turn.

Recipes by Elinor Klivans

The allure of the sweet and sticky starts young. Remember your first caramel apple? Or that gooey caramel roll? These desserts have those same irresistible qualities. Seasonal ingredients are at the heart of each one, but they're pushed to maximum appeal with thick fillings, sauces and syrupy glazes. These recipes are perfect for Thanksgiving, but why wait? Fall is a deliciously long season … and any other time of year would work great too.

Apple Cake with Maple-Walnut Glaze

This moist cake explodes with fall flavors: maple syrup, apples, cinnamon and walnuts. Because maple syrup is a dominant taste, be sure to choose a high-quality one labeled pure maple syrup, not maple-flavored syrup. The cake absorbs the glaze as it stands, making it even moister a day or two later.

CAKE
- 2¼ cups all-purpose flour
- 2 cups sugar
- 1½ teaspoons baking soda
- 2 teaspoons ground cinnamon
- ¾ teaspoon salt
- 1 cup vegetable oil
- 4 eggs
- ¼ cup pure maple syrup
- 1 teaspoon vanilla extract
- 3 cups grated peeled tart apples (about 3 apples)
- 1 cup golden raisins
- 1 cup chopped walnuts

GLAZE
- 2 tablespoons cornstarch
- 2 tablespoons water
- 1½ cups pure maple syrup
- 2 teaspoons vanilla extract
- 1 cup chopped walnuts, toasted*

1 Heat oven to 350°F. Grease bottom and sides of 10-inch tube pan (do not use tube pan with removable bottom). Line bottom with parchment paper; spray paper with nonstick cooking spray.

2 In large bowl, whisk together flour, sugar, baking soda, cinnamon and salt until blended. Stir in oil until dry ingredients are moistened. Stir in eggs, ¼ cup maple syrup and 1 teaspoon vanilla until blended. Stir in apples, raisins and 1 cup walnuts until combined. Spoon batter into pan; smooth top with spatula.

3 Bake 1 hour or until top feels firm and wooden skewer inserted in center comes out moist but clean. Cool in pan on wire rack 15 minutes. Run knife around edge of pan and center tube to loosen cake. Invert onto wire rack; remove parchment. Turn cake top side up to cool completely.

4 Meanwhile, in small bowl, stir together cornstarch and water. Place 1½ cups maple syrup and cornstarch mixture in medium saucepan; bring to a boil over medium heat. Reduce heat to medium; boil 3 minutes, stirring frequently, or until mixture thickens slightly. Remove from heat; stir in 2 teaspoons vanilla. Reserve ¾ cup glaze; cool to room temperature. Stir 1 cup walnuts into remaining glaze; cool to room temperature. Spoon over top of cooled cake, letting glaze drizzle down sides. To serve, spoon reserved glaze over each slice.

TIP *To toast walnuts, place on baking sheet; bake at 350°F. for 6 to 8 minutes or until pale brown and fragrant. Cool.

12 servings

PER SERVING: 720 calories, 33 g total fat (4.5 g saturated fat), 8 g protein, 103 g carbohydrate, 70 mg cholesterol, 330 mg sodium, 3.5 g fiber

Coffee-Fudge Blondies with Chocolate Sauce and Coffee Whipped Cream

This rich, buttery dessert is totally decadent. The secret to the bars' gooiness is to underbake them slightly. They'll sink as they cool and become quite flat. But don't worry; when topped with whipped cream and a warm chocolate sauce, these blondies become a dessert extravaganza.

BLONDIES
- 2¼ cups all-purpose flour
- 1 teaspoon baking powder
- ½ teaspoon salt
- 3 tablespoons instant coffee granules
- 1 tablespoon hot water
- 1 cup unsalted butter, softened
- 1 cup sugar
- 1⅔ cups packed light brown sugar
- 3 eggs
- 2 teaspoons vanilla extract

WHIPPED CREAM
- 1 cup whipping cream
- 2 tablespoons powdered sugar
- 1½ teaspoons instant coffee granules
- ½ teaspoon vanilla extract

SAUCE
- ¾ cup whipping cream
- 1½ cups semisweet chocolate chips
- ½ teaspoon vanilla extract

1 Heat oven to 350°F. Line 13x9-inch baking pan with foil, letting foil extend over edges. Spray foil with nonstick cooking spray.

Baking Answers

Why toast nuts? When you toast nuts, they brown and dry out a bit, resulting in a more intensely nutty flavor. Toasting also mellows the slightly bitter tannins in some nuts, such as walnuts and pecans. It's an effective way to boost the impact of nuts, whether they're mixed into a batter or filling, used in a frosting or topping, or sprinkled over food as a garnish (see Apple Cake with Maple-Walnut Glaze and Caramel-Pecan Tart). There are several ways to toast nuts; one of the easiest is in the oven, but watch them closely. They can go from toasted to burned in a very short time. When the nuts become fragrant, they're usually done.

Why whisk together dry ingredients? You might think whisks are all about wet, useful only when mixing egg whites, creams or other liquids. But they have a dry side, too. When a recipe has several dry ingredients—flour, leavening and various spices, for example—using a whisk to blend the ingredients ensures the spices are evenly and quickly distributed (see Apple Cake with Maple-Walnut Glaze and Sticky-Top Pumpkin Cake with Brown Sugar Sauce).

Why use parchment paper? If you've ever had a cake or quick bread stick to a pan when removing it, even after greasing and flouring the pan, you'll appreciate parchment paper. Lining a pan with it gives added insurance that the cake will release intact (see Sticky-Top Pumpkin Cake with Brown Sugar Sauce and Apple Cake with Maple-Walnut Glaze). To cut the paper to size, trace the pan's bottom on the paper. Cut the paper slightly smaller than the tracing. Grease the bottom of the pan (this helps to hold the paper in place), and place the paper in the pan.

2 In medium bowl, stir together flour, baking powder and salt. In small bowl, stir together 3 tablespoons coffee granules and hot water until granules are dissolved.

3 In large bowl, beat butter, sugar and brown sugar at medium speed 1 minute or until smooth and blended. Beat in coffee mixture, eggs and 2 teaspoons vanilla until blended. (Mixture may look curdled.) At low speed, beat in flour mixture until incorporated and batter is smooth. Spread batter in pan; smooth top with spatula.

4 Bake 30 to 35 minutes or until dark golden brown and toothpick inserted in center comes out with a few moist crumbs attached. Cool completely in pan on wire rack. (Blondies will sink in center as they cool.)

5 Meanwhile, in another large bowl, beat all whipped cream ingredients at medium-high speed until soft peaks form. Cover and refrigerate while preparing sauce.

6 To make sauce, place ³/4 cup cream in medium saucepan; heat over medium heat until hot (about 150°F.). Remove from heat. Add chocolate chips; let stand 1 minute. Stir until chocolate melts and sauce is smooth. Stir in ¹/2 teaspoon vanilla.

7 Lift foil and cooled bars from pan; cut into 12 pieces. Cut each piece diagonally into 2 triangles. Place 2 triangles on each plate, overlapping pointed edges. Spoon whipped cream over one side and warm chocolate sauce over other.

12 servings

PER SERVING: 635 calories, 34 g total fat (20.5 g saturated fat), 6 g protein, 81 g carbohydrate, 130 mg cholesterol, 185 mg sodium, 2 g fiber

Caramel-Pecan Tart

This twist on pecan pie introduces a rich, buttery caramel filling in place of the usual custard. And the pecans are toasted for extra-deep, nutty flavor. Brushing the sides of the saucepan with a damp pastry brush while the caramel

Caramel-Pecan Tart

cooks helps inhibit the formation of sugar crystals, which can make the caramel grainy.

CRUST
- 1 cup all-purpose flour
- ½ cup cake flour
- 1 tablespoon sugar
- ½ teaspoon salt
- 6 tablespoons unsalted butter, chilled, cut up
- 3 tablespoons shortening, chilled
- 3 to 4 tablespoons ice water

FILLING
- 1 cup whipping cream
- 2 tablespoons unsalted butter, cut up
- 1⅓ cups sugar
- ½ cup water
- 1 tablespoon corn syrup
- 2½ cups pecan halves, toasted*
- 2 teaspoons vanilla extract

TOPPING
- 1 cup whipping cream
- 1 tablespoon powdered sugar
- ½ teaspoon vanilla extract

1 Place all-purpose flour, cake flour, 1 tablespoon sugar and salt in food processor; pulse to combine. Add 6 tablespoons butter and shortening; process until mixture resembles coarse crumbs with some pea-sized pieces. Add 3 tablespoons of the ice water; process just until dough begins to form, adding additional water 1

teaspoon at a time if necessary. (Dough also can be mixed by hand using a pastry blender or two knives.) Shape into flat round; cover and refrigerate 45 minutes.

2 On lightly floured surface, roll dough into 12-inch round. Line 10-inch tart pan with dough; trim to ½ inch beyond edge of pan. Turn edge of dough under, even with edge of pan; crimp. Freeze 30 minutes or until firm.

3 Meanwhile, heat oven to 375°F. Line crust with foil; fill with pie weights or dried beans. Bake 15 minutes; remove foil and pie weights. Bake an additional 20 minutes or until crust is golden brown. Cool on wire rack.

Sticky-Top Pumpkin Cake with Brown Sugar Sauce

4 To make filling, place 1 cup cream and 2 tablespoons butter in small saucepan; heat over medium heat until butter melts and mixture is hot. Remove from heat; cover to keep warm.

5 Place 1 1/3 cups sugar, 1/2 cup water and corn syrup in large saucepan; cover and cook over medium heat, without stirring, until sugar dissolves. Uncover; with pastry brush dipped in water, brush down any sugar crystals on side of saucepan. Increase heat to medium-high. Bring to a boil; boil until sugar turns golden brown, watching carefully. Remove from heat; slowly add hot cream mixture. (Be careful as mixture will bubble up.) Stir until boiling stops and mixture is smooth. Stir in pecans and 2 teaspoons vanilla.

6 Let stand 15 minutes to cool slightly. Pour into baked crust. Cool completely on wire rack, at least 3 hours or until set but still soft.

7 In medium bowl, beat all topping ingredients until soft peaks form.

Serve tart at room temperature with whipped cream. Refrigerate leftovers.
TIP *To toast pecans, place on baking sheet; bake at 375°F. for 4 to 6 minutes or until slightly darker in color. Cool.

8 servings

PER SERVING: 770 calories, 57.5 g total fat (23 g saturated fat), 6.5 g protein, 62.5 g carbohydrate, 95 mg cholesterol, 175 mg sodium, 3.5 g fiber

Sticky-Top Pumpkin Cake with Brown Sugar Sauce

The pièce de résistance of this irresistible pumpkin dessert is the caramel sauce. It bakes into a sticky glaze on top of the cake and also is poured over each serving. Cold, fresh cream provides a silky, crowning touch.

CAKE

- 1½ cups all-purpose flour
- 1 teaspoon ground cinnamon
- ¾ teaspoon baking powder
- ¾ teaspoon baking soda
- ¼ teaspoon salt
- ¼ teaspoon ground nutmeg
- ⅛ teaspoon ground cloves
- ½ cup unsalted butter, melted, cooled slightly
- 1 cup sugar
- ¾ cup canned pure pumpkin
- 2 eggs
- 1 teaspoon vanilla extract

SAUCE

- 6 tablespoons unsalted butter, cut up
- 1¼ cups packed dark brown sugar
- 1 cup whipping cream
- 1 teaspoon vanilla extract

TOPPING

- 1 cup whipping cream

1 Heat oven to 350°F. Grease bottom and sides of 9x5-inch loaf pan. Line bottom of pan with parchment paper; grease paper.

2 In medium bowl, whisk together flour, cinnamon, baking powder, baking soda, salt, nutmeg and cloves until combined. In large bowl, beat melted butter, sugar and pumpkin at medium speed until blended. Beat in eggs and 1 teaspoon vanilla until smooth. At low speed, beat in flour mixture until blended. Pour batter into pan; smooth top with spatula. Bake 30 minutes or until top feels firm (cake will be partially baked).

3 Meanwhile, place 6 tablespoons butter, brown sugar and 1 cup cream in medium saucepan. Cook over medium heat 5 minutes or until butter melts and sugar dissolves,

stirring occasionally. Increase heat to medium-high; boil 2 minutes, stirring constantly. Remove from heat; stir in 1 teaspoon vanilla.

4 Remove cake from oven. Carefully pour ½ cup of the sauce over top of cake; reserve remaining sauce. Return cake to oven; reduce oven temperature to 250°F. Bake 35 minutes or until sauce is bubbling gently and wooden skewer inserted in cake comes out clean. Cool in pan on wire rack 10 minutes. Run knife around edges to loosen cake from pan. Invert onto serving plate; remove parchment paper. Turn top side up. Serve warm or at room temperature.

5 To serve, warm reserved sauce over low heat. Cut cake into ¾-inch-thick slices; cut each slice in half. Place 2 halves on each plate. Spoon remaining sauce over each serving; drizzle with 1 cup unwhipped cream.

12 servings

PER SERVING: 465 calories, 27 g total fat (16.5 g saturated fat), 4 g protein, 54 g carbohydrate, 115 mg cholesterol, 195 mg sodium, 1 g fiber

Elinor Klivans is a cookbook author based in Camden, Maine. Her next book, *Big Fat Cookies* (Chronicle), is due out this fall.

General Index

There are several ways to use this helpful index. First — you can find recipes by name. If you don't know a recipe's specific name but recall a main ingredient used, look under that heading and all the related recipes will be listed; scan for the recipe you want. If you have an ingredient in mind and want to find a great recipe for it, look under that ingredient heading as well to find a list of recipes to choose from. Finally — you can use this general index to find a summary of the recipes in each chapter of the book (techniques, ethnic cooking, main dishes, savory ingredients, sweet ingredients, and desserts).